SHAKERS near LEBANON state of N YORK.
their mode of Worship. *Drawn from Life.*

*The Scarecrow Press, Inc.*
*Metuchen, N.J., & London*
*1980*

*edited by*
*Gairdner B. Moment*
*& Otto F. Kraushaar*

# UTOPIAS:
## the American experience

## Acknowledgments

Frontispiece from the collection of the Library of Congress; illustrations on pages 13 and 33 from Charles Nordhoff, The Communistic Societies in the United States; on pages 46, 64 and 77 from Constance Noyes Robertson, Oneida Community, An Autobiography; on page 123 from Charles Morse Stotz, The Early Architecture of Western Pennsylvania, courtesy of the University of Pittsburgh Press, copyright © 1936 by the Buhl Foundation; on pages 110, 112, and 116 from John William Larner, Jr., "Nails and Sundrie Medicines: Town Planning and Public Health in the Harmony Society, 1805-1840," Western Pennsylvania Historical Magazine (June 1962); on page 197 from G. B. Lockwood, The New Harmony Movement.

Library of Congress Cataloging in Publication Data
Main entry under title:

Utopias, the American experience.

Includes index.
1. Collective settlements--United States--Addresses, essays, lectures. 2. Utopias--Addresses, essays, lectures. I. Moment, Gairdner Bostwick, 1905- II. Kraushaar, Otto F.
HX654.U86                    335'.9'73                79-25068
ISBN 0-8108-1277-0

Manufactured in the United States of America

# TABLE OF CONTENTS

# PREFACE

It is with genuine satisfaction that we record our gratitude for the cooperation of the authors whose essays comprise this book. The diversity in outlook, academic training, interests, and style exemplified by the group, taken as a whole, reflects the varied expectations that contemporary men and women have of the shape and form of a more humane and more rationally ordered society, as well as the widespread concern within the academic community over the imbalances, the dangerous drift, and the injustices prevalent in existing society. The diversity of points of view and style of our authors also reflect the fact that utopias grow out of despair as well as out of hope; and that they are conceived as the dreams and experiments of a glorious past or as a consummation yet to be achieved in the future.

Given this variety, and the firmness with which our authors hold their beliefs, it was a foregone conclusion that the task of the editors was not one of negotiating agreement on basic issues. We believe, rather, that the chief virtue of this book lies in just this variety of standpoints and approaches.

It is a pleasure to acknowledge the initial sponsorship and support of the Alumnae Association of Goucher College, the continuing encouragement of the college administration, in particular of Dean James Billet, and the aid of a small grant for the preparation of manuscripts from the Faculty Committee on Research and Publication.

Finally, we recognize that the publication of a multi-authored book of this kind presents more than the usual share of problems to the publisher and its editors. For the patience and sympathetic assistance we have received from the editors of the Scarecrow Press we record our gratitude.

Gairdner B. Moment          Otto F. Kraushaar

iv

# ABOUT THE AUTHORS

BAKER, JEAN HARVEY. Chair, Department of History, Goucher College. A. B. , Goucher College; A. M. , Ph. D. , Johns Hopkins University. Historian. Author: The Politics of Continuity, 1973; The Maryland Know-Nothings: A Case History, 1979; Ambivalent Americans (The Know-Nothings), 1979.

BELFORD, FONTAINE MAURY. Associate Professor of English and Director, Goucher Center for Educational Resources. B. A. , Hollins College; M. A. , Yale University; Ph. D. , University of North Carolina. Comparative Literature. Futurist. One-time student at the Sorbonne and in Munich. Teacher, Friends School, Ram Allah, Jordan. Member: World Future Society (U. S. affiliate of The Club of Rome); Institute for Theological Research. Archaeologist at Jericho. Author: Molière's Le Misanthrope and Bergson's Le Rire; Comedy's Play: A Prelude to a Metaphysics of Comedy; A Once and Future Time: The Theological Response to Global Crisis (editor); articles in The Sewanee Review, The Churchman, Christian Century, etc.

BRADFORD, JEAN L. Associate Professor of Psychology, Goucher College. A. B. , Ph. D. , University of Minnesota. Humanist Psychologist. Formerly Child Psychologist, Johns Hopkins Hospital. Author: Sex Differences in Anxiety; A Psychological Lexicon: A Clinical Psychology Monograph (co-author).

CHAMBERLAIN, JOHN V. Chair, Department of Religion, Goucher College. A. B. , Florida Southern College; A. M. , Ph. D. , Duke University. Special interest in religion in North America. Trained as a carpenter. Temporary factory worker. Author: An Ancient Sectarian Interpretation of the Old Testament Prophets: A Study of the Qumran Scrolls and the Damascus Fragments; other works on the Qumran Scrolls and their meaning.

DOUGLAS, PAUL H. Associate Professor and Coordinator, American Studies Program, Towson State University, Baltimore, Maryland. B. A., University of Connecticut; M. A. University of Oregon; Ph. D., George Washington University. Winner of various awards, including Fellow, Smithsonian Institution and Winterthur Museum; Fulbright Lecturer, Hacettepe University, Ankara, Turkey. Author: "Seneca, Sandstone and the Smithsonian," The Smithsonian Journal of History, 1968; Those Inventive Americans (two chaps. ); "The Material Culture of the Harmony Society," Pennsylvania Folklife, 1975. Systematic visitor to nineteenth-century American communes (whether restored or still functioning).

GREEN, CLIFFORD. Chair, Program on Ethics and the Professions, Goucher College. A. B., Sydney University; B. D., Melbourne College of Divinity; graduate studies in London and Geneva; S. T. M., Ph. D., Union Theological Seminary, New York. Author: numerous works on the theologian Dietrich Bonhoeffer, including Bonhoeffer: The Sociality of Christ and Humanity; articles on Tillich, Barth, and Marx; Critical Issues in Modern Religion (co-author).

HEDGES, WILLIAM L. Chair, American Studies Program, Goucher College. A. B., Haverford College; Ph. D., Harvard University. American Literature. Author: Washington Irving: An American Study, 1802-1830; Land and Imagination: The Rural American Dream (co-author and co-editor with Elaine R. Hedges).

KILCHENSTEIN, MARY L. Graduate student, University of Maryland, College Park. A. B., Goucher College. Catholic Working-Class Optimist. Participant in contemporary communes.

KOLMERTEN, CAROL A. Assistant Professor of English, Hood College. Ph. D., Purdue University. Author: "Women and Work," Georgia Review; "Frances Wright," American Women Writers; Women in Utopia (forthcoming).

KRAUSHAAR, OTTO F. President Emeritus, Goucher College. A. B., A. M., State University of Iowa; Ph. D., Harvard University; LLD., Smith College, Dickinson College, Brandeis University, Johns Hopkins University, Goucher College, College of Notre Dame; Litt. D., Wartburg College; L. H. D., Elmira College; D. H., Washington College. Philosopher. Teacher. College President. Author: "Kierkegaard in English," Journal of Philosophy, 1942; "Josiah Royce," in Fisch, M. H., ed., Classic

American Philosophers, 1951; "The Landscape Teaches Too, " Landscape Architecture, 1961; American Nonpublic Schools: Patterns of Diversity; Private Schools: From the Puritans to the Present; Baltimore's Adopt-a-School Program: A Fruitful Alliance of Business and Schools.

KRIEGER, RONALD A. Chair, Department of Economics, Goucher College. A. B., University of Colorado; M. S., Ph. D., University of Wisconsin. Economist, The World Bank, 1965-67. Senior Economist, First National City Bank of New York, 1969-72. Economics Editor, Business Week, 1972-73. Author: The Mexican Economy; Brazil: An Economic Survey; Inflation and Growth in Latin America; contributor to Robert Puth's Current Issues in the American Economy.

MOMENT, GAIRDNER B. Professor of Biology Emeritus, Goucher College; Guest Scientist, National Institutes of Health. A. B. Princeton University; Ph. D., Yale University. Biologist, Animal Development. Secretary-General XVI International Congress of Zoology, 1963; Associate Program Director, National Science Foundation, 1960-61; Voice of America, Program Organizer for Biology; Continuing Teacher, American Institute of Biological Sciences film series. Author: numerous research papers on animal development; co-author with Kirtley Mather, Wm. E. Hocking, et al., Science and the Spiritual Nature of Man, 1958, Member Corporation Bermuda BioStation.

# I. INTRODUCTION

## Otto F. Kraushaar

The essays comprising this book are the outgrowth of a series of lectures on American utopias given during the American Bicentennial year under the auspices of the Continuing Education Program sponsored jointly by Goucher College and Johns Hopkins University. "The great expectations of 1776," stated the lecture brochure, "when our forefathers believed they were creating 'a new order of the centuries' (as we still say on our dollar bills) have been realized only in part. Somehow we have fallen short of establishing the 'Heavenly City.' In the belief that we have something to learn from the bright visions of our past, or at least can enjoy the contemplation of past follies, a group of Goucher scholars of widely different training, philosophies, ages and life styles will undertake to examine the long series of model societies which have marked our history from 1776 to 1976."

The essays based on the lecture series were augmented by contributions from a number of scholars from other colleges who were known to be writing on one or another aspect of American utopias. So the book as it stands reaches out quite beyond the confines of the Goucher College family.

No special pattern or developmental plan lies behind the essays other than their focus on American utopian thought and experience as seen from a variety of approaches and points of view. No attempt was made to impose any kind of uniformity of treatment or approach on the authors. Most are (or have been) college teachers; but the disciplines they are at home in range over philosophy, psychology, history, English, religion, theology, economics, biology, American studies, and futurism. Their degree of involvement in utopian experiments ranges all the way from detached descriptions, comparisons, and analysis done in a scholarly spirit, to firsthand accounts of life lived in contemporary communes,

1

to passionate avowals of a burning need to transform American society in order to stem the deluge.

While utopias are objects of perennial and never-ending interest to students of the human scene, the human crisis confronting Western civilization in the closing decades of the twentieth century is such as to drive people to reflect on the past and present visions of better society in a mood approaching desperation. In many respects the world we live in is far better than at any earlier time. The miracle of placing men on the moon dramatically epitomized the swift, giant strides of modern science and technology. But the same forces that have brought the modern consumer a bewildering glut of conveniences and gadgets, useful and pernicious, have also pushed the rate of change to such frenetic proportions that a growing segment of the population is unable to cope with it. As a result life in America is filled with signposts to oblivion as well as to utopia. We have the best of medical care ever--provided you can get it at all and afford to pay for it. We live longer, provided we are not cut down on the highways, by murderous assaults, or by ingesting one or another of the panoply of chemical poisons that filter into our food, our streams, and our fields. And we have the means to provide a better education and to be better informed than ever, but the spread of functional illiteracy is a national scandal, while ordinary citizens struggle daily to sift a few grains of truth from the cascade of trash that flows into their living rooms and mailboxes. And most alarming of all, we live with the knowledge that more people have been killed in the wars of this century than in all prior human history combined, and that available weaponry is now capable of incinerating whole nations.

Such reflections fuel the belief that there must be a better way, that there must be a more humane and less threatening vision of the human future than that now in prospect. The turbulence of the late 1960s was a clear signal of widespread discontent with things as they are, especially among young people. Though it subsided with surprising rapidity, it left in its wake a host of communes or experimental communities. Several of these are described in subsequent chapters. They differ, quite naturally, from the nineteenth-century utopias in that they are attempts to overcome the social, economic, and spiritual problems peculiar to our time, just as the earlier ones bore the imprint of the conditions prevailing at the time of their founding. Many of the recently founded communes had weak and shallow roots and soon perished. "To get away from it all" is a motive that many can sympathize with, but it is not of itself strong enough to provide a solid base for a new community possessing high survival potential.

Before delving farther into that interesting question it may be useful to consider some of the variable meanings attached to "utopia" and "utopian." The latter is often used in a pejorative sense as meaning "impossible of fulfillment," or "unrealistic," "impractical." Contemporary reformers bent on trying to improve the functioning of some aspect of society avoid the label "utopian" like the plague. Nevertheless, reform clearly implies the recognition of a gap between the actual and some attainable ideal. Certain organizations --the Quakers are a good example--are active in promoting the concept of a non-political community needing no police force or military establishment but trusting the regulation of community concerns to a developing consensus, as in a Quaker meeting. Such a vision has much in common with many separatist utopian enterprises, although the Quakers do not think of themselves as such. The reason is clear. The Quakers are dedicated to dwelling in, influencing, and making terms with the open societies in which they reside, rather than withdrawing in order to found separate ideal communities of their own. Whether or not Quakers think of themselves as utopians, there is no denying that their ideal of life contains strong utopian tendencies. For this reason an essay on "John Wollman and the Quaker Utopian Vision," by William L. Hedges, finds a place in this book. Wollman's faith would not permit him to turn his back on injustice, oppression, or exploitation, but prompted him to call upon the resources of the Inner Light, to espouse pacificism, to oppose slavery, to support equal education for women, and to be active in diminishing human conflict and resentment and in promoting charity toward all.

Without quarreling with this broad signification of "utopia" and "utopian," most of the essays in this volume are concerned with distinct and separate ideal communities. Several such are described on the basis of firsthand experience. Chapter 11, "Ambiguities of Community: A Koinonia Experience," describes a two-year stay of author Clifford J. Green and his family in the community located in Baltimore's Green Spring Valley.[1] Here, too, the members do not think of themselves as utopians and prefer not to be classed as such. The group's original mission was to serve as a Christian training center for world service, which, since it is a task requiring a good measure of hard-nosed realism, would rather dissociate itself from the pejorative connotations of utopia.

Illustrating the great diversity of present-day communes, Chapter 10, "Extremes of the Contemporary Communal Frontier," by Mary Isabelle Kilchenstein, describes the life and ideals of two contrasting communes: The Farm at Summertown, Tennessee, a large rural community under the charismatic teachership of a single leader; and the Philadelphia Life Center, a much smaller urban collective with a democratic-socialist form of organization.

The solid and positive core of meaning of "utopia" is exemplified by idealistic, visionary enterprises of this type. In the words of Rosabeth M. Kanter, they represent "humankind's deepest yearnings, noblest dreams, and highest aspirations come to fulfillment, where all physical, social, and spiritual forces work together, in harmony, to permit the attainment of everything people find necessary and desirable."[2] Such early utopias as Campanella's City of the Sun and Sir Thomas More's Utopia were essentially sustained exercises of the literary, political, and spiritual imagination, which in their very conception served as both a criticism and challenge to all the ills of the established order. The long succession of famous books--from Plato's Republic to Karl Marx's Das Kapital and beyond--attest to the perennial interest in this subject. Although Marx spurned utopianism in favor of his concept of scientific socialism and world revolution, his writings were the font of a renewed and sustained interest in the creation of a more perfect society.

America was seen from the beginning as a haven for utopian communities. In fact the notion that America has a God-given mission to be the cradle of a more perfect social order and an example to the rest of the world remains deeply embedded in our national consciousness. Chapter 2, "America: Symbol of a Fresh Start," examines some of the reasons why this country came to be thought of in these utopian terms. For the original settlers the virgin land gleamed as a new heaven and a new earth, a new moral and spiritual vista with the decadence and depravity of Europe left far behind. The process of founding utopian societies began early in our national history. One of the earliest was the Labadist community founded at Bohemia Manor, Maryland, about 1680 by the followers of Jean de Labadie, the influential French Catholic mystic who became a Protestant dissenter. It was a deeply religious community dedicated to simple, pious living and to holding goods and children in common. But it was during the late eighteenth and all through the nineteenth centuries that the utopian movement gathered momentum as like-minded groups, seeking a refuge from the wickedness and injustices of the world, braved the wilderness in search of a better life. They soon penetrated beyond the New England and Middle Atlantic States to the Middle West and beyond into the Dakotas, Texas, Utah, Oregon, and California. By the end of the nineteenth century, the number of separate utopian communities ran into many hundreds. And now that our time is witness to a renewed proliferation of communes, the total number of such societies may well be numbered in the thousands.

Rosabeth Kanter suggests that the impulse to the founding of ideal societies is basically three-fold. The early ones drew their inspiration mainly from the Christian religion, using the Bible as their spiritual guide and mentor and the communism of the early Christian church as the model for their political and economic organization. Seventeenth-century Europe was full of heretical Christian separatist sects that found both the ecclesiastical and the political order of the prevailing world corrupt and immoral and that undertook to live as groups apart under the precepts of the Sermon on the Mount. Once America was colonized, many of these groups fled to the new land in the hope of finding a refuge from persecution, war, and class struggles and a place to live in peace and harmony. Because of William Penn's benign and tolerant Quaker rule, Pennsylvania in particular was a magnet to these religious societies. Dunkards, Moravians, the Amish and Mennonites, the Shakers (or Shaking Quakers), Seventeenth-Day Baptists, and other sects were attracted to Penn's domain. Once acclimated there they soon began founding new societies in other areas. The celibate Shakers were particularly successful in recruiting new members by means of the religious fervor generated at their great revival meetings. By 1830 they had founded eighteen societies embracing fifty-eight families with a total membership of over 5000.

The second major impulse to the founding of model communities is politico-economic. This type of motivation became a potent force in the mid-nineteenth century, as the Industrial Revolution with its mechanization, factory system, urbanization, labor exploitation, pauperism, and the despoilage of the environment became ever more apparent. While the spark of charismatic leadership was most often the power of fusion in the religious communities, ideas and social theory played a growing role among those groups whose primary aim was a juster and more humane social and economic order.  The intellectual and ethical ferment created by Rousseau's essays on the natural goodness of people and by the writings and tracts of the anarchists, socialists, and syndicalists--from Saint Simon and Fourier to Karl Marx and beyond--set people to thinking in new ways about property, community control of the means of production, equality, sharing, brotherhood, and a host of related social issues.

The third and historically most recent urge to the founding of ideal communities or communes as they are now known is, in Kanter's analysis, psycho-social.  The prevailing society is seen as forcing people to live an unnatural, competitive, depersonalized, and alienated existence that destroys the truly human potential in them.  The critique of "the establishment" sees it as sick and essentially dehumanizing, forcing people into roles that lead too often to neuroses, desperation, and suicide.  Contemporary communes undertake to start afresh by creating a new physical and social environment, one that attempts to eradicate the barriers to untrammeled human development and fosters a life of greater social intimacy and individual fulfillment.  The new social organism usually takes the form of an extended family.

While it is instructive to see the historical development of utopias in terms of successive stages defined by the predominating impulse--the first religious, followed by the politico-economic, and then the psycho-social--the dynamics of history always tend to overrun any such categorial interpretations.  The religiously founded utopias, whether early or late, obviously had to make some sort of provision for making a livelihood, and they were concerned also with establishing a viable, just, and caring interpersonal basis for community life.  On the other hand, many of the nineteenth-century utopias, which are studied today mainly for their politico-economic and social characteristics, were religious in inspiration.  The Rappites, the Oneida communities, the followers of Charles Fourier, and the Amana Colonies are cases in point.  The religious motivation is present also in many contemporary communes.  The Koinonia Farm near Americus, Georgia, founded by Clarence Jordan, a theologian-farmer, is an example, as is the other Koinonia referred to above.  In fact the religious element is seldom totally absent in the conception, founding, or conduct of ideal societies.
In Chapter 8, "The Spiritual Impetus to Community," John

Chamberlain makes a strong case to the effect that American utopias of the nineteenth and twentieth centuries, irrespective of whether the generative idea behind them was religious or secular, all owe their hope for a better society, wittingly or unwittingly, to the Biblical tradition, with its stress on the Kingdom of God to come and its vision of a new heaven and a new earth.

One of the ancient but still controversial problems that many utopias grapple with is the role of women. Some ideal societies undertake to redefine the sexual roles of men and women, the responsibilities and opportunities available to women, as well as the arrangements for the rearing, care, and nurture of children. Two of the essays in this volume are devoted to this timely subject. In Chapter 4, "Women in Utopia: The Nineteenth-Century Experience," Jean Harvey Baker probes the way in which three different utopian communities altered the conventional role of women and traces some of the consequences: the mandate of total celibacy among the Shakers, the shared sexuality and complex marriage practiced in the Oneida communities, and polygamy as practiced by the Mormons. And in Chapter 5, "Unconscious Sexual Stereotyping in Utopia," Carol Kolmerten undertakes to show that however much various utopias tried to restructure the institutions of marriage and the family, they were seldom able to escape for long the stereotype of "true womanhood" embedded in the established order, a point that is well illustrated by selected quotations from the rhetoric of Robert Owen's New Harmony Gazette.

Another topic of special interest in the literature of utopia is the role and influence of science in the conception, organization, and governance of ideal communities. From Sir Francis Bacon's New Atlantis to B. F. Skinner's Walden Two, advocates of science have urged the utilization of the vast body of scientific knowledge in the construction and management of utopias. But just how, and in what connections and to what end, this is to be done remains a matter of dispute. To many students of utopias, George Orwell's 1984 is a more probable assessment of the future application of science and technology than is Walden Two. Biologist Gairdner Moment undertakes to show in Chapter 3, "Man the Maker," the uses and limits of scientific knowledge as it applied to utopias and points to some extrapolations of scientific truths that should be taken into account. He points out that one cannot simply renounce the fruits of science and turn the calendar back to earlier, simpler ways, but must

learn how to apply and use them for humane and beneficial
ends.

The extent to which the town plans and architecture
of utopian communities afford special insights into their social philosophy is explored by Paul Douglas in Chapter 7,
"Town Planning for the City of God." He examines the
physical layout of the three villages occupied in succession
by the followers of George Rapp, known as the Rappites or
Harmonists, over the century from 1805 to 1904. An analysis of the three sites and the grouping, disposition, and
interrelationships of buildings devoted to housing, work
places, and community-wide functions at each site reveals
the significant social changes this utopian community under-
went through its long and generally prosperous history. The
author points out that the Harmonists, unlike other utopians
who aimed to cut their ties with the world they wished to
leave behind, realized from the start that in order to pros-
per the community must of necessity interact commercially
with the larger world. So the sites chosen for the villages
took into account not only the desire for a pleasant abode,
but the demands of a vigorous agriculture (they were chiefly
wine-growers) and of maintaining a vigorous two-way river
commerce.

A reminder that utopian thinking is not confined to
the conception and creation of small separatist ideal societies but is involved also in reformist economic thinking and
planning for nations and the world is found in Chapter 12,
"The Economics of Utopia," by Ronald Krieger. In it he
reviews various current theories of economic individualism
and collectivism in order to assess their potential for creating an internally consistent idealized system applicable to
society at large.

Similarly, in Chapter 9, "Imaginings and Dreams for
the Future," Jean Bradford, finding the blueprints for utopias too abstract, asks what kind of psychological changes in
human attitudes and in moral values are needed in order
that people in their daily concourse in the here and now can
achieve a deeper and more satisfying realization of their potential, both as individuals and as members of society. In
an intensely personal statement she delineates what she, as
a psychologist, considers to be requisite, personally and
communally, for the building of a good society.

That utopian experiments are not immune to a peculiar

pathology all their own is brought out by Gairdner Moment's chapter "From Utopia to Dystopia: The Jonestown Tragedy." Did this murderous episode mirror the savagery latent in the modern psyche or was it just a hideous freak of history? Utopias of the past and present that are inspired and held together by the personal power of a charismatic leader are peculiarly vulnerable because of their total dependence on the state of mind of a single person in the absence of any countervailing democratic power or sanction lodged in the community or its representatives. Moment assesses the grisly events at Jonestown, how and why they transpired, and what this horror of a utopia turned inside out signifies for the utopian movement as a whole.

The concluding essay, by Fontaine Belford, "Yester-day's Dream, Tomorrow's Necessity," raises the ominous question whether we have already set in motion those forces that will call the human experiment to a close, and whether we have lost the capacity to dominate our destiny. She points out that the literature of the past fifty years "has been marked by the emergence of a new sub-genre, the dystopian." And she sees vision and visionary activity not as a kind of gratuitous and dispensable pursuit--like day-dreaming or fantasy--but as the only force capable of carry-ing us to a world that is informed by new values and a new understanding of being.

"The history of these experiments," wrote Mark Hol-loway in summarizing two centuries of American utopian communities,

> is one of few successes, many failures, and con-stantly renewed endeavor. Only three or four communities have lasted longer than a hundred years. Many vanished within a few months of their foundation. But all have contributed some-thing of value, not only to the fund of experience upon which succeeding experiments of the same kind have relied, but also to the history of Ameri-can society. When they failed, going down before the advance of large-scale industry and "scientific" socialism, one of the most valuable qualities of revolutionary man suffered an eclipse from which it has not yet emerged.... It is better, perhaps, to be slightly mad with a sound heart, than to be sane without one. [3]

## Notes

[1]Not to be confused with an older community of the same name, founded on a farm near Americus, Georgia, in 1942.

[2]Commitment and Community--Communes and Utopias in Sociological Perspective (Cambridge, Mass.: Harvard University Press, 1972), p. 1.

[3]Heavens on Earth: Utopian Communities in America 1680-1880 (New York: Library Publishers, 1951), p. 19.

## II.  AMERICA:  SYMBOL OF A FRESH START

Otto F. Kraushaar

One of the salutary effects of the recent Bicentennial celebration, with its strange mixture of froth and substance, is
the thoughtful reflection it evoked about the American past--
the birth of the nation and its two centuries of tumultuous
history--all reviewed as a prelude to speculation about what
lies ahead.  The Bicentennial found Americans in a singular-
ly impressionable state of mind, rendered so by the sobering
memories of the Vietnam War and the constitutional crisis
precipitated by the Watergate affair.  It is a good time to
reflect on the innate human tendency to dream of a more
perfect world and to dwell on American dreams and blueprints for a better society.

I shall leave it to my colleagues in subsequent essays to delineate and interpret the visions and goals of specific utopian schemes.  My aim here is to ask why America
and Americans provided such a fertile soil for the germina-
tion and flowering of utopian ideas and communities.  What
was there about the American history and outlook that made
our people so hospitable to optimism and utopian dreams
and raised such great expectations?  Why did the millions
of immigrants flocking to these shores come here expecting
a new life, a brighter future, a better chance?  It is a
large and many-sided question; I can do no more than suggest some approaches to an answer.

Dreams of a better world, free of the imperfections,
the finiteness, and the corruptibility that hamper earthlings,
are as old as history.  Most often they have taken the form
of religious or utopian beliefs in a glorious afterlife, re-
served mainly for heroes and legendary figures worthy of a
lasting reward.  Thus, Homer's Elysian Fields, Plutarch's
Island of the Blest, the Mount Mero of Hindu lore, the El
Dorado of Spanish longing, the Happy Hunting Ground of the

11

American Indian, and the Shangri-la of recent popular fantasy. Others visualized the perfect world as a Golden Age
belonging to the hallowed past. In Plato's Dialogues Socra-
tes speaks of the lost island of Atlantis, renowned as the
cradle of civilization and supposed to have existed somewhere
westward beyond the pillars of Hercules. But by far the
most influential image of a more perfect past is presented
in the Old Testament. Adam and Eve are pictured living in
the Garden of Eden in a state of perfect innocence, enjoying
a spiritual plenitude and freedom from material concerns
never again realizable after the Fall. But there was also
the notion of the Promised Land of Canaan, "the land of
milk and honey," envisaged by "the chosen people" as the
hope of paradise to be regained, but only by dint of purifying suffering and moral striving.

Among the first of the utopian visionaries of modern
times who transmuted the myth of Eden into the dream of a
terrestial paradise was Sir Thomas More. As he was writing his Utopia in 1516 life in the England he knew was mis-
erably insecure and corrupt, and the common people had
little hope of a better life, other than the Christian promise
of life after death. Even that afforded little consolation, for
complementing the idea of a heavenly paradise for the saint-
ly was the idea of hell painted in lurid, fiendish colors--a
fit depository for souls consigned to the torment of eternal
damnation. The sixteenth century was a period of theological strife and severe economic maladjustment, and the possibility that life on earth could be made more secure and
rewarding seemed remote.

Realizing that a frontal attack on the evils of government and society would be useless, More resorted to political satire. His ideal commonwealth is a picture of England
as it should be, but situated on an imaginary island, westward beyond the setting sun, to which he gave the Greek
name "utopia," meaning literally "nowhere" or "no place."
The institutions and conduct of the utopians are in effect an
attack on avaricious tyrants, the exploitation of labor, the
acquisitiveness of the rich, the inequities of the criminal
law, religious dogmatism and intolerance, and the perfidy
of international diplomacy.

The melancholy assessment of the human prospect
prevailing during the sixteenth century brightened dramatically during the seventeenth and eighteenth centuries, and in the
process the pursuit of terrestial happiness and material

Amana, a general view

welfare became detached from its former religious associations. A sense of the magnitude and importance of this shift in human attitudes respecting the future may be gained from this passage of a letter written by Benjamin Franklin during the Revolutionary War to his English scientific friend, Joseph Priestley: "It is impossible to imagine," he wrote, "the heights to which may be carried, in a thousand years, the power of mind over matter. We may perhaps learn to deprive large masses of their gravity and give them absolute levity, for the sake of easy transport. Agriculture may diminish its labor and double its produce; all diseases may by sure means be prevented or cured, not excepting that of old age, and our lives lengthened at pleasure even beyond the antediluvian standard." Then he adds, "O that moral science were in a fair way of improvement, that men would cease to be wolves to one another, and that human beings would at length learn what they now improperly call humanity."[1]

As we know, Franklin's confidence that the march of science would revolutionize humanity's control over its environment and thus reduce human toil and render life healthier, longer, pleasanter, and more secure has been confirmed in large part long before the expiration of "a thousand years." That interesting bit of speculation about neutralizing the force of gravity has thus far escaped the scientists, although rocket ships, space exploration, and air transport generally are a close approximation to what Franklin evidently had in mind. The caveat in all this remarkably prescient optimism is the nature of humanity itself, and in this, too, Franklin was truly prophetic.

The detailed delineation of how the momentous shift in the human outlook took place, from the melancholia of the late medieval period to the confident hope of better days ahead as typified in Franklin's optimism, fills many large volumes in the history of ideas. But it is of such importance in lending perspective that I propose to dwell, even if sketchily, on selected highlights of this pregnant transition. Three broad developments that help to explain the growth of optimism and utopian expectations are singled out: first, the image of the New World as it appeared during the Renaissance and later; second, the continuing role of religion in the development of utopian schemes; and third, how the rise of science affected the outlook for the human future.

The image of the New World that was current during the Renaissance arose out of strange and wonderful accounts of explorers returning from voyages of discovery. In a book entitled O Strange New World Howard Mumford Jones suggests that the cultural history of America begins with the letter Christopher Columbus wrote on a pleasant February day in 1493 during his homeward journey aboard the Niña. Published in Barcelona, it was soon translated, illustrated, and circulated widely in the capitals of Europe. The voyages of Columbus were the culmination of two centuries of maritime exploration, all guided by the shadowy geography and speculative cartography of the time. Long before Columbus sailors returned from uncharted seas bearing tales of dreamlike islands in the vastnesses of the Atlantic. The island stories often pictured inhabitants who enjoyed great wealth and superior wisdom and lived together in perfect innocence and concord. In the embroidery of these stories the islanders live longer and are happier, drudgery is unknown, the soil is more fertile, the weather is more salubrious, and the inhabitants are nearer God than are the peoples of the known world.

The picture of arcadian bliss that Columbus and other explorers, such as Amerigo Vespucci, painted of life on the island of Hispaniola, the modern Haiti, and elsewhere, had a profound effect on the European imagination. Whatever virtues Columbus may have possessed, reportorial accuracy was not among them. His account of the native "Indians," as he called them in the belief that he had landed somewhere in Asia, as he had intended, is a melange of classical, pastoral, chivalric, and biblical virtues read into the tribal folkways of primitive island people. Columbus even reported the singing of nightingales, a species unknown in the New World. But the picture of the naked, innocent, guileless, generous, peaceable, happy natives of the West Indies lingered for centuries in the European mythology of the New World.

There was, of course, another less felicitous side to the American image that came to light. The mirage of fabulous riches awaiting the voyager soon tarnished the picture of perfection. Wild tales of gold, silver, pearls, and precious stones to be had palpably for the mere labor of gathering them, aroused the greed of Europeans and propelled adventurers into coarse and murderous forays under the leadership of daring conquistadors. As these are related in the pages of Prescott's romantic histories of the conquest of Mexico and Peru, they constitute a record of treachery, cruelty, enslavement, and degradation that casts a sinister shadow over the earthly paradise. Even so, the association of fabled wealth with the New World persisted for centuries. It was crassly used in promotions designed to lure immigrants to America even in the eighteenth century. And it lingers on in the belief abroad that all American tourists are rich.

Second thoughts about the New Eden were provoked also when it became evident that by no means all the aborigines lived in blissful innocence and harmony. Encounters with cannibals, ritual human sacrifice, torture, treachery, and massacre were inevitable as the European culture came into conflict with the mores of primitive tribes. To most American settlers the unpredictable Indians became objects of permanent distrust, and it was only after the tribes had been cruelly despoiled of their land and driven into reservations that the Indian became once again "the noble savage."

The fear and terror of the Indian was augmented by tales of weird, horrendous phenomena in the seas and on the land of the New World. The sightings of huge icebergs, giant tortoises, immense predatory fish, as well as sudden violent storms, struck terror into the hearts of even the most intrepid sailor. Evidently the legendary Bermuda Triangle was giving a good account of itself, then as now. And those who ventured into the trackless interior brought back reports of crocodiles and other loathsome reptiles, of roaring rivers and thundering waterfalls, of dark and impenetrable forests and immense open spaces, of debilitating extremes of heat and cold, and of tornados, earthquakes, and a blood-red Aurora Borealis. America seemed to the fainthearted a land where everything goes to dangerous extremes, a land of strange, hideous, and monstrous natural phenomena.

The powerful anti-image of America repelled and terrified but also fascinated European observers of the American scene during the Renaissance and the ensuing centuries. It helps to explain why the colonization of even the temperate eastern shores of the New World was so slow in getting under way. The anti-image persisted, with changing forms and symbols, as the United States evolved into a radical democratic republic spanning the continent and then into a major world power. European visitors, such as Mrs. Trollope and Charles Dickens, saw the America of the mid-nineteenth century as a vulgar, lawless, avaricious, crude, provincial society utterly lacking in refinement and cultivation, and with few redeeming features. The United States was viewed abroad with something of that mingled feeling of hope and revulsion that we nowadays reserve for the Soviet Union. And at home the repellent anti-image was interpreted by literary critics as a pre-Freudian premonition of that dark night of the American soul that is reflected later in the works of Poe, Melville, Hawthorne, Henry James, and William Faulkner.

Whether the New World was regarded as a wondrous new dawn of hope and fulfillment or as a squalid, desperate nightmare, it is plain that people were ready to be credulous about America, one way or the other. The early settlers and the immigrants who followed naturally inclined to the benign myth rather than the nightmare. "They were," in the words of Marcus Lee Hansen, "Americans before they started." Once the years of extreme hardship and privation were behind them and life became more secure and expansive, they rejoiced in the opportunity to build a new life in untrammeled surroundings. And though they felt culturally inferior to the older nations of Europe, once the Constitution was in effect they were quick to contrast the liberty of the New World with the despotism of the Old.

The contrast between the Old and the New was a dominant theme in the populist literature of the Revolution and persisted until well into the twentieth century. Europe, Catholic Europe in particular, was presented as the fallen

land in contrast with the New World paradise. Europe is
denounced as the seat of effete refinement, arid intellectual-
ism, of degenerate monarchy, and of corruption and debauch-
ery. Thomas Jefferson, steeped as he was in French culture, nevertheless warns against sending young Americans to
Europe to be educated. "No American should come to Europe," he wrote, "under thirty years of age: and [he who]
does, will lose in science, in virtue, in health and in happiness, for which manners are a poor compensation, were we
even to admit the hollow, unmeaning manners of Europe to
be preferable to the simplicity and sincerity of our own
country.... "[2] Jefferson envisaged America as an agrarian
utopia, a nation exemplifying simplicity in its government
and undergirded by the virtues of the free, sturdy yeoman.
These sentiments were echoed not only by many of his contemporaries, such as Tom Paine, but later by Ralph Waldo
Emerson, who in his influential lectures and essays enjoined
his fellow Americans to "flee the courtly muses of Europe."
By that time the contrast between Europe as a special kind
of artificial and decadent hell and the heaven of free, self-
reliant American individualism had been transmuted into a
fundamental article of national faith and the premise of
America's messianic mission: The Redeemer Nation, charged
with the regeneration of humankind by spreading the gospel
of democracy.

The inner thrust of this American idealism is the
commitment to the idea of the indefinite perfectibility of
men and women. It was an aspect of the American ideology
that provided a fertile soil for utopian thinking and for social, political, and economic reform. Alexis de Tocqueville,
the most open-minded of the many European commentators on
American democracy, maintained that while the idea of perfectibility is "as old as the world," in the United States it
had taken on a new character as a result of its association
with the ideal of equality. "In proportion as castes disappear
and the classes of society draw together," he wrote, "as
customs and laws vary, because of tumultuous intercourse of
men, as new facts arise, as new truths are brought to light,
as ancient opinions are dissipated ... the image of the ideal
but always fugitive perfection presents itself to the human
mind." And he concludes: "Aristocratic nations are naturally too liable to narrow the scope of human perfectibility;
democratic nations, to expand it beyond reason. "[3]

We have dwelt thus far on certain traits of the developing American image that attracted millions to these

shores and stimulated them, once here, to dream of human betterment. The utopians in the precise sense have been at all times only a tiny fraction of the whole. The early settlers came here not so much in search of utopia as from a desire to worship as they pleased or for economic gain. The hardships imposed by life in colonial America quickly dispelled any hope they might have entertained of utopia as an immediate goal. Among the immigrants who arrived during the eighteenth and nineteenth centuries, the number who were interested in experimental communities was always a small part of the total, and most of these were members of religious communities. As the problems of industrialization in the second third of the nineteenth century mounted, Europe became alive with schemes of human betterment. Some of these, such as Robert Owen's ideal industrial community and Fourier's phalanxes, became blueprints for utopian communities in the United States. After the Civil War, however, utopian schemes were largely homegrown affairs, and their authors or instigators were native, or second or third generation Americanized progeny of immigrants.

The point is worth stressing because of the long-standing view that the immigrant population in the United States has been and continues to be the main source of radical ideas. In The Immigrant in American History, Marcus Lee Hansen shows persuasively this is a misreading of recent American history. Relatively few of the immigrants who came to these shores after 1850 showed any interest in the experimental communities. The typical immigrants were radical only in their belief in individualism. What they wanted above all was the freedom to seek opportunity, wherever it beckoned, and to make good. They were all for free enterprise. Native Americans, however, had seen enough of unregulated free enterprise and resulting social imbalances to set them to thinking about better ways. And while European reformers sought a remedy in socializing the state, American utopians were more inclined to long for a return to the simple agrarian life.

Another facet of American life that strongly affected the nature and direction of utopian thinking was the religious factor. Most of the utopian schemes proposed during the eighteenth and nineteenth centuries were religious in inspiration. The aim was commonly that of building a perfect community exemplifying Christian principles, or the way of Jesus. Naturally, all such communities had to make provision for a livelihood, and so they became involved in economic planning. The religiously inspired communities had somewhat greater staying power than those whose main concern was the building of a more equitable economic order, chiefly because religious communities succeeded better in controlling human selfishness and greed, which were most commonly the undoing of utopias that relied on human reason, moral enlightenment, or community loyalty alone.

For example, New Harmony, Indiana, founded in 1825 by Robert Owen, the British philanthropist, socialist, and reformer, had only a brief and rather inharmonious career. But the seven colonies of the Amana Society, settled in 1855 near Iowa City, Iowa, by members of the Community of True Inspiration, an offshoot of a seventeenth-century German religious sect, is still in existence, though in modified form. Beginning as a closed, communal, agrarian society devoted to sheep raising and weaving the well-remembered Amana blankets, it has evolved recently into an industrial corporation that manufactures and markets air conditioners, refrigerators, and microwave ovens under the Amana label.

What was there about religious life in America that attracted so many utopian thinkers and experimental communities? To begin with, from early colonial times until recently America has been dominated by a strong Protestant majority. This fact was of particular importance in defining the character and ideals of American institutions. Protestantism, it will be recalled, began in Martin Luther's defiance of papal authority and his defense of the right of the individual conscience. What he protested against was the immense authority of Rome, which at the time was blamed for all the ills of society, social and moral, as well as religious. But Luther's dramatic refusal to recant had long-range consequences that he did not foresee. Others, too, could challenge authority, including Luther's, on the basis of conscience, and soon did so. A century after Luther's death there were some 180 Protestant sects and denominations, each dogmatically justifying its position on biblical authority. The basic principle of Protestantism soon spilled over into other life concerns and the Protestants thus played a leading role, often willy-nilly, in the growth of free thought, the rise of democracy, the sponsorship of education, and the spread of the industrial revolution.

In America the impact of Protestantism in these areas was delayed by the circumstances of the colonial

settlements. Some Protestant sects, persecuted in the Old
World for their religious convictions, migrated to America
in order to worship in freedom. But once settled in politically organized communities of believers they brooked no
heresies and persecuted nonconformists. The banishment
of Roger Williams and Anne Hutchinson, and the persecution
of Quakers and Catholics by the Holy Commonwealth of
Massachusetts and other colonies, are prime illustrations.
Only under William Penn's benign rule in Pennsylvania was
there a semblance of religious toleration. The colonies
taken together did not constitute a truly pluralistic society;
they were more like a collection of separate and somewhat
hostile sectarian nations eyeing each other at a safe distance.

But by the eve of the Revolution sectarian groups had
become so numerous that even the established churches were
failing dismally to control dissent. With the ratification of
the First Amendment and the disestablishment of the old
colonial church-states, the shape of American Protestantism
changed radically. Bereft of the sanction of public authority, the denominations were cast in the role of voluntary
associations having to resort to persuasion and aggressive
proselytizing in order to survive. As a consequence sectarian groups became dynamic agents in the spread of education and in schemes for human betterment and social reform. In the freer air of toleration the fissioning of American Protestantism into more and more denominations and
sects went on apace. Many of the groups thus formed became important centers of social action and initiative.

One outcome of this splintering process was the
emergence, during the nineteenth century, of the so-called
"third force" in Christendom, a group of adventist, fundamentalist, and holiness sects owing their origin usually to
special revelations, visions, or sudden conversions, or re-
birth through evangelical revivals. They are receiving some
unaccustomed publicity just now because of the public's interest in Jimmy Carter's religious convictions. The "third-
force" label points to the fact that they do not identify with
either Catholics or Protestants, though historically most are
departures from or schisms of Protestant bodies. Of special interest in this connection is the belief in and confident
expectation of an approaching apocalypse that will usher in a
glorious millennium. The millennialist faith in the coming of
a New Heaven and a New Earth tended to coalesce with
utopian dreams of a golden age for the Republic. The feeling

that great and wonderful events were impending penetrated
deeply into the national consciousness, far beyond the confines of the various millennialist religious groups.  The
apocalyptic trumpet sounded its most stirring note in Julia
Ward Howe's "The Battle Hymn of the Republic," filled with
the imagery and metaphors of a titanic struggle with a glorious outcome in prospect:

> "Mine eyes have seen the glory of the coming of the
>     Lord:
> He is trampling out the vintage where the grapes of
>     wrath are stored;
> He hath loosed the fateful lightning of his terrible
>     swift sword:
> His truth is marching on. "

Believers in the millennium were divided between
those who, like the Millerites, Shakers, Jehovah's Witnesses, and Mormons, believed God's direct intervention would
establish a divinely ruled state, and the so-called "progressive millennialists, " who believed that the good is destined
to triumph according to God's plan and that this world will
thus fulfill the Christian mission.  Millennialists of the first
kind believe the world to be inherently evil and the role of
the faithful is to succor its victims until the great day of
Redemption arrives; while the progressive millennialists are
fundamentally optimistic about the earthly course of events.

Spurred by the Homestead Act of 1862 millennialist
groups joined the massive westward movement, doubly motivated by the search for a new Zion and for the garden
utopia that haunted the imagination of writers about the New
West.  The linkage of Christian utopian groups with agrar-
ianism is not surprising in view of their long tutelage in the
Bible.  The Hebrew tribes of the Old Testament were simple agrarian folk, elevated to the role of a chosen people by
virtue of a covenant with God, under which they would enter
the Promised Land of Canaan.  In the Garden of Eden all is
innocent nakedness in an arcadian setting, reflecting the
agrarian orientation of the Hebrew peoples and their distrust
of sophisticated urban cultures.  From the mouths of the
prophets issue severe indictments of cities:  Sodom, Gomor-
rah, Babylon, the Egyptian cities, the old Jerusalem even;
all are symbols of lust, wealth, corruption, and sinfulness.
And in the New Testament, Jesus, the son of a carpenter,
is born in a manger in rural Bethlehem, and as he matures
he associates much with fishermen, shepherds, and children.

The animals that appear in the imagery of the Old and New Testaments are the guileless kind: lambs, donkeys, doves, hares, and fawns. A snake appears as the very personification of evil. It is small wonder, then, that for devout Christians caught up in the westward movement the idea of utopia would necessarily take on the agrarian mode of life described in the Bible. "He maketh me to lie down in green pastures: he leadeth me beside the still waters."

Another respect in which Protestantism influenced the visions of utopia, as it did the social outlook of Americans generally, is through the well-known Protestant Ethic of hard work, thrift, piety, and sobriety. The Christian dream of an earthly paradise was not so much one of material abundance to be enjoyed as of a stress on diligent labor in the Lord's vineyard. In the context of Calvinism work was seen as a means not only of furthering good and useful ends, but as a way of meriting God's grace. Since hard labor was in any case an unavoidable necessity in new communities bent on hewing a living out of the raw wilderness, Calvinism was well adapted to their needs. And since the burdens of toil in a communal utopia are usually expected to be shared by all, a doctrine that lent dignity and divine sanction to even the humblest work served as an added spur above and beyond the imperatives of survival.

What can happen when such higher motivation is lacking is amusingly illustrated by Hawthorne's experience at Brook Farm. An unlikely candidate for such an experiment, he did spend some months there after losing his job at the Boston Customs House, and made some wry comments about his experiences. After a month devoted to spreading manure from what seemed a never-ending pile, he wrote his Sophia: "That abominable goldmine! Of all hateful places, that is the worst.... It is my opinion, dearest, that a man's soul may be buried and perish under a dung-heap or in a furrow of the field, just as well as under a pile of money."[4]

The basic traits of religiously founded utopias in the United States are exemplified by the odyssey of the Mormons, or more correctly the Church of Jesus Christ of the Latter-day Saints. The Mormons are not commonly thought of as utopians, partly because they encountered so much tragedy during their fifteen-year wanderings from Palmyra, New York, to the valley of the Great Salt Lake, not unlike the wandering tribes of Israel in search of the Promised Land. It began in 1831 with a succession of divine revelations

opened to Joseph Smith, a farmer's son, disclosing to him
the golden tablets containing the Book of Mormon. After
gathering converts rapidly and organizing his church, the
group began the perilous journey in search of the New Zion,
where Christ would reign after his return to earth. They
settled first at Kirtland, Ohio, moved thence to Jackson
County, Missouri, and from there to Nauvoo, Illinois, en-
countering at each stay a growing degree of hostility from
their neighbors, based partly on the practice of polygamy,
though there were other grounds also. Finally, at Nauvoo
Joseph Smith and his brother were assassinated by an angry
mob, and the group was threatened with extermination if it
remained.

At that point Brigham Young came forward as the
second prophet-leader. His proposal to migrate to the Far
West beyond the reach of an unfriendly civilization met with
joyful acceptance, and in early 1847 a picked band of stal-
warts set out as a scouting party in search of the New Eden.
They reached the Salt Lake flats by midsummer and set to
work at once tilling the soil and making ready for those who
had been left behind, who soon joined them. Seeing that
many more hands were needed in addition to the 1500 survivors of the overland journey, the elders of the church
dispatched missionaries to the eastern states and Europe to
make converts and bring back helpers.

Brigham Young soon displayed a remarkable talent
for leadership and the administration of economic affairs.
Steering a steady course between the pitfalls of communism
and the hazards of disruptive individualism, Young directed
the community to a degree of material prosperity far beyond
that of other similar ventures. Speculators and profiteers
were firmly restrained, and effective blocks were placed in
the way of the accumulation of large private fortunes by establishing a cooperative commonwealth, including a commonly owned store and irrigation works, with profits going into
a common fund to finance new ventures. The community as
a whole, even after being exposed to all the temptations of
western life and the brawling ways of the gold-rush adventurers passing through, was marked by industry, sobriety,
frugality, temperance, and moderation.

But as the Mormon utopia became a success story
and the people spread to many parts of the country, the
pentacostal fervor of the early days subsided, the Mother
Church grew rich, and individual Mormons amassed large
fortunes and became worldly minded.

The third major historical development that conditions the conception and goals of American utopias is the scientific revolution. As the nineteenth century wore on, science and associated advances in technology, invention, and industry conjured up bold new hopes of a golden age in the Here and Now rather than in some far-off divine event. Marvelous developments in mathematics, new instruments of navigation, the printing press, machines for spinning and weaving cotton, the steam engine, and a flood of other inventions raised the hope that a totally new dispensation in human affairs lay just ahead. Machines would alleviate toil, conquer time and space, minister to human comfort, health, and leisure, and enable humanity to control its environment. And in time an even more promising hope of progress lay in the expectation that the application of the scientific method would bring about advances not only in the tools and machines men and women use, but in men and women themselves, by improving not only their nurture but their very nature.

These heady expectations grew out of the fundamental reinterpretation that the early scientists and Enlightenment savants made of the concepts of Nature and Reason. Nature, which in the Christian scheme of salvation carried connotations of imperfection and potential evil, was transformed into a benign concept by the Enlightenment philosophers. Sir Isaac Newton demonstrated convincingly that in the realm of cosmology Nature works according to elegantly simple mechanical laws. By means of Reason he transmuted the "music of the spheres" of the ancient philosophers into a system of mathematical notation. And John Locke undertook to show that a reasoning approach to humankind and its social institutions can clear up the superstitions, false assumptions, and unfounded beliefs that stand in the way of progress.

These ideas, filtering down into the minds and thoughts of people coping with their everyday problems, provoked a powerful sense of optimism regarding the future potential of human life. Not only were they basic to the philosophy of the American Declaration of Independence and the Constitution, they functioned as a new charter of freedom in assessing the future of humankind.

Sir Francis Bacon, a herald of the scientific revolution, was also one of the first to sketch a utopia in which science would reign supreme and scientists would usurp the place of the philosopher-king in Plato's Republic. The brave new world of Bacon's New Atlantis (1627), an engineer's

dream, envisaged a state organized and governed by experts
who have at their disposal the latest in mechanization and
invention. The Lord Chancellor prophetically anticipated
airplanes, submarines, clocks, engines, drugs for various
uses, and other marvels for the conquest of nature. Drawing on his experience in the world of administration, Bacon
stressed the need for a plan of action for scientific development. He foresaw subsidized research, scientific specialization, professional journals, international congresses, and
other paraphernalia for the promotion and propagation of
science. And he saw the scientists of the future as forming
a community transcending class, nation, and religious loy-
alties. But it was not in Bacon's makeup nor in the spirit
of his time to be greatly concerned over the lot of the common people. Doubtless, they too would be beneficiaries of
scientific progress, but only as those living in the benign
dictatorship of their more gifted superiors.

More than two and a half centures later Edward
Bellamy was advocating a more domesticated version of a
utopia that would capitalize on the intervening advances in
science and industry. Bellamy spoke not as a scientist but
as a humanist with a village mentality, a man with a lively
appreciation of the pathos of everyday life. In his novel
Looking Backward--2000-1877, published in 1888, he undertook to awaken his contemporaries to a sense of the democratic progress that might be realized through a more
equitable, systematic, and planned use of the nation's resources and inventive talents. The book was read by millions of people in this country and abroad and is still in
demand. Bellamy wrote as an idealist with an abiding faith
in the moral potential of the average man and woman and a
deep sense of compassion for the poverty and suffering he
saw around him. Although he was experienced neither in
economics nor in politics, he was a lifelong student of both,
schooled by the need to delineate and then to defend his
utopia from a host of critics.

For those who may not be familiar with Looking
Backward, let me say that it tells the story of Julien West,
a young and affluent Bostonian who hibernates for 113 years.
Awakening in the year 2000 still in the full vigor of youth,
he gazes in amazement at the simplicity, efficiency, and
humanely administered justice of the new system that developed during his long sleep. Explanations of the workings
of the new order, and the weighing of its basic virtues in
contrast with the misery of the world of 1887, constitutes

the heart of the book. Since the year 2000 now looms
ahead as the object of so many turn-of-the-century conjec-
tures and assessments, Bellamy's utopian fantasy once again
holds a peculiar interest.

While there is not time to describe Bellamy's proposed reorganization of society adequately, a brief characterization may be in order. He finds the key to a more
equitable, just, and humane society in the redistribution of
wealth and labor. Starting from the premise that equality
is the vital, basic principle of democracy, he traces existing inequalities--wealth and poverty, leisure and toil, superiority and subservience--to the competition inherent in the
capitalist system as he knew it in 1887. He proposes in its
place a thoroughly socialized national state using as its pro-
totype or model the modern military system, redirected to
meet human needs with clock-like perfection. People are
allotted work on the basis of ability, but all alike are paid
the universal state stipend of $4000 per year. Such was
Bellamy's faith in the inherent decency of the common people, he believed that once the root of social inequalities had
been destroyed, the concern for the common good and love
of duty would motivate them to devote their best energies
unselfishly to the assigned tasks. The approach to utopia
is through education, which Bellamy sees as something owed
to the community, so that each citizen may develop his or
her talents to serve the public good most effectively.

Bellamy's democratic socialism is of the homegrown
American variety. There is no evidence that he read even
a page of Karl Marx or other socialist works by the time
he wrote Looking Backward. The book so captured the imagination of a large segment of the American middle class
that "Bellamy Clubs" sprang up in all parts of the country.
It is said that a few still exist. One of their first objec-
tives was the nationalization of the public utility companies.
The Populist uprisings of the nineties and the swing toward
government regulation of banking, commerce, transportation,
communication, the stock market, and monopolies generally
owed much to Bellamy's inspiration.

To some conservatives of 1976 Bellamy's United
States of the year 2000 probably looks more like a national
chamber of horrors than a utopia. It is not surprising that
he raised a chorus of critics, satirical novels, and other
literary outbursts. But one is prone to miss the point if
Bellamy's keen sense of the dire need for social and economic

reforms in his time is left out of the reckoning. The
Americans of Bellamy's generation were passing through an
exceedingly troublesome period. Agrarian revolt was in the
air; the South was moving backward from Emancipation to
Jim Crowism; strikes, labor unrest, and violence were common; monopolies and "malefactors of great wealth" were
running wild; corruption in government was widespread; and
for the rank and file the time was hard and frought with
critical uncertainties. Samuel Eliot Morison said about the
time, "American society appeared to be in a state of dis-
solution."[5] Something had to be done.

The progressive philosophy of government that lay
behind Theodore Roosevelt's "Square Deal," Woodrow Wilson's "New Freedom," and Franklin Roosevelt's "New Deal"
was a response to the fact that, as industrial production became more complex, interdependent, and indispensable,
limits to the free action of powerful individuals and corporations had to be set by the government in the interests of
justice and social harmony. Bellamy's utopian reflections
were instrumental in raising and defining the problem, even
though his ultimate solution may strike some critics as a
benign version of George Orwell's dystopian 1984.

From the perspective we now have in looking back
over the events of the turbulent twentieth century, we can
see that Bellamy's solution--a superstate that would regu-
late life down to its minute details--has not only lost its
appeal but looms as a serious threat to the freedom men
and women cherish. The advent of totalitarianism provided
a grisly demonstration of how the fruits of science and
technology, which in earlier times were hailed as instruments of human liberation, can be turned against people
and make of existence a hellish nightmare. The literature
of the world since the Second World War owes more to disillusionment than to dreams of utopia, and so dystopias and
anti-utopian novels abound. B. F. Skinner's Walden Two is
one of the exceptions, but because of its reliance on behavioral engineering, even though it be in a beneficent cause,
the book enjoys only a limited appeal. The books that capture the public's attention are more often novels of lost illusions, betrayal, and cynicism. The theme is not so much
progress decried, as progress realized; like the place re-
served in Dante's Hell for the damned who get exactly what
they most zealously desired, only to find it is all ashes.
And so, as a character in Orwell's 1984 says, "The earthly
paradise had been abandoned exactly at the moment when it
became realizable."

I believe, nevertheless, we can affirm with a good measure of confidence that today's world is in many respects a better world than that of our ancestors. The world we live in, so much of which we take for granted, would surely be a world of miracles to our forebears-- miracles of communication, of speedy transport, an unprecedentedly high standard of living for most (though not all), of accessibility to health and education, and to a wide and rich range of cultural experiences. But the human appetite grows by what it feeds on. Every step forward in the march of progress provokes a reassessment and a raising of the sights. And so our dreams always outdistance those not only of our forebears, but our own of yesterday, simply because every actualization evokes new dreams of possibilities.

And there is another fly in the ointment. The realization of our dreams seldom yields to the full the anticipated satisfaction. Either our anticipations prove to have been exaggerated, or we are quickly satiated and take the new benefits for granted, or--and this is the greatest hazard of all--we find that each new achievement disturbs the old balance and thus exacts a price in the form of adjustments, some of them painful.

And that, I suppose, is why so many Americans, outwardly living lives that our forebears could only envy, feel let down, frustrated, cheated, outraged, or resentful. The garden that America once was in our romantic idealization of the past, and the New Eden that science and progress were to bring, turn inexorably, like Oscar Wilde's picture of Dorian Gray, into a loathsome wasteland.

But this is only another way of saying what the philosophers have said since ancient times: It is the pathos of human existence to strive for perfection, while in our finiteness we are condemned to fall always short of our aim.

## Notes

[1]Quoted in Charles A. Beard and Mary R. Beard, The Rise of American Civilization (New York: Macmillan, 1930), Vol. 1, pp. 455-56.

[2]Quoted by H. M. Jones, op. cit., p. 297.

[3]Democracy in America. Edited by Phillips Bradley (New York: Alfred A. Knopf, 1945), Vol. II, p. 34.

[4]The Heart of Hawthorne's Journals, Newton Arvin, ed. (Boston and New York: Houghton Mifflin, 1929), pp. 3-4.

[5]The Oxford History of the American People (New York: Oxford University Press, 1965), p. 795.

## Bibliography

Jones, Howard Mumford. O Strange New World (New York: Viking, 1964).

Parrington, Vernon Louis, Jr. American Dreams, 2nd ed. (New York: Russell & Russell, 1964).

Sanford, Charles L. The Quest for Paradise (Urbana: University of Illinois Press, 1961).

Tuveson, Ernest Lee. Redeemer Nation (Chicago and London: University of Chicago Press, 1968).

### III.  MAN THE MAKER

Gairdner B.  Moment

Humankind has been characterized in innumerable ways.
Charles Darwin in his Descent of Man called us "the wonder
and glory of the universe." A contemporary writer sees us
as "naked apes" and rather vicious ones at that. For an
ordinary zoologist the designation of humans as "toolmakers"
serves well. Perhaps "fire makers" would be an even better definition, because the use of fire as a tool makes a
cleaner break between us and our animal relatives, some of
whom can be said to use tools. Jane van Lawick-Goodall,
for example, has observed chimpanzees using a piece of
straw to catch edible ants. Although human tool making is
also the outgrowth of a mind, brain if you insist, it is the
outgrowth of a mind that so far surpasses all others that
we constitute an evolutionary breakthrough into a new order
of existence.

We are also as inescapably social as a swarm of
bees or a troop of baboons. "A lone baboon is a dead
baboon" runs an old African proverb. The same holds for a
bee. The human condition was well put by John Donne: "No
man is an island ... every man is a piece of the continent,
a part of the main." But there is an enormous gulf between
human societies and those of even our nearest primate relatives, "our little brothers" as St. Francis would have called
them. Their social structure is characteristic of a species
with minimal flexibility. There is no such thing as an "intentional society." Rousseau's "social contract" is incon-
ceivable among them.

Look at the primates, the most diverse order of
mammals, and the one to which Homo sapiens belongs.
Compare chimpanzees with gibbons. The chimps are gre-
garious, very loosely organized, promiscuous, somewhat
rambunctious, and with a very vague, if any, feeling for

territoriality.   In marked contrast the gibbons live in solitary pairs.   Each pair is widely separated from the others
and will fight off intruders of either sex.   Compare these
two species with baboons, which live in tightly organized
troops each ruled by a clique (committee is too polite a
term) of dominant males who cooperate with each other to
maintain themselves in power.   Then there are the well-
studied howler monkeys of tropical America, which live in
female-led packs and are highly conscious of territoriality.

To what extent these species differences are due to
genetically inherited behavioral factors and to what extent to
the social environment in which the young are raised is unknown.   What is known is that these social patterns are not
the subjects of symposia or protest marches among these
non-tool-making primates but remain characteristic of each
species.   They are not the products of intentional planning
or design.   Much the same appears to be true of primitive
human societies, defined by Margaret Mead as societies
without the use of metals or a written language.   Their
potential for assimilating or adopting alternative cultures of
course is very great.

The major evolutionary event of the present age is
the confluence, or collision, of the toolmakers' creative
minds and the unthinking traditional society in which they
live.   It has been so at least since Plato was resident in
Athens, which to an evolutionary zoologist is a mere yesterday afternoon.   This turning of the manipulative intellect to
focus on society appears to a zoologist as the central
biological fact about the present human situation, not some
question about a territorial imperative, the universality of
peck orders, the omega point of evolution, or whether we
are men-apes or ape-men.

## The American Scene

America has long been a symbol of a new and better life
for those who came to our shores.   It was here that the
mind of the toolmakers seemed to have a golden opportunity
to fashion a society closer to their highest aspirations.
Yet somehow the great expectations of our forebears, who
believed they were bringing forth "a new order of the centuries" in 1776, has been realized only in part.   We still
make that claim, though obscured in Latin, on our dollar
bills, but somehow the passionate conviction has cooled.

True, many people from diverse parts of the world have greatly improved their fortunes in the New World. More important, we enjoy a measure of freedom of expression in the arts, religion, and science and in social and economic opinions that is quite impossible in many areas of our planet. Yet it remains painfully obvious that, in this turbulent world, we have fallen far short of establishing the "Heavenly City."

A widely pervasive fact of contemporary life is a profound, even violent, dissatisfaction with things-as-they-are combined with an astounding explosion of scientific knowledge and technology with more to come. We may not be about to enter a new era of human history, as Barbara Tuchman and some other historians believe, but there can be little doubt that the future will differ widely from the past. Most modern historians, while admitting the inevitability of change, seem even less able to guide us or predict the future than the Oracle at Delphi. She at least offered us conundrums. The sad truth is that too many historians follow the nihilistic tradition of Charles A. Beard. Specifically, they hold that history is essentially subjective, a fascinating tale, but what is told changes with every generation because every generation sees the past in a different way. A natural scientist would reply yes, of course, what any investigator in any field looks at and sees is determined by a host of factors that will vary from individual to individual and from age to age. Nevertheless, who can doubt that science is not only open-ended but also cumulative? Even Newton said very plainly that his achievements were possible only because he stood on the shoulders of a host of predecessors. The whole scientific enterprise is founded on the firm conviction that it is possible to learn from past experience.

Happily, Americans have had a long and diverse experience with communities established to bring into being the ideal society. One of the earliest was begun in the 1630's, when Roger Williams and Anne Hutchinson left the Massachusetts Colony to found a new community on the shores of Narragansett Bay in what is now the state of Rhode Island. This community was based on the new principles of religious freedom and of the democracy of one man, one vote. It was a tiny group, but, significantly for this study, what they did there has had a profound influence on American history ever since. And ever since, Americans have been busy founding ideal communities. In the light of the influence of the little

Map showing location of communistic societies

Rhode Island experiments, it seems reasonable to suppose that important insights for the future welfare of us all might be gained from examining the experiences of our grass-roots utopias.

## Two Persistent Questions

Before considering these natural experiments in the ideal social order, there are a number of important issues that must be discussed.   No one can talk very long about utopias to other people without confronting two insistent questions that cut deep into the enduring problems of human existence.

First of all, what is an ideal community?   One person's utopia might be another's nightmare.   Consider a statement about the Ephrata Cloister, an ideal community established in Colonial times.   A leaflet, published by the Ephrata Cloister Associates, an organization "dedicated to the restoration of the life and times" of this eighteenth-century religious community near Lancaster, Pennsylvania, says, "As you walk along the shaded paths prior to the Vorspeil (religious choral music) observing selected restored crafts ... and bow your head as you pass through the low doorways of the 'straight and narrow path of virtue and humility' you too will know the sense of peace and unworldliness such as the self-disciplined celibates of the community knew.   You will be guided into a world you have never known but have always longed for. "

It is easy to imagine people who have not always longed for a quiet, well-ordered, and celibate life. There are many who rejoice in the most turbulent competition, even those who endorse the terrible words of Mussolini, "Better to live a day like a lion than a thousand years like a sheep."

A cursory examination of utopias both past and present will reveal an enormous range of opinions about what the character of an ideal community should be. To choose but a single example, most modern communes emphasize shared work, including menial physical work as did the Benedictines, both as a source of shared communal life and for the spiritual benefits to the individual. In marked contrast Sir Thomas More's Utopia includes in the work force slaves who have been captured in war or have been convicted of heinous offenses. The point is clear enough. What is perceived as the ideal social organization is rooted in the philosophical beliefs of the beholders and in their position in the wide range of human variability. The case of Jack Spratt and his wife can never be ignored.

The second question is one of the most frequently asked. Was this or that community a success? This is a very slippery question indeed! More's word "utopia" (from either the Greek outopos, no place, or eutopos, true or good place) can be taken to suggest that an ideal community is impossible, a view welcomed by considerable numbers of people, some reactionary, some soured. Indeed, if utopia is defined as a visionary impracticality, then any community that succeeds cannot be utopian by definition. Thus the Mormons are often not thought of as living in utopia. The same holds for the Amish and the Mennonites. In evaluating our little home grown utopias success is commonly defined in terms of duration. Certainly few would call Brook Farm, the ideal community formed outside of Boston in the 1840's by a group of New England transcendentalists, a success. It may have been, in the words of Isaac Hecker, one of the members, "the greatest, noblest, bravest dream of New England," but it endured only a scant six years. However, even in such a case who can measure the influence this vivid though brief experience had on the thinking of Nathaniel Hawthorne, Ralph Waldo Emerson, the Alcotts, or Charles Dana, editor of the New York Sun, and others who participated? Or how far, through them its influence may be extending?

If human diversity is anything like as great as it

appears to be, it can be expected that a given utopian community will be successful for some people, unsuccessful for others. Perhaps the best way to measure success or failure is to attempt to determine the extent to which life in any particular community enables the members to achieve the ends for which the community was established. This is a usable criterion, but it should be remembered that by this standard communities that must be rated successful would be condemned by many of our contemporaries. For example, few moderns would approve of militaristic Sparta with its famous black broth or of the Shakers with their complete celibacy (and the potential extinction of the human race on earth).

## Scientific Extrapolations: Valid and Invalid

Any utopia, if it is to fulfill its mission in the lives of its members, must be based on the value judgments, on the religion, broadly defined, of those members. To design such a New Jerusalem--whether in New Harmony, Indiana, or anywhere else--is a psychological, political, and economic problem, and one with an important biological dimension. Thus, it is conceivable that the substitution of some of the empirical outlook of the natural sciences for the dogmatic theologies of capitalism and communism might make what now seems impossible possible. This emphatically does not mean that raw biological facts or principles can be applied directly to human affairs. What is important to remember is that human life, including social life, has to be lived as much within the laws of biology as within the laws of physics. Unfortunately, biologists themselves, some authentic professionals, some not, have too often failed to apply the same critical acumen they use in their own work when they attempt to bring biological knowledge to bear on social problems.

One such widely known attempt takes territoriality, which is widespread but not universal among vertebrates, and elevates it to the status of the dominant force in human life--the "Territorial Imperative." The scientific justification for such a theory is supposed to be some immutable law of animal behavior. What is the actual validity of such an extrapolation from animal to human behavior?

In general, the farther from the cellular level, the more difficult it becomes to extrapolate from one species to another. The nerve cells in the brains of all mammals are just about the same, and valid extrapolations are possible. Except in very closely related species the brains composed of these cells are markedly different in different mammals. In behavior, extrapolation is often quite impossible between even closely related species. The red fox is so highly territorial that it is almost impossible to drive it out of its home turf. That is why it is such a satisfactory species for the fox hunter. The closely similar gray fox, when chased by the hounds, runs in a fairly straight line mile after mile until the hunt ends up so far away that no one can get home for dinner. Recall the highly territorial gibbons with the more or less indifferent chimps. Remember the male-dominated societies of the baboons and the female-led ones of the howlers.

How then can it be said that by some biological law humankind is predominantly territorial? Or, for that matter, that men are biologically the natural leaders rather than women? In fact, the expressions of territoriality from fish to primates varies from virtually zero to high intensity. The members of no utopia should feel under any scientific imperative whatever to believe that territoriality is central or even of great importance in human life.

Another widely read work proposes that men and women are really "naked apes" and rather vicious ones at that. Everyone already knows only too well that people can be vicious as well as kind and loving, so what is added to the sum of knowledge by pointing to the fact that we are primates with deficient hair? In this respect we are almost as badly off as the porpoises and other cetaceans. The naked-ape theory takes such a low view of human nature that one is reminded of the old Christian hymn, "From Greenland's Icy Mountains to India's Coral Strand," wherein are the lines, "Where every prospect pleases, And only man is vile."

If we are to be compared to apes, let us remember that the primates have some fine qualities as well as deplorable ones. From the scientific point of view a strong argument can be made for Louis Bolk's theory that we are not naked apes but fetal apes; in fact a far stronger argument than could have been made in Bolk's time nearly a century ago. Simplifying a bit, the large relative size of the brain found in Homo sapiens is characteristic of all fetal, as opposed to adult, mammals. The higher primates

are exceptions, with humanity the most extreme by far.
The relatively flat face of humans, as contrasted with the
long snout of dogs, horses, porpoises, and adult mammals
generally, is another fetal trait.  Humankind is much re-
tarded compared with our relatives in the age at which teeth
erupt and bony sutures of the skeleton fuse.  Our very lack
of hair is another fetal trait.  Most important is the prolonged period during which learning is possible.  The extensive work of the animal psychologist John Paul Scott has
shown that the old adage that you can't teach old dogs new
tricks is pretty much true, especially in regard to socialization.  Harlow and Zimmerman at the University of Wisconsin have shown a very similar thing in monkeys.  Students
of bird behavior have demonstrated that it is easy to teach
nestlings and young birds new songs but fully mature adults
cannot learn.

The attainment of sexual maturity while still in a
larval or fetal state anatomically, technically called neoteny,
is well known in various salamanders and some other animals.  It is now believed to have played an important role
in major new developments in evolution.  The presently accepted view among historical evolutionists is that the vertebrates arose by neoteny from the elongate swimming larvae
of sedentary animals (tunicates) living in the mouths of rivers.  Insects are believed to have arisen in the same way
from larval millipeds.  Our fetalization may well explain
our ability to learn far into adult life.

Akin to the "Naked Ape" is The Selfish Gene,
by Richard Dawkins.  The anthropomorphic title suggests a
bias we have already met above.  The book is indeed an
interesting tour de force because it is essentially a restate-
ment of Darwin's theory of natural selection and Weismann's
theory that the germ plasm  (i. e. , DNA) is the only biological inheritance transmitted from one generation to the next,
yet the idea manages to seem new!  As Samuel Butler, author of Darwin Among the Machines and of the well-known
utopian novel Erewhon, put it over a century ago, "A hen
is an egg's way of making more eggs. "  Even the more
knowledgeable and up-to-date work on "sociobiology" by E.
O. Wilson has raised a storm of controversy among his
colleagues at Harvard precisely because he has attempted
to extrapolate too freely results from the study of social
organizations in lower animals to human beings.

It may fairly be asked whether writings of the naked-
ape sort are essentially more valid than extrapolations

running in the opposite directions that attribute human meaning to animals. Recall the medieval zoology that asked why
the pigeon has red feet. The answer: because the dove
represents the Church, which is stained by the blood of the
martyrs in its march through the ages; its eyes are yellow,
the color of ripe grain, because they represent the ripe wisdom with which the Church looks out on the world. The organic analogy in which the state or society is compared with
a unitary living organism surely holds much truth. Society
is a highly interdependent organization. However, any such
analogy must be used with extreme caution, as the history
of this idea shows. Thus John of Salisbury, writing in the
middle of the twelfth century, asserts in his Policraticus
that the king is the head of the state; the heart represents
the senate, from which proceeds the initiation of good works
and ill; the sense organs correspond to judges; the hands are
the soldiers, the intestines financial officers; and so on down
to the feet. In modern times this organic analogy, as it has
been termed, has played havoc with European political philosophies. It can be as dangerous as naive racial theories.

The attribution of human ills to some sort of biological predestination and the calling on biological science to
support our meanest prejudices continue to appear. Indeed,
they continue to have a certain popularity for both obvious
and obscure reasons. To be sure, Thomas Hobbes had
plenty of facts to justify his devastating view of human life
as "solitary, poor, nasty, brutish, and short," but there is
nothing presently known about our biological inheritance to
suggest that we are forever doomed to such a condition.
Quite the contrary. The central fact is that biological evolution has furnished the ground substance out of which human
cultural development has emerged. As a toolmaker and as
a thinker, if not quite the lord of creation, humanity as a
species has achieved a new level of existence much as the
warm-blooded vertebrates achieved a new dimension of mastery over their cold-blooded ancestors. So great is the gap
between Homo sapiens and our closest relatives that it can
be compared to the difference between water and the hydro-
gen and oxygen of which it is composed. The properties of
water are neither the sum nor the average of the properties
of the two gases, but something new.

## Dollo's Law and the Principles of Similarity

The enormous difference of human culture from the usual
subject matter of biology does not mean that utopian com-

munities have nothing to learn from biological methods and discoveries. To begin with one of the older principles of biology, Dollo's law that evolution is irreversible appears to have a cultural equivalent. This law does not state that improvement or change of any kind will occur but only that once it has occurred, it is irreversible. Single reverse mutations are well known among animals, but that is a very different thing from, say, horses evolving back into small creatures resembling dogs, five toes on every foot. In the hundreds of millions of years of the history of life recorded in the rocks, nothing like that has ever been discovered. Apparently, the web of circumstances in historical events is too complex ever to have recurred in the same way. The mutations, or in human affairs the cultural inventions, will be different or appear in a different sequence, the climate may be different, and, possibly most important, the other plants and animals that serve as food or are competitors will be different, since they have been evolving also. To a biologist it looks as though we did not need to worry very much about Santayana's famous dictum, "Those who do not know the past are condemned to repeat it." We can't repeat it. Even Mahatma Gandhi at the very time he was campaigning to lead India back to a simpler, earlier life wore an American-made watch attached to his clothes with a modern safety pin. The Amish and Mennonites on their farms have managed to remain in the technological state at which they began with considerable but not complete success. It takes a heroic traditionalist indeed not to seek the services of a modern dentist in the face of a good toothache. And these people have never returned to any earlier condition, as is clear if you compare their farming equipment, the harnesses of their horses, or their carriages with those of any century previous to the time they left their native Germany.

The significance for a commune of the human counterpart of Dollo's law is simple and should be welcomed. Except for a few special items the answers to present-day problems cannot be sought in a return to the life of the past. The answers lie rather in utilizing the tremendous body of modern knowledge to construct a more humane social life for everyone.

Another evolutionary principle that overlaps both biological and cultural evolution concerns the ways different animals and animal societies have met similar problems. Over and over again in the long history of life on this planet similar problems have been met in closely similar ways or

in only a very few ways that have been evolved in very different groups of unrelated animals. Other problems of
course have been met in a great variety of ways. Examination of our utopias should enable us to learn something about
the problems for which there is only a limited number of
solutions and those that can be met in a great variety of
ways. The explanation for similarities may be common descent, but it also is due to the fact that for many problems
faced by living creatures there is only a finite, and sometimes very small, number of possible solutions imposed by
the laws of physics, chemistry, and mathematics.

No more elegant example of the way physical laws
impose limitations on how animals solve common problems
can be found than in a comparison of the eyes of vertebrates
with those of mollusks, which were chosen at the turn of the
century by the philosopher Henri Bergson to illustrate this
principle. Without agreeing with his explanation, it is true
that for light-perceiving organs these two great groups of
animals, completely unrelated in their evolution, have developed eyes that are the same in overall anatomy and in
many details all the way down to fundamental similarities in
visual pigments (a fact unknown in Bergson's day). In both
Homo sapiens and the octopus the eye consists of a transparent cornea, a colored iris, a crystalline lens, and a
chamber behind the lens filled with a transparent gel backed
by a cup-shaped surface of photoreceptive nerve cells, the
retina, on which an inverted image is projected from the
lens. A standard camera ("camera" equals "chamber" in
Greek) is constructed on exactly the same plan, and for the
same reasons. A similar eye with lens and simple retina
is found in some of the oceanic worms and jellyfish! Among
the mollusks there is found in different species a complete
series of simpler and simpler eyes all the way down to a
pinhole-type camera. In all the vast panorama of the animal kingdom only one other way of seeing images is found,
the compound eye of insects and crustacea. And although
organized differently from the vertebrate-mollusk-jellyfish
eye, these eyes also possess lenses, gels, pigments, and
of course photo-sensitive cells.

Convergent evolution is a related and also widespread
evolutionary phenomenon and should be instructive if found in
our utopias. The shape of a shark, of a porpoise, and of
some of the extinct marine reptiles are so similar that
swimmers sometimes mistake a friendly porpoise for a shark.
Nevertheless, all three are quite unrelated and have evolved

separately into the same shape due to the laws of hydro-
dynamics, which all three must meet.


## Science and Our Modern Utopians

Among many contemporary Americans interested in the return, as they see it, to a simpler and more natural life
style within a community based on mutual respect and cooperation, the sciences are suspect.  The technologies that
flow from them are viewed as unnatural and sometimes even
with a kind of self-righteous hatred.  The result is too often
a rejection of the tools that could help enormously to make
"the Valley of Love and Delight" possible.  Such a rejection
greatly diminishes the value such communities could have as
beacons and guides for the larger society.

The world at large will not, indeed cannot without
unthinkable upheavals, renounce the fruits of science.  A
wealthy, urban John Ruskin could berate the newly introduced
railroads as not meaningful for the attainment of the good
life, yet those despised iron horses proved to be a key factor in alleviating the severe local famines that have brought
death in many lands throughout the centuries.  In affluent
regions people may condemn family planning.  In the vast
poverty-stricken barrios of Latin America--for example,
around Mexico City, where the birth rate exceeds that of
any other part of the world including India--first-hand accounts testify that the women in these deserts of deprivation
are desperately anxious not just to be able to plan their
families but to avoid having their sixteenth child.

That scientific knowledge can be used for diabolical
purposes is only too obvious.  But it is important for utopians to remember that evil did not enter the world with the
invention of the electric light or even of gunpowder.  When
the Romans sacked and burned Carthage in 146 B. C. and put
to death every man, woman, and child, they were doing
something that had been and would be done to the inhabitants
of hundreds of cities in other centuries.  Regardless of how
reprehensible and ghastly was the dropping of that atom
bomb on Hiroshima, the destruction of the city and its inhabitants was by no means as complete as the destruction
of Carthage.  We should all remember that Cain did not
need a revolver to commit murder.

What explains the anti-scientific bias among so many

intelligent people, people committed to building a better world? In part this bias is soundly based on a clear perception of the rampant irrationalities of our times. The way soul-stunting drudgery in the fields day after day after day for years on end with no hope for any diversity or creativity is exchanged for an equally monotonous drudgery in a production line. These modern utopians are acutely aware of the worldwide link of heavy industry with the military establishment, against which Dwight Eisenhower warned in one of his last speeches as President. They see almost any sort of project, whether needed or not or even wanted, justified on the grounds that it makes jobs. They live in a hungry world where the U. S. government pays farmers not to plant crops. They see tobacco farmers subsidized at the same time the Department of Health, Education and Welfare fights lung cancer and heart disease with an anti-smoking campaign. Some know that a similar paradox exists in France, that old symbol of logical organization, where the government runs the tobacco industry alongside the ministry of health's anti-smoking campaign. They witness the destruction of young lives by lack of employment. It is enough to make the strong weep, even those who do not wear their hair like Samson in his prime.

In part the bias against the sciences arises from a pervasive mindset derived largely from the Romantic poets. This is not to say that anyone who read this poetry became a convert to the cult of Nature as good and beautiful in all her moods. Many true believers may not even be aware of such writings, but well down into the present they have been part of high school curricula and were apt to appear on College Entrance Examination Board tests in English Literature. They are part of the sacred scriptures of the back-to-nature movement, just as is the lingering myth of the "noble savage" of the eighteenth century. Listen to Wordsworth:

> One impulse from a vernal wood
> Can teach thee more of man,
> Of moral evil and of good
> Than all the sages can.

Of course many people do experience a sense of spiritual renewal in the world of nature. It can lift the heart to walk through the deep silences of a grove of immemorial redwoods or along the ocean's edge with nothing but sand and sea and sky. However, it is not known that

the great beauty of the Caribbean Islands did very much for
the moral uplift of the ruthless pirates who once infested
that region.    The law of the jungle is commonly perceived
as something very different from that of the gentle English
Lake Country.    Modern history affords a terrible example
of what magnificent scenery can do.    Superb alpine views
served as an unfailing source of inspiration for Adolf Hitler.
Clearly, contact with the world of nature evokes from the
human soul what is already there and magnifies it.    Lovers
of Wordsworth's poetry will be glad to know that in his maturity he recognized that these early effusions of love and
delight in nature were far indeed from the whole truth.
Unfortunately, his correction never caught up with his message.

Not surprisingly, Shakespeare knew better, as is
clear to anyone who has read the last verse of his familiar
forest song in As You Like It.

> Under the greenwood tree
> Who loves to lie with me,
> And turn his merry note
> Unto the sweet birds throat,
> Come hither, come hither, come hither!
>   Here shall he see
>   No enemy
> But winter and rough weather.

> Who doth ambition shun
> And loves to lie in the sun....

To which the melancholy Jaques replies,

> If it do come to pass
> That any man turn ass,
> Leaving his wealth and ease
> A stubborn will to please,
>   Here shall he see
>   Gross fools as he,
> An if he will come to me.

In part the anti-science bias arises from forgetting
that science is not only or even primarily concerned with
good plumbing, the attainment of unlimited sources of energy, or the relief of pain.    Aristotle put it well in the first
sentence of his Metaphysics.    "All men by nature desire to
know."    This obviously does not mean that everyone desires

to know everything about everything all of the time, but an almost incurable curiosity is a basic primate trait. We do not know what our cousin apes think about the results of their investigations, but we do know that they investigate. From the very earliest times and in many cultures human-kind has sought explanations for rainbows. And among moderns who is there who has not at least once looked up at the night sky and wondered about what might lie beyond the outermost stars or what discoveries await within the heart of the atom? To renounce science is to deny a central part of our humanity.

Below the surface the anti-science and even anti-technology feeling may not be anything like as strong as it appears. I have been led to this belief by long conversations with college and university students who were oriented towards the simple life in close harmony with Nature, with the earth, Mother of us all. The picture was the same in Maryland, in Ohio, and in California. Perhaps my sample was not sufficiently randomized to be statistically impregnable, and it was certainly small compared with the total number of American students. Nonetheless, the samples were widely scattered and the results highly consistent. Put briefly, these idealists, when specific questions were put to them, were not interested in abolishing the technology of the wine press and certainly not that of its lineal descendant, the printing press. They didn't even want to abolish the mimeograph machine. They would readily acknowledge the obvious fact that humans are tool-making and tool-using animals and that to deprive us of our tools is to deprive us of part of our humanity. What truly concerned these students, who are as much realists as idealists, is how technology is used and how that use is organized.

Almost all would agree that there is a remarkable creative element in scientific activity and that, once you think about how one discovery is built on previous ones, it is one of the most intensely social of human endeavors. Many came to agree with a Nobel-prize-winning physicist, the late Percy Bridgman of Harvard, who stands in the orthodox tradition that extends back through the Middle Ages into classical antiquity, when there was no distinction between a scientist and a philosopher. This tradition explains why a physicist is awarded a Ph.D., a Doctor of Philosophy. In this view there is no such thing as a special scientific method. The method of science, says Bridgman, "is nothing more than doing one's damnest with one's mind, and no holds barred. " Thus, science is not a thing apart but the source of knowledge that is based on experience that can be shared by any tool maker who has the facilities and is willing to devote the time.

Two additional facets of the relation of science to our intentional communities require at least brief mention. The motivations of the founders and recruits of our utopias were undeniably spiritual. At the same time, especially in the case of the millennialists, the motivations were scientifically based in that the inhabitants were acting on what they believed to be true about the nature of the physical universe. The Rappites, for example, had definitely identified Napoleon with one of the beasts mentioned in the book of Revelations and deduced that Europe was about to be destroyed. Hence, some of them very sensibly migrated to Russia and others to the United States. In what ways does such action differ from that of people who move away from the base of Vesuvius or a geologic fault in San Francisco? The whole problem of the interconnectedness of beliefs about the external universe and the inward reality of religion is involved, but that is far too large a subject to be treated here.

The infant science of psychology deserves a place second to none in the concerns of intentional communities because it covers the area where intention and fulfillment overlap. Many contemporary utopians cherish the belief of St. Paul's, as expressed in his epistle to the Corinthians, that love alone is truly important and knowledge of but little account. Many present-day utopians hold the view that if only people are free, free to "do their thing," free to "be themselves," all will be well. One is reminded of the naive way both Karl Marx and Lenin believed that once a communistic state was set up, the government would gradually wither away. But who can say that a Stalin or a Hitler was not doing his thing as truly as was Gandhi or Pablo Casals? You do not need to have read William Golding's Lord of the Flies to know that children can be exceedingly cruel to each other. Anyone familiar with very young children knows how much insight and skill as well as love is needed to resolve the fierce sibling and peer-group rivalries that are now so often part of growing up. Beyond them lie the frustrations inherent in human finitude so unforgettably portrayed in the story of Moby Dick and Captain Ahab. The wellsprings of "love and delight," of creativity as well as the far reaches of the human mind and spirit, lie still largely unexplored. The thrust of the sciences proclaims that the deepest and most sincere concern for human welfare must be firmly grounded in knowledge, or the most beatific vision of utopia will remain forever exactly that, "such stuff as dreams are made on."

## American Utopias--Selected Examples

Perhaps because over the past two centuries and more America has appeared to hundreds of thousands of Europeans as the promised land, this country has been a hotbed of little utopias. So many social activists hell-bent on setting up their ideal communities had swept across upper New York State by the middle of the nineteenth century that it was referred to as a "burnt over region." Today the number of communes, rural, suburban, and urban, is variously estimated as between 2500 and 3500, enough so that the U.S. Census Bureau plans to include them in the 1980 census.

The roster may be said to begin with the Plymouth Colony founded by what historians Morison and Commager call a group of "left wing Puritans from East Anglia" via Holland. We have already mentioned the Rhode Island settlement of the 1630's and Ephrata toward the end of the

The children's hour, Mansion House, Oneida Community

eighteenth century.   Early in the nineteenth century a group
of German immigrants under one Father Rapp settled on the
banks of the Wabash in Indiana at a site they called Harmony.
With much hard work, music, and freedom of opinion the
colony flourished until it was sold and the Rappites moved to
Pennsylvania.   The new owner, Robert Owen, a wealthy mill
owner from Great Britain, renamed the place New Harmony
and recruited many notables amid much excitement.   Owen
was even invited to speak before the U. S. Congress.   For
several reasons the community at New Harmony soon fell
apart.   The place has now been restored, and Indiana University has produced a handsome full-length film about this
attempt.

One of the largest and most "successful," as well as
most written about, of our utopias was the Oneida Community in the Mohawk valley of New York.   By now it has
evolved, "degenerated" is perhaps an equally valid word,
into a silverware manufacturing company listed on the New
York Stock Exchange.   Equally well known are the Shakers,
who established many flourishing agricultural communities
in New York and other states.   The short-lived Brook Farm
outside of Boston in the 1840's is probably best known today
because of the illustrious Boston Transcendentalists it attracted.   The Pennsylvania Mennonite, Amish, and Dunkard
farmers and the Mormons are sometimes not considered as
utopians, but there seems no reason to exclude them.   In
fact Pennsylvania was established by royal charter to William Penn primarily as a place where Quakers could follow
their own life style and religious beliefs.   The Amana community in Iowa, founded of course much later, is now known
for its refrigerators and microwave ovens.

In the closing years of the last century and continuing
for several decades there was a spate of utopias in California.   Theosophists (Annie Besant for example) and others
interested in new approaches to religion, notably Buddhist
and Hindu, built handsome domed temples, Greek amphi-
theaters, and elegant houses complete with Tiffany-glass
windows in Point Loma on the Pacific, in Ojai Valley, and
elsewhere.   At the opposite end of this California spectrum
was the "Holy City" of William Riker, dedicated to a bizarre
mixture of white supremacy, fundamentalist Christianity,
honky-tonk, and socialism of sorts.

To select any of the present-day communes as representative would be futile, so much do they vary.   Of special

note, however, are Twin Oaks, founded under the inspiration of B. F. Skinner's Walden Two and located in central
Virginia; "The Farm" in Sumertown, Tennessee, and a
Quaker group scattered in a particular area of Philadelphia,
in the world but not exactly of it.

## A Comparative Approach

Some comparative anatomists begin with the outside of the
body, the skin and its derivates; others with the innermost,
the skeletal system. Likewise, comparative biochemists
may begin with DNA or with the cytochromes, the molecules
at the end of the respiratory process. Yet all roads lead
to the same place. In scrutinizing our native attempts to
reach and live in what the New Harmony people called "the
Valley of Love and Delight" certain features continue to re-
appear.

To begin with economics, metabolism so to speak,
most utopian communities have a "cash crop." In Twin
Oaks it is handwoven hammocks, very well made ones sold
retail through Pier 1 and other stores. In other contemporary communes it is soybeans, honey, or other specialized
items. A century earlier the Oneida Community became
prosperous by making steel traps that one of their members
had invented. Earlier still the Ephrata group was famous
for its bread (George Washington sent there for bread for
his army). In some cases the cash source may be specialized services to surrounding communities. This is true at
Twin Oaks, where members go out as carpenters.

The recurrence of such income-producing activities
emphasizes the wisdom so well put by John Donne, "No man
is an island." Twin Oaks, for example, needs electricity,
metal tools, glass for windows, improved strains of vegetables and field crops--the list is a long one. And because
communes need these things, they need the past all the way
back to the first glassmakers in Egypt. It is the kind of
selection that utopians make from the past and the way they
use it that makes them significant.

Unfortunately for our utopians, or perhaps for the
rest of us, the very fact that society is such a highly inter-
reactive whole has presented tough problems for our social
pioneers. The founders of Rhode Island were chased out of
Massachusetts. The Mormon experience was far more

severe.    Joseph Smith established the Church of the Latter-
day Saints in upstate New York,  sent missionaries to both
Indians and Americans of European descent,  and set up
colonies around Independence,  Missouri,  and elsewhere.    It
was not long before they were driven out with some blood-
shed.    In the 1840's about 15, 000 moved to Nauvoo,  Illinois,
on the eastern bank of the Mississippi River.    Here again
the "gentiles" became jealous,  so it is said,  of the prosperity and political influence of the Mormons and were outraged
by their belief in "polygamy. "    They were again attacked,
their houses and fields set on fire,  and Joseph Smith jailed.
After a mob stormed the jail and shot Smith,  the Mormons,
under Brigham Young,  began the long trek to Utah.

     John Humphrey Noyes founded what was to become
the Oneida Community in Putney,  Vermont,  from which they
were driven to New York State because of their "Bible communism" and practice of "complex marriage. "    In more recent times the Kaweah Cooperative Commonwealth in California,  which called itself an example of "Christian Anarchy, "
ran into trouble,  although in their photographs the inhabitants
look like hardworking examples of respectability,  the men
with picks and shovels,  the women wearing long dresses,
and on occasion both playing croquet.    However,  they were
evicted from what is now part of Sequoia National Park and
their Karl Marx big tree renamed General Sherman.

     Today,  if you sit and talk with the local people in the
crossroads store nearest the Twin Oaks commune,  you will
learn of the deep apprehension they felt when they learned
that such a group had bought a large tract of land in their
countryside.    You will also learn that they have found the
Walden Two inhabitants to be the hardest working,  cleanest,
and best-ordered men and women they have ever seen.

     Another recurring attitude toward these social pio-
neers has been ridicule.    Utopia has frequently been used
in a scoffing pejorative sense.    Such scorn has often been
meted out to innovators and inventors--until their projects
succeed.    Perhaps it is not too important.    In any case
some of these utopians have been very easy to poke fun at.
Father Rapp,  for example,  intending to confer a high compli-
ment,  wrote that "the power of God is revealed in the crocodile,  in the hippopotamus,  and in Alexander Hamilton. "    One
can only surmise how the haughty Hamilton felt about being
bracketed with the hippopotamus and the crocodile.    In what
is probably the ultimate anticlimax,  the members of the

Oneida Community pledged themselves to "seek a more perfect union with Christ and with Mr. Noyes," the founder.
For some of the women this meant the ultimate physical
union.

A far more important and possibly essential feature
of utopias is the leader possessing a charisma, to use a
theological term, a gift of grace and inspiring leadership.
Roger Williams, Anne Hutchinson, Joseph Smith, John H.
Noyes, Richard Owen, and Annie Besant were all such.
Skinner's reputation through his writings is enormous, but
he has kept away from Twin Oaks, where his program has
been considerably modified as the result of experience.
The Farm in Summertown, probably the largest and most
prosperous of our contemporary communes, was founded
and still led, dominated some would say, by Stephen Gaskin,
who found the drug culture of San Francisco unrewarding and
led a busload or two of so-called hippies and flower children
eastward. The lives and thoughts of these charismatic mes-
siahs would make an interesting study.

The actual governance, the real control, of utopian
communities has varied widely. Most contemporary ones
are run on more or less democratic principles with much
discussion. There has also been, in the past especially but
by no means exclusively, a tendency for the charismatic
leader to behave like a certain type of university administration, permit complete freedom but only so long as the students do what the administration believes to be right. This
syndrome dominates the leadership of the two great com-
munisms of our time and is certainly related to the conviction that "the national interest" places limitations beyond
which no citizen may go. It was precisely this "Mother
knows best" attitude of the Massachusetts colonists, who
themselves had come to the new world seeking freedom,
that forced out the Rhode Island dissidents. In some of the
utopias the legal ownership is vaguely known by most of the
members and the final decision-making process obscure.
Happily, loving concensus appears to be the rule, but it
should be remembered that these groups are self-selected
and anyone is always free to leave. It should also be remembered that the old, old problem of who shall guard the
guardians remains unsolved in the modern world. In Plato's
utopia, The Republic, the philosopher kings ruled in part by
lying to the people.

The question of human exploitation, both economic and

psychological, arises in communes, although certainly no more than in a factory-owned town. In contemporary communes like The Farm or Twin Oaks everyone works hard and long. Twin Oaks provides its members with a weekly work schedule with a square for every hour of every day of the week from 8:00 a. m. through 11:00 p. m. so that everyone can schedule their forty hours of work per week at the times most suited to their personal wishes. All work counts the same except for making the hammocks, for which extra credits are awarded. Most entrants into communes bring little with them except their hands and good will. They may also bring personal problems. If they leave they carry away little more than pocket money in material wealth. Some communities have become wealthy. The Oneida Community became so long before it turned to manufacturing silverware. Twin Oaks has recently purchased a large additional tract of land. The Farm has become a $1.5-million business. Under such circumstances the opportunity for exploitation exists, which is not to say that it occurs.

The personal rewards can be very great for both leaders and owners and all other members, far transcending any possible monetary recompense. Being part of what is perceived as a noble and important human enterprise is a deeply rewarding experience. Losing oneself in such an endeavor can furnish the key to finding new meaning in life. Others find an inexpressible sense of self-realization and inner peace and strength, as in the old Methodist hymn, "content to let the world go by, to know no gain nor loss," and are thus enabled to follow a life-style of simple, or at least human-sized, tasks and happy companionship. Those that leave communes like Twin Oaks carry with them a renewed faith in their own worth and a sounder sense of values on which to base a more permanently satisfying life.

Within American communes the emotional tone of daily living has varied widely. Ephrata and the Rappite colony were notable for music, especially choral music, certainly a potent force to develop group morale. The Oneidians were encouraged to be happily studious, and there are many photographs of croquet games, very fashionable at the time, and, more important, of eager-looking work groups--berry-picking "bees," sewing bees, gardening bees, and the like. The Shakers are still known for their vigorous stamping songs and dances with men and women facing each other on opposite sides of the room. Fortunately, some of the last surviving Shakers have recorded on sound

film some of these routines and demonstrated the stamping
while they "shake, shake, shake" and "stamp, stamp,
stamp," shaking out the dross and evil. It must have had
something in common with hard rock music, for at the end
some of the dancers would fall to the floor exhausted. Music, both live and recorded, is reported from many contemporary communes, Twin Oaks included. There have
been complaints that some communities are overly serious
to the point of being grim. Perhaps that is the reason at
least one group schedules special days for clowning.

The relationships between the sexes as a cause for
the persecution of some of the early communities in this
country is discussed in detail in chapters four and five.
Certainly, a very wide range of beliefs and practices have
existed and exist today. In Rhode Island the status of wom-
en was high, as shown by the prominent role of Anne Hutchinson. Joanna Southcott, a Devonshire countrywoman who
heard "Voices," became a prophetess of the Owenites before
they came to this country. Women played a very prominent
role in the turn-of-the-century California communes, where
Annie Besant was only one of a number of women leaders.
The situation among the Mormons and the Oneidians was
much different. The latter practiced what they termed
"stirpiculture," a form of eugenics based largely on the
personal judgment of the charismatic Mr. Noyes, who fa-
thered most of the resulting children. Infants and children
have been lovingly nurtured and educated, albeit often in un-
conventional ways. There is a charming picture of a children's dancing class of Owenites while still in Scotland with
parents sitting around the edge and large paintings of African
animals on the wall.

A major problem has been to inspire a second and
third generation to want to continue in the commune. The
young Oneidians are said to have been healthy, smart, and
ambitious in a career-minded way. Perhaps stirpiculture
had worked too well. In any case many of them left to join
the mainstream of American life, to go "where the action
is," to use a common phrase. There are two aspects to
this problem, both equally important. Children born and
raised within a utopian community have had a very different
experience from their parents. The parents may have been
raised in a poverty-ridden mill town or among affluent su-
burbanites whose lives have become a desperate and unre-
lenting struggle for place and power, where spontaneity is
crushed by stuffy formalities and no time left "to be oneself."

The other aspect concerns the nature of any communal life that will be permanently satisfying to all sorts and conditions of men and women. The parents could experience the pull and excitement of being part of a great pioneering movement and of finding it possible to live in a way that particularly suits them. The children take the commune for granted, where nothing to stir the blood of the more unimaginative ever seems to happen. As the Romans knew long ago, we do not live by bread alone, but by something more, whether it be circuses or a transcending spiritual awareness.

Many of our utopias, especially the long-lasting ones, have been founded and sustained by religious convictions. Many have been founded on millennialism, i. e. , the belief that the thousand years of terrestrial bliss mentioned in the twentieth chapter of the book of Revelations, when Christ shall reign on the earth, is about the begin. One is reminded of the approaching Age of Aquarius, which some young contemporaries have sung about. The communism so often present also has a Biblical basis often explicitly taken from Acts 2:44--"And all who believed were together, and had all things in common. " It is enough to make most genteel Christians blush, or at least feel a twinge of embarrassment.

In many instances the founders and the members of our utopias had undergone an intense religious experience. This was notably true of Joseph Smith. John Humphrey Noyes testifies in his diary, "I went home with a feeling that I had committed myself irreversibly, and, on my bed that night, I received the baptism which I desired and expected. Three times in quick succession a stream of eternal love gushed through my heart and rolled back again to its source. 'Joy unspeakable' filled my soul. " How could the prophesy of such a man fail to be self-fulfilling? Despite Joanna Southcott's "Voices," Robert Owen does not seem to have had any comparable divine inspiration. The Owenites, including William Maclure, one of Owen's closest associates, spoke freely of experimentation. Nevertheless, for anyone to invest hugh sums of money or commit a large segment and perhaps all of one's life's work to some utopian community requires conviction of a high order, whether based on divine guidance, reasoned throught, or visceral faith. Whatever the inner motivation behind our utopias, from the outsider's point of view they constitute natural experiments, just as did the voyages of Columbus on which Queen Isabella wagered the crown jewels. The role of commitment is one of the things to be looked at in such diverse communities.

What then is to be learned from these experiments? No doubt many insights can be harvested and will become evident in subsequent chapters. Two salient features are clear. One is the existence of an unquenchable determination in humankind, generation after generation, to reach what John Bunyan called the "Delectable Mountains." All through our history there have been courageous men and women who refused to believe that the terrible view of human life expressed by Thomas Hobbes is our inescapable destiny. On the contrary, we can so organize our collective lives that a new and far better "order of the centuries" will dawn.

Equally significant is the demonstration in many, perhaps most, of our present-day communes, as well as those of the past, that the eternal verities are just that, still eminently viable. It was well said by Ruskin in his Modern Painters, "All real and wholesome enjoyments possible to man have been just as possible to him, since first he was made upon the earth, as they are now; and they are possible to him chiefly in peace. To watch the corn grow, and the blossoms set; to draw hard breath over ploughshare or spade; to read, to think, to love, to hope, to pray, --these are the things that make men happy...." Importantly, our utopians have added a dimension that Ruskin denounced and rejected, the use of the fruits of science for the enhancement of human life. It is in this growing reconciliation of the creative mind of the toolmaker with the loving intentions of a St. Paul that our best hope lies.

## Bibliography

Bestor, Arthur E., Jr. Backwoods Utopias: The Sectarian and Owenite Phases of Communitarian Socialism in America, 1663-1829 (Philadelphia: University of Pennsylvania Press, 1950).

Bridgman, P. W. Reflections of a Physicist (New York: Philosophical Library, 1950).

Carden, Maren L. Oneida: Utopian Community to Modern Corporation (Baltimore: Johns Hopkins University Press, 1969).

Harrison, J. F. C. Quest for the New Moral World. Robert Owen and the Owenites in Britain and America (New York: Scribner's, 1969).

Kagan, Paul. New World Utopias: A Photographic History of the Search for Community (1870-1975) (New York: Penguin, 1975).

Lockwood, George B. The New Harmony Movement (New York: Appleton, 1905; rpt. New York: A. M. Kelley, 1970).

Mumford, Lewis. The Story of Utopias (New York: Boni and Liveright, 1922).

Nordhoff, Charles. The Communistic Societies of the United States (New York: Hillary House, 1960).

Robertson, Constance Noyes. Oneida Community: An Autobiography 1851-1876 (Syracuse, N. Y.: Syracuse University Press, 1970).

Swift, Lindsay. Brook Farm: Its Members, Scholars, and Visitors (New York: Corinth Books, 1961).

# IV.  WOMEN IN UTOPIA:
## THE NINETEENTH-CENTURY EXPERIENCE

Jean Harvey Baker

In 1893 two American women, Alice Ilgenfritz Jones and Ella Merchant, published a now-forgotten novel, Unveiling a Parallel:  A Romance.  A female vision of a better world, the book described two kinds of utopias.  While in both women were equal to men, in one women not only occupied important political and financial positions, but they smoked, drank, fought, and sought sexual gratification in gardens of prostitution staffed by seductive young males.  In a word, they acted, for better or worse, like men.  A parallel utopia depicted a community wherein the greedy aggressive urges of all human beings have given way to a physical, moral, and spiritual nirvana.  Here women--long on nurturing, loving instincts--have led the way to a better world, and human aggressiveness has been replaced by cooperation and harmony.

Perhaps even more unsettling to readers of late-nineteenth-century fiction was another feminist utopia--Mary Lane's Mizora, ominously subtitled "A Prophecy."  In Mizora, the author described an idyllic paradise under the North Pole.  Whatever visions nineteenth-century Americans held of the quality of life on the Pole, life under it, at least in Lane's hands, fulfilled every expectation of perfection.  Clearly, Mizora was the ultimate feminist utopia, a misanthropic paradise, created by a race of women scientists.  Unable to compete--or even survive--in an environment of love and cooperation, men, like Darwinian ganoid fish, were ill-adapted for peaceful Mizora.  In fact, after a series of inter-male wars caused by their innate greed and aggression, men have become extinct.  Meanwhile, scientific advances have assured the asexual reproduction of women, and while Lane, very much a Victorian, was suitably vague as to the specifics of her fictional parthenogenesis, hers was a maleless utopia where "mizora"--or happiness--reigned for all women.

56

Neither Unveiling a Parallel nor Mizora made the best-seller lists of the 1890's. Most reviewers and readers of utopian literature preferred safer delineations of sexual arrangements and instead savored Edward Bellamy's popular Looking Backward, in which women were granted more equality, at the same time that the typical and therefore contradictory sexual divisions of labor prevailed. But both Mizora and Unveiling a Parallel serve as prophetic introductions to the wishes and dreams of a neglected species--American women in the nineteenth century. Both novels raised the essential and recurring questions of the women's movement. Should women view their quest for liberation as a catalyst for improving all society or should they settle for a lesser goal--equality of opportunity with men in a less-than-perfect society? To what extent was equality possible within a male-oriented society? What chance was there for autonomy within marriage and its burdensome cycle of childbearing? In their literary statements of a perfect society all three authors hoped that women would serve as the vanguards of societal change, but it was Lane who gave the most radical answers. Her rejection of male dominance presaged the positions of feminists a century later. But all three women confronted the forgotten issue of what utopia might be--not as filtered through the eyes of men, but as delineated by women themselves. Too often blueprints for the perfect society were defined by men who could not, in a sexually repressive world, speak for all humans any more than the best-intentioned whites could define freedom for blacks.

Throughout the nineteenth century Americans of both sexes not only wrote endless novels about their "heavens on earth," but they acted out their dreams in a myriad of communities. The United States had always served as a natural environment for the testing of utopian ideals, and by the early nineteenth century acceptance of the doctrine of perfectionism, the existence of free land, an earlier tradition of communitarian settlements, and the growing need for reform combined to stimulate the organization of utopian ventures. By 1870 the peripatetic John Humphrey Noyes counted over a hundred such communities, varying in size, duration, and purpose from the ephemeral Yellow Springs, Ohio, community of six members to the durable Shaker settlement at New Lebanon, New York. Yet all these societies shared certain characteristics--they were efforts to establish a new social pattern based on a vision of the ideal community; they were initiated by those who believed that disharmony and disequilibrium derive from the environment; they were set apart from the outside society, and they expected to serve as models for humankind to follow. In the United States, perhaps more than other nations, Yeats's prophecy that "the unseen world is no longer a dream" was practiced by a dedicated few.

Given their diversity, the only realistic generalization about these utopian societies is that they included both men and women. As always, there were exceptions--Martha McWhirter's Women's Commonwealth began with Bible readings in Belmont, Texas, and ended with a celibate community of Sanctified Sisters living in a District of Columbia boarding house. But only this all-woman community comprised of former Texas housewives attempted to establish the ultimate female supremacy of Mary Lane's Mizora. Yet even in bisexual communities the position of women altered drastically, and was the most striking characteristic of many utopias. While it was possible to find work, spiritual life, and even physical surroundings little changed from the outside world, few communitarians found that their previous sexual and familial arrangements survived efforts for a better society. Thus, during a time when the roles of women in the United States remained glacially consistent, inside most utopias the women's lot changed dramatically. Such alterations often became a badge of commitment, a mark of distinction, and a lever of cohesiveness for the community itself. While the degree of change necessary for a better world was a depressing comment on woman's position in the real world, inside the utopian societies the altered woman's role was a telling statement on the ethos of nineteenth-century communitarianism. A closer examination of three communities, the Shakers, Oneidans, and Mormons, establishes these points.

## The Shakers

In 1774 nine members of the United Society of Believers emigrated to America from England. As was so often the case with utopian communities, their leader, Mother Ann, was a charismatic figure who believed that, as the female counterpart to the male Christ, she was God's special instrument. Strengthened by such a conviction, she--and her successors James Whittaker and Frederick Evans--kept their community together and despite the difficult process of resettlement in a new world began to attract converts. Soon the Shakers, as they were universally known, had communities from Maine to Kentucky, and by 1870 some 2500 Americans enjoyed the austere life of the United Believers.

In part, Mother Ann's zeal came from a vision she had while imprisoned in England for her radical Quaker beliefs. Like so many other heretics imprisonment only reinforced her dissent, and in Mother Ann's case a revelation experienced while in jail established her special role as God's representative of His own female nature. Armed with a fervent commitment to end human corruption, Mother Ann dedicated herself to erasing its source--lust and sexuality. She had no difficulty accepting such views, for, as the former Ann Lee Stanley, she had suffered an unhappy sexual relationship with an alcoholic husband, as well as the death of four children. Sentiments of celibacy came easily to such a woman, who could chant with special fervor the Shaker hymn:

> In the church of Christ and Mother
> Carnal Feelings have no place.
> Here the simple love each other
> Freed from everything that's base.

Under Mother Ann's direction the Shakers developed a theology based on the view that God was bisexual, Christ male, and the Holy Spirit female. As millennialists, Shakers believed that the day of resurrection began with the founding of their church, and while they rejected physical resurrection, they accepted Mother Ann as a holy force. Accordingly, the future was derived from the female part of God's bisexuality. Such beliefs contradicted the familiar interpretations of Genesis and Corinthians, which provided useful theological justifications for woman's subservience in nineteenth-century America. Instead, Shakers believed men and women were equal in God's world and must forego fleshly contamination. To do so required a separate and distinct community dedicated to love of God, spiritual association, celibacy, and communal sharing.

To achieve their goals Shakers practiced rigid sexual segregation. Men and woman ate at different tables, worked at different jobs, and even used separate stairways to their dormitories, where, needless to say, they slept apart. In time Shakers spent a good deal of time checking on each other. To prevent any violation of these rigid codes of sexual apartheid and to provide evidence of their celibacy, they often traveled in twos--two men and two women. Only rarely

was conversation permitted. One occasion was the Sunday
service in the large assembly hall found in every Shaker
community. Here, seated on sturdy wooden benches, men
and women faced each other during a ceremony that included
hymn-singing and an address. Then began the lively activities that earned Shakers their nickname, as the men and
women filed from their seats and began marching around the
room--shaking, twitching, clapping, and chanting in an effort to get rid of the Devil: "there's a great spirit on you."
Outsiders' reaction to this ritual varied. John Humphrey
Noyes found it an important manifestation of spiritualism;
Charles Nordhoff declared it a remarkable ceremony, but
Alexis de Tocqueville's traveling companion, Gustav de
Beaumont, dismissed it with Gallic finality as "mad," and
de Tocqueville himself compared the Shakers to "trained
dogs who are forced to walk on their hind legs." All observers agreed that the ceremony was one of ecstasy and
heightened emotionalism, and in the Freudian world modern
observers have interpreted the ritual as a mechanism of
release for a sexually repressed community.

For Shaker women the implications of celibacy were
immense. Certainly, chastity was a sacrificial practice for
both sexes, and as such bound the believers to their society.
But for women it meant much more. Removed from their
traditional roles as wife, mother, and housekeeper, Shaker
women no longer could be identified in traditional nineteenth-
century terms as the wife of their husband, the mother of
their children, and the keeper of their hearth. Those of
course were the primary reference points for most
nineteenth-century women, and they were traded for a rough
equivalency with men in the Shaker world. Thus, even after
Mother Ann's death women continued to share political power
with men, and in every one of the twenty-seven Shaker communities women filled the posts of deaconness and eldress.
Such equality was reflected in the communities' dress, for
Shaker men and women resembled each other. The women
cropped their hair and wore neat bonnets and simple gowns
quite different from the increasingly narcissistic garb of
American women in the nineteenth century. In so doing they
followed the directions of Mother Ann "to dress in modest
apparel such as became the people of God."

Yet even in this androgynous world of sexual equality
there were clear divisions of labor between the sexes.
Shaker women worked in kitchen and house; men in the fields.
Women did all the sewing and laundry and were assigned a

particular brother's dirty linens.    Although based on a traditional view of sexual roles, this economic division of labor
made little difference, for there were no wages, and property was owned by the community, not by individuals.    Whatever discriminations such a system imposed were those of
unshared labor, rather than unequal pay.    Thus, the usual
objections to labor division based on sex did not apply, for
everybody owned everything and each owned nothing.    Actually, there was little to own, for the Shakers were unremit-
tingly simple.    Their fulfillment did not require even the
limited consumer products of the nineteenth century; they
neither drank, smoked, nor ate meat or, in some cases,
animal products.    Indeed, the only official stratification that
influenced Shaker life was between Novitiates, new members
who had been married in the outside world; Junior members
who had not; and Church-Order or Full Members.

In such a religious community Shaker women achieved
a rough equality with men; in part because all were seekers
after God, but also because women were freed from their
roles as mothers and wives.    In an age that lacked efficient
forms of artificial contraception and rejected them philosoph-
ically, the average nineteenth-century American woman produced six children and was in her late fifties before her old-
est child left home.    The task of food-making and housekeep-
ing, so easily accomplished in the machine age, consumed
endless energy and time in individual households.    But in a
communal arrangement Shaker women were freed from such
demands and accordingly could spend more time in the spiritual communications and silent prayers that marked their
society's life.    Furthermore, women--whom Shakers found
more likely to experience the trances, swoonings, and "super-
induced conditions" that marked spiritualism--gained an added
status.    Thus, while women were more often in charge of
the rearing of the young orphans who provided the necessary
human legacy in this celibate society, and while women were
more likely to run the schools, they were released from the
natural forces of nineteenth-century oppression--husband,
children, and home.    In a community that accepted a bisexual God and revered a female prophet, women were spared
the ideological sources of oppression.    As Frederick W.
Evans, one of Mother Ann's successors, explained to a visitor: "Here we find the women just as able as the men in
all business affairs and far more in the spiritual ones. "
Shaker women were more explicit in their explanations:

To plainly tell the truth, we do not rue,
The sober godly course that we pursue,

But 'tis not we who live the dronish lives,
But those who have their husbands or their wives.

By denying the two-person intimacy that characterized
American monogamy Shaker leaders expunged one of the possible threats to the universalism of their community. Like
other utopian societies they successfully submerged the intense, particularistic, nuclear family into a larger more
general collectivism. Celibacy provided a lever of commitment all Shakers could share, and the authoritarian system
of public control over members served to bind the communitarians to their utopia. Clearly, the growth and longevity
of Shaker communities, as well as their simplicity, suggested that both women and men felt fulfilled in such efforts "to
walk with God. "


## The Oneida Community

Also based on perfectionist principles, the Oneida community differed from the Shakers in two significant ways: its
shorter life as a utopian society and its inability to expand
beyond a main center at Oneida. Even at its height in the
1870's there were only two hundred Oneidans, and a small
society at Wallingford, New York, lasted only a few years.
But Oneida shared with the Shakers other characteristics--
it, too, had a charismatic organizer in John Humphrey
Noyes; it, too, was based on the belief that people were
neither originally nor irrevocably depraved but rather that
their environment had tainted them; and it, too, radically
altered the position of women--although in a quite different
way than had the Shakers.

Certainly John Humphrey Noyes was as improbable a
leader as Mother Ann. The son of a banker, the Vermont-
born Noyes had studied in the schools of America's elite--
Dartmouth, Yale, and the Andover Theological Seminary.
As a young man he had undergone a conversion experience
that had convinced him that, however sinful his behavior,
God forgave his motives. Such a revelation led Noyes to
accept his own salvation, although his public proclamations
of such an exalted state offended his New England neighbors,
who accepted Calvinist determinism and who considered
Noyes's theology the brashest form of spiritual "hubris. "
Soon Noyes was expelled from a ministry that did not accept his doctrine of grace. Yet even when his license to
preach was revoked Noyes did not waver in his belief that
fate was not determined by some deistic game of chance

that consigned some to heaven and others to hell. Rather, Noyes believed that men and women must be removed from the materialistic competitive culture of the United States to an environment where private property was abolished, where they would seek not consumer goods, but right behavior.

Certainly, there was nothing unusual about such beliefs; they were in one form or another the basis of many intentional utopian experiments. Noyes, however, extended his communalism to argue that monogamy was based on jealousy and exclusivity. The institution of marriage was "selfish love"--a position Mother Ann would have had no difficulty accepting. Yet here all resemblance between Shaker and Perfectionist view ended, for Noyes believed that sexuality was an essential God-given part of the human condition. In its most exalted form love was the reciprocal and satisfied attraction of two kinds of desire--physical and spiritual. There was no shame or sin in sex, only that which developed as a result of the misuse of the earthly passions. While Noyes admitted the expediency of monogamous marriage in the ancient world, Christ's Second Coming--after the destruction of the Jewish Temple in A. D. 70--meant that new sexual arrangements must be developed. Thus, like the Shakers the Oneidans believed Christ's Second Coming had already taken place, and their millennial expectations required a progression toward Christ's heaven on earth. The replacement of marriage represented one aspect of Christ's anticipated perfect world. Accordingly, Noyes used Biblical injunctions that none were married in Heaven as the theological basis for his condemnation of monogamy.

From such views Noyes developed his view of "complex marriage," an arrangement where all males and females were married to each other. Accordingly, sexual intercourse between different consenting partners was encouraged by the community, and the exclusivity of an intimate relationship forbidden. What the Shakers called "sparking" and the outside community "love marriage" violated the community intentions of Oneidans, who accepted the sharing of both property and sexuality.

As was the case with the Shakers the application of such views greatly affected women. For the first time in American history they were given equal access to men. Gone was the double standard that inhibited female sexual contacts and made nubile women into prostitute and wanton seductress at the same time that it tolerated the sexual

Library of Mansion House, Oneida Community

adventurings of males. Instead, Oneida women enjoyed sexual intercourse with any man, provided that he agreed and
that their contacts were made through an intermediary. In
fact, men continued to initiate these contacts, circumstances
that doubtless demonstrate conditioning by the outside world.
As is too often the case in women's history, there are few
extant documents about the reaction to complex marriage, although several women acknowledged the successful fusing of
physical and spiritual love.

But in the world outside Oneida, complex marriage became a synonym for lascivious free love. Noyes himself
was continually harassed, both in his first community at Putney and later in Oneida. On one occasion he was charged
with adultery and on another with rape--both complaints coming from outside the community. Oneidans, like other communitarians, soon learned that it was far easier to change
work arrangements than to change sexual behavior, and the
granting of sexual freedom to women struck hard at one of
the great shibboleths of nineteenth-century America--female
chastity.

Yet, if sexual promiscuity is defined as violating society's sex codes, then Oneida was as pure as Mother Ann's
celibate Mount Lebanon. In both instances women traded the

privacy of control by husband for that of mutual submission by men and women to the community--or more realistically Noyes himself. Indeed, one of the most striking character- istics of the Shakers, Oneidans, and Mormons was the de- gree of control exerted by the community over what the out- side world considered private affairs. There were few devi- ants from Noyes's strict sexual code, and those who did mis- construe the intent of his views were subjected to the most searing condemnation in the groups' frequent sessions of mu- tual criticism. Thus, from the time of a woman's initiation into heterosexuality--usually with an older man--sex life was administered by the community. And when Noyes began his famous eugenic experiment of stirpiculture after the Civil War, his belief that the best men and women should bear children was only a natural extension of collective sexuality.

Even reproduction was controlled at Oneida, for Noyes forbade what he called the "random procreation" that led to so many unwanted children and unhealthy women. At a time when most Americans made no distinction between procrea- tional and recreational sex, Noyes insisted on male contracep- tion. His personal life had convinced him of the biological agonies of American women; his legal wife in the period be- fore his commitment to complex marriage had been pregnant five times in six years and had borne four stillborn children. Even in her twenties Harriet Holton Noyes suffered from a seemingly endless--but typical--series of disorders associated with her pregnancies. To prevent such illness Noyes devised a theory of male continence, based on the division between amative and propagative love. According to his view the propagative function of the male (that is the expelling of se- men) could be controlled, while the amative function contin- ued. Said Noyes: "It is as foolish and cruel to expend one's seed on a wife merely for the sake of getting rid of it, as it would be to fire a gun at one's best friend merely for the sake of unloading it." In plain talk, he believed that men could engage in orgasm and exercise self-control over ejaculation, and he frequently illustrated his point by using the metaphor of a man rowing a boat in a stream above a waterfall: "The skillful boatman may choose whether he will remain in the stillwater or venture more or less down the rapids or run his boat over the fall. But there is a point on the verge of the fall where he has no control over his course." Such an unusual view nonetheless developed at a time when the conception of conserving energy was applied to male sexuality throughout the United States--what Ben Barker-Benfield has called "the spermatic economy." But

if male continence was nurtured in common attitudes,
Noyes's handling of it was, to say the least, startling.

Certainly his ideas had a striking impact on the lives
of women within the community. While not all men successfully applied male continence--and hence the nursery and
Children's House were never empty--still the birthrate at
Oneida was one-third that of nineteenth-century America.
Furthermore, the emphasis on birth control, the effort to
make men responsible for conception, and the division of
sex into its recreational and procreational aspects relieved
some of the biological oppression of women. Indeed, gyne-
cological studies testify to the physical well-being of Oneida
women, and a few women even noted the disappearance of
chronic maladies while in the community.

In most other aspects of their life Oneida women were
also equal to men. Certainly, the community worked hard
to install sexual equality in work arrangements: men learned
to sew, women to hoe; men cooked; women gathered the ber-
ries and fruits. Both men and women worked in the animal-
trap factories, kitchens, and nursery. In the latter the
special attachments of parents toward children were discouraged, for Oneidans traded the particularism of the
nuclear--or even extended--family for the universalism of
the community. Both men and women shared the political
and administrative functions that ran the increasingly successful economic life of Oneida. But ultimately it was the
patriarch Noyes who held the benevolent despot's power.

As they moved closer to men biologically and economically, women came to dress more simply and practically.
Visitors to the community noted the loose trousers under
their tunics, and Charles Nordhoff, admitting his own prejudices in such matters, complained that Oneida women lacked
grace and beauty. But others like T. W. Higginson found the
women "healthy and cheerful, cordial and with inoffensive
manners." Oneida women insisted that it was impossible to
wear the elaborate bustles, crinolines, hairdos, and tight
girdles effected by American women. The ease with which
Oneida women divested themselves of the artificial flummery
of the Victorian Age suggested that they found their identity
in what they did, not what they wore.

Yet, for all their equality of condition Oneidans did
not accept the theoretical equality of men and women. Noyes
himself believed in an ascending fellowship--in which men

outranked women.    Indeed, the male architect of the community never varied in his belief that men were more com-
petent in most functions than women.    This view of male
superiority explained his own commitment to male continence.
Such beliefs spilled over into the educational training of young
Oneidans.    While boys and girls received equal schooling,
boys went off to the best male colleges and girls for the
most part stayed home.    But perhaps this iniquity was as
much the failure of the outside world to provide higher education for women as it was an illustration of Oneidan discrimination.

## The Mormons

Both physically and ideologically far removed from Oneida,
the Mormons nonetheless shared certain characteristics with
both the Shakers and Oneidans.    Too often omitted from
studies of utopias, the Mormons nonetheless fill the criteria
for nineteenth-century communes:  they were intent on establishing a new social pattern based on their conception of
an ideal community; they separated from the community at
large to practice their vision, and they hoped to provide a
model for all mankind.    Even their westward movements--
from Ohio to Missouri to Illinois and finally to Utah--were
classic efforts to settle beyond the limits of established communities and to avoid both the harassment and contamination
of nineteenth-century America--the Mormon's Babylon.    Their
religion was also based on a vision--in this case one that
came to the young Joseph Smith, who found himself "seized
by a power which overcame him--a brilliant light announcing
all existing faiths were false."    As delineated in the Book of
Mormon the faith of the Latter-Day Saints was based on several variations of orthodox Christianity.    God, for example,
did not create the world out of nothing; rather, both humanity and God were a part of eternity.    In such a doctrine the
distance between God and humanity is diminished, the former
representing the latter perfected.    People are not eternally
damned but rather redeem themselves by faith and good
works.    Such a recognition of perfectability and the importance of human efforts at salvation drew on the same philosophical and environmental sources as had the Oneidans and
Shakers.    Furthermore, the need "to gather together" in a
community that would create a congenial heaven on earth was
shared by all three of these chiliastic groups.    But by the
time Mormons had settled near Salt Lake in the early 1840's
they had become identified--and indeed identified themselves--
by a practice foreign to the Shakers and Oneidans--polygamy.

Such a practice, however titillating to outsiders, drew on Mormon beliefs, not just the obvious need to increase the society's numbers in the hostile American West. Accepting the existence of an eternal soul in three states--a spiritual state before its admission to earth, a mortal state within the human body, and finally a celestial state after death--Mormons sought to bring as many souls as possible to earth. But according to Mormon doctrine supply had outdistanced demand. Hence, millions of souls in the spiritual state waited to obtain bodies on earth. In a sentimental evocation, perhaps directed at their wives, Mormons argued that these souls longed for good parents to produce children for them to inhabit. Thus, the duty of Mormons was to prepare tabernacles for souls, and because monogamy limits birthrates, Mormons practiced a system whereby men took as many wives as they could afford. Added justification for their concept of polygyny came from the Old Testament practice of ancient patriarchs, like Abraham. Polygyny also rested on a third base--Joseph Smith's vision which authorized the taking of several wives.

Commonly called polygamy by friend and enemy alike, the Mormon concept was in fact polygyny, i.e., a plurality of wives. Only a male-ordered society could fail to distinguish between permitting males several wives and denying females several husbands. Indeed, in the early days of the society, Mormon women petitioned that they be allowed plural husbands. If this had been granted the Mormons would have practiced true polygamy, but as it was, their system--consistent with the intended goal of high birthrates, not female equality--was polygynous. Actually, Mormons preferred the term "celestial marriage" for their sexual arrangements, and this meant that only the married could enter the soul's third state where a man's kingdom would be proportionate to his earthly progeny. Yet only one wife could accompany him to heaven; hence, Mormons produced two kinds of marriages--those for time on earth and those sealed for eternity.

The implications for Mormon women were obvious--competition to be sealed to a patriarch, status accorded from childbirth, and uncertain position in a household that might be increased by younger wives and their offspring. In the mind of Brigham Young such circumstances took on a specifically anti-female dimension, and the stratification of Mormon society soon was one of wealth and sex. "It is women's God-given role to bear children, to receive, conceive, bear and bring forth in the name of the Lord," said

Young. And when angry Mormon wives complained of their
continuing demotion the patriarch replied that they must obey
their husbands: "Let the wives and children say Amen to
what he the head of the family says and be subject to his
dictation not ever trying to govern him." Much of the rhetoric directed at women sought to gain their acceptance of
polygyny. An Easterner traveling in the West, for example,
visited a Mormon clinic and heard a doctor encourage wom-
en to obey and love their husbands. This, the doctor insisted, would end their pains.

In practice it was not always the fact of plural marriage, as much as its possibility, that affected women.
Certainly, some women suffered specific humiliation; one
"old" wife found herself moved into a chicken shed and her
husband's newer, more favored wife abruptly installed in
her former bedroom. Others suffered the personal indignity
of anonymity. On one occasion Brigham Young failed to
recognize one of his wives--perhaps understandable for a
man who had seventy. But few Mormon men could afford
more than two wives, and only ten percent of the community
ever had more than one wife. Yet, the ideal of polygyny
remained a goal and colored the relationships between men
and women in the community.

In such a society it was not surprising that women
were denied public roles. The all-male, self-perpetuating
Council of Fifty helped Brigham Young run the community.
Nor did women have economic power; their role and position was restricted to the family--a much-vaunted institution among the Mormons. Thus, in Utah as nowhere else
in America, woman's biology was her destiny. If she was
barren, she had failed; if a monogamous relationship was
unsuccessful, she stood to lose status and position. It was
not surprising that unlike the Shakers and Oneidans the reaction of many Mormon women was bitter, and while some
doubtless enjoyed the certainty of their subservience, for
others the utopia at Deseret was hell.

## Summation

Thus, the experience of women in nineteenth-century communal movements is a mixed one, and like so many other
aspects of nineteenth-century utopianism, defies generalization. If, as Frank Manuel says, utopian visions indicate the
sharpest anguish of an age, then women were nineteenth-

century America's special agony. In both the literary
statements of women who wrote about utopias, and in the
actual blueprints for these societies, the positions and roles
of women altered dramatically. In the case of the celibate
Shakers and pantagamous Oneidans, these changes moved
women toward equal rights and gave them more opportunity
to fulfill their potential. Among the Mormons the substitution of polygyny made women even more subservient than
they were elsewhere. Perhaps less isolated than in a
nuclear household, Mormon women nonetheless became splen-
did sacrifices to the radical Mormon Calvinism. But in all
three communities women traded the household of a man for
the family of a group and exchanged the privacy of one family for the public life of a collective. But nowhere did they
gain the personal autonomy they would later demand.

Inside the communities themselves sexual arrangements became a central point of identification. Shakers
were known for their celibacy, Oneidans for their "complex
marriage," and Mormons for their polygyny. Such concepts
served to bind members to the community and heighten
group solidarity and recognition. Finally, while there were
vast differences between the woman's role in all three, the
Shakers, Oneidans, and Mormons recognized that a more
perfect society required a basic rearrangement of sexual
roles and position. In all three, statements of what this
arrangement should be violently assailed nineteenth-century
practices. While utopians varied in what they said and did,
they joined the intrepid women authors of utopian novels in
recognizing that a new and better world must confront the
women's issue. It is a point worth remembering a century
later.

## Bibliography

Carden, Marian Lockwood. Oneida: Utopian Community to
    Modern Corporation (Baltimore: Johns Hopkins Press,
    1969).

Egbert, Donald Drew, and Stowe Persons, eds. Socialism
    and American Life (Princeton, N.J.: Princeton Univer-
    sity Press, 1952).

Hinds, William. American Communities and Co-Operative
    Colonies (Chicago: Charles Kerr, 1908).

Holloway, Mark. Heavens on Earth: Utopian Communities in America 1680-1880 (New York: Library Publishers, 1951).

Jones, Alice Ilgenfritz, and Ella Merchant. Unveiling a Parallel: A Romance (Boston: Arena, 1893).

Kanter, Rosabeth Moss. Commitment and Community: Communes and Utopias in Sociological Perspective (Cambridge, Mass.: Harvard University Press, 1972).

Lane, Mary. Mizora: A Prophecy (New York: G. W. Dillingham, 1889).

Muncy, Raymond. Sex and Marriage in Utopian Communities (Bloomington: Indiana University Press, 1973).

Nordhoff, Charles. Communistic Societies of the United States (New York: Hillary House, 1960).

Noyes, John Humphrey. History of American Socialisms (New York: Dover Publications, 1966).

O'Dea, Thomas. The Mormons (Chicago: University of Chicago Press, 1957).

Tyler, Alice Felt. Freedom's Ferment: Phases of American Social History to 1860 (Minneapolis: University of Minnesota Press, 1944).

## V. UNCONSCIOUS SEXUAL STEREOTYPING IN UTOPIA: A SAMPLE FROM THE NEW HARMONY GAZETTE, 1825-1827

Carol A. Kolmerten

The natural tendency of most people when studying utopian communities has been to look for what the experiment attempted to change, what structure and assumptions of the mainstream culture it challenged. In nineteenth-century America hundreds of intentional communities were created that challenged every mainstay in American life, from its modes of production to its methods of worship; but perhaps the most controversial communities, and thus the ones most likely to be judged "progressive" when set against the mainstream culture, were those that questioned the basic foundation of society--marriage and the family. [1]

The community of New Harmony, in southern Indiana, founded in 1825 by Robert Owen, attempted the first secular communal restructuring of familial roles in America, and, predictably, comments on New Harmony have focused on its "experiments in the unique and untried."[2] George B. Lockwood, whose The New Harmony Movement was the first book-length study of the community, also approached New Harmony as it differed from mainstream America; it was, in his and Robert Owen's words, "a new moral world," a world dedicated to egalitarianism.[3]

One reason it has been so difficult to perceive New Harmony other than through this "progressive" lens is that Robert Owen's expansive rhetoric on social reforms abets this perspective. In his first address to his fledgling community Owen optimistically prophesized: "I am come to this country, to introduce an entire new state of society; to change it from the ignorant, selfish system, which shall gradually unite all interests into one, and remove all cause for contest between individuals" (New Harmony Gazette: October 1, 1825).

72

To implement this "New Moral World" Owen leveled an attack against the middle-class family, which he considered the bastion of private property and selfishness. His criticism of marriage, in which women were regarded merely as property, as well as his firm belief that women, as well as men, needed financial independence, led him to conceive of New Harmony as a "Community of Equality," where women and men were to have equal rights and opportunities. Although Owen's theories were not all put into practice,[4] some real reform did occur at New Harmony: girls, as well as boys, were educated in the highly acclaimed community schools, and women were not dependent upon their husbands for economic support.

Despite these reforms, focusing only on how different New Harmony was from the society around it can lead to erroneous exaggerations about the changes that did occur.[5] More importantly, it can blind us to the immutable "givens" found in New Harmony as well as in the mainstream culture, which I contend are just as significant, if not more so, as the actualized reforms.[6] Although New Harmony did encourage its women to wear a practical loose-fitting tunic with trousers (which most women quickly rejected as "unseemly") and did offer educational opportunities to women in the community, real sexual equality was impossible, because in New Harmony, as in the mainstream culture, women were regarded as more pure, more moral, more delicate than their male counterparts. As Barbara Welter has concluded from her comprehensive examination of popular culture, the all-encompassing "Cult of True Womanhood" permeated every crevice of mid-nineteenth-century America; the True Woman, everywhere the ideal for feminine behavior and attitudes, embodied purity, submissiveness, domesticity, and self-sacrifice.[7] Even in New Harmony, an experimental community where women were ostensibly freed from cultural stereotypes, neither the reformers who verbally demanded equality nor the members of the community themselves could escape their semi- or unconscious beliefs about the "true" nature of woman.

The official voice of New Harmony, the weekly New Harmony Gazette, is an ideal place to find both Owen's "progressive" rhetoric of equality and its unconscious contradiction. The Gazette was not a "news" paper, except for its last page of notices; rather it contained a collection of liberal essays, editorials, and reviews. Each week a serialized central essay, usually written by an ideological

leader, such as Robert Owen, opened the paper. Without
exception during the first two years of the Gazette's publication (the two years that New Harmony was a functioning communal enterprise) this lead essay and the following "major"
essays promulgated a true "Community of Equality." But
following the opening essays shorter articles and a brief
section of notices, poems, and aphorisms exposed how firmly and unquestioningly the New Harmonyites and their leaders
accepted nineteenth-century notions about the nature of woman. [8]

In its first years of publication, the Gazette published
numerous articles that extolled woman's equal place in
Owen's forthcoming "Social System" and her limited functions in the "old immoral world." The anonymous author of
"Mental Capacities of Females," a major article in the
March 29, 1826 Gazette, finds it not "at all surprising that
females seldom shone very conspicuously on the stage of
life," because "man withheld from them that rank and influence which their sex demanded and which nature intended."
The argument continues by blaming the inadequate training
women receive for their lack of knowledge: "Woman has a
mind equal in every respect to man; though it may, and often does, lie under partial neglect, it by no means implies
that women have not adequate understanding, or that they
can never be brought to the same perfections as those of
the male sex." The argument concludes with examples of
the accomplishments possible if women are allowed to develop their mental capabilities, because "in the past" women
have "governed states, presided at council, adjusted dis-
putes, headed armies ... the female mind has been found
capable of reasoning on the hypothesis of Locke--of commenting on the various positions of Reid--and of expatiating on a
proposition of Euclid.... This woman can do, this woman
has done."

In another unsigned lead article the absurd customs
women have been taught to believe are ridiculed in the rational, Enlightenment-like rhetoric found so often in the writings of the New Harmony reformers. "Females," the article
on "Fashion" begins, have always "imagined themselves much
more dependent upon public opinion, whether rational or irrational in its dictates, than men. Yet there appears no just
cause or reason why a woman should sacrifice her better
judgment to that of her neighbor's any more than her self-
styled lord and master is called upon to sacrifice his."
Blasting away at cultural conditioning that limits women to
passive roles, the author points out that

independence of character is considered unfeminine, and the right of female self-judgment, though it be recognized in theory by the voice of reason, is yet condemned in practice by the voice of the public.... And what is the consequence? This--that a foolish habit, or an irrational custom, or a silly practice, once adopted among the fair sex, is perpetuated from generation to generation, because forsooth, though females may initiate folly, they may not originate reason (November 29, 1826).

The invective continues by berating the stupidity of permanently diminishing the capacity of the chest because of "fashionable" stomach boards and tight lacings. Three weeks later, in a follow-up article on "Ladies Beauty" [sic], the standards of the Chinese are criticized: "It does certainly seem a strange perversion of nature to admire female feet contracted to deformity" (December 20, 1826).

The importance of a good education, that all-encompassing equalizer in Robert Owen's schema, is constantly reiterated in Owen's ideological tracts published with great regularity in the Gazette, for it was a "primary object of the Community to give the best physical, moral and intellectual education to all its members."[9] A humorous insertion entitled "Female Education," in the March 29, 1826 edition furthered Owen's ideas:

> A young girl was presented to James I as an English prodigy because she was deeply learned. The person who introduced her boasted of her proficiency in ancient languages. "I assure your majesty," said he, "that she can both speak and write Latin, Greek, and Hebrew." "These are rare attainments for a damsel," said James, "but pray tell me, can she spin?"

The many articles in the Gazette on the vital importance of education for women suggest that the asking of such a question would be amusing to New Harmonyites.

Just as it was necessary for women to receive an excellent and equal education, so it was also necessary, according to Robert Owen's theory, to alter marriage and the family. On July 4, 1826 Robert Owen delivered his famous "Declaration of Mental Independence," which censured the "trinity of the most monstrous evils"--private property, irrational religion, and marriage. Marriage, Owen believed, reinforced the isolation and the selfishness of the family in relation to society; moreover, it relegated the woman (as a wife or daughter) to a subservient position as the "property" of her husband/father. A good marriage could occur only when there was affection between the spouses, which, in turn, could occur only when women were treated equally in the marital relationship. [10]

Concomitantly, Owen extolled a simple divorce procedure that would "prevent the increasing evils which must arise to those who are compelled to live together when they no longer retain the affection for each other which is necessary to their happiness."[11] Throughout the Gazette "statistics" and anecdotes accentuated Robert Owen's attitude toward traditional marriages. [12]

Despite these attempts to posit new assumptions about education, marriage, and divorce, which could liberate women from the familial chains that bound them to a servile position, the New Harmony reformers themselves held unthinking and unanalyzed assumptions about women. Although they might speak eloquently for sexual equality, the reformers also believed that women were very different beings from men, not "equal partners" in any way. The resulting tension between the rhetoric of equality, placed sporadically but prominently in lead articles on the first pages of the paper, and its subtle but constant contradiction, appears first in the editorial commentary. The first editors of the Gazette, William Owen and Robert L. Jennings, say in an afternote to a review of Mary Wollstonecraft's Vindication of the Rights of Women:

> It is, we believe, contemplated in Mr. Owen's system, by giving our female population as good an education as our males, to qualify them for every situation in life which, consistently with their organization, they might be placed. We have several instances on record which demonstrate, that, properly educated, they equal our sex in legislative ability, and in the lighter paths of literature they probably excel.... In the next generation, when our females have from infancy been properly educated, we shall have a fair opportunity of ascertaining whether their general organization is such as to admit of their participation in the legislative proceedings of their country (November 23, 1825).

Though Owen and Jennings admit that women have not had a comparable education to men in the past, women are "others" with natures different from those of men.  They are the beings who excel in the "lighter paths of fiction," who may or may not have the "general organization" that would allow them to cast a ballot.

Because women were "others," they were the sex that were advised, lectured, and admonished by the editors of the Gazette.  Nowhere in the New Harmony Gazette were men ever advised; nowhere were there articles on "Men's Nature" or on "How to Capture a Wife," but women were advised by the male editors at every turn.  Selecting an essay on the importance of a "silent example" being set by women in order to persuade their "obstinate husbands," William Owen and R. L. Jennings suggest in an editorial commentary that "the following advice may not be unacceptable to our married females, for whom it is particularly selected."  The advice itself instructed women to manipulate their husbands by subterfuge:  women should never lecture or admonish, rather they should only "hint" of a problem; thus, "by an artful train of management and unseen persuasions, having at first brought him not to dislike, and at length to be pleased with, that which otherwise he would not have borne to hear of, she would then know how to press and secure this advantage, by approving it as his thought and seconding it as his proposal" (November 5, 1825).

Oneida Community kitchen

Women were also advised on how to get and keep a husband. During the editorship of William Owen, he included in the Gazette several essays from other newspapers to help counsel women. In order to "enchain the heart of a husband with those golden fetters which only death can sever," an article on "Female Beauty and Accomplishments," proclaimed the necessity of a woman to be not only "as beautiful as one of the celestial beings," but also to be able to unite the external charms of her person "with her refined accomplishments and sublime sentiments of an elegant mind" (January 15, 1828). Once a woman "enchained" her husband with those "golden fetters" she was then advised in "Whisper to a Wife," extracted from Mrs. Coluin's Weekly Messenger, of her "sacred and important" duties to fulfill. These duties included asking, "How shall I continue the love I have inspired? How shall I preserve the heart I have won?" The answer to these questions was simple for a self-sacrificing True Woman; she was only to:

> Make yourself amiable and pleasing to him.
> Study your husband's temper and character; and
> be it your pride and pleasure to conform to his
> wishes. Check at once the first advances to con-
> tradiction, even of the most trivial nature....
> And the woman, who after a few years are gone
> by can say, "My husband and I have never yet had
> a loud and angry debate," is, in my opinion, bet-
> ter entitled to a chaplet of laurels than the hero
> who has fought on the plains of Waterloo (Decem-
> ber 19, 1827).

The advice given during William Pelham's editorship agreed with that of his fellow editors. Pelham patiently explained to his readers that "no anger or irritation ought to be felt towards female members [of the New Harmony community] when they brawl or quarrel, because they have been taught to believe that loud talking is an effectual way of giving force to what they have to urge in their own favor," though Pelham quickly added, in complete agreement with the "whispers" given to a wife, that "nothing tends more to distort the female character than loud and stormy disputations. It is contrary to the course which nature meant them to pursue" (April 19, 1826). In order to eradicate the "wish of finery and pretty baubles in women," Pelham includes in the June 28, 1826 Gazette a poetic "Address to the Ladies":

No more ribbons wear, nor in rich dress appear ...

This do without fear, and to all you'll appear
Fine, charming, true, lovely, and clever
Though the times remain darkish--
Young men will be sparkish
And love you more dearly than ever.

Even in New Harmony, women were cajoled out of their
"innate" wish for finery by promises of young men's love.

Robert Dale Owen, the Gazette's popular editor from
October 1826 to May 1827, reiterates his colleagues' attitudes
toward women despite his personal commitment to sexual
equality. In criticising a fellow editor's praise of a quilting
party, the young Owen's tone, just like the tone of all the
editors when addressing women, is patronizing:

> A brother editor expresses pleasure at a Mrs.
> Carr's bedquilt ... a great feat of some 4,572
> pieces.... Now ladies, ... such a contest is, at
> the best, but a childish one unworthy of your good
> sense. We ourselves would be ashamed to engage
> in any such.... We ought ... not to encourage by
> publicity an idle and girlish ambition, which seeks
> to put as many stiches as possible in a given
> space, and to spend the greatest possible amount
> of labor to produce nothing, or, it may be, to
> create an object fit only to gratify a silly vanity....
> Scarcely any useful inventions have been made by
> you; yet, your inventive powers are at least equal
> to ours; and if we had possessed good sense enough
> to direct these powers as they ought to have been
> directed, we should have been able to give publicity
> to exertions more creditable to your sex and more
> useful to society than Mrs. Carr's bedquilting
> (November 29, 1826).

Men, it would appear, need to direct women's inventive
powers, otherwise women will occupy their time with child-
ish feats such as quilting--the very domestic tasks that
"True Women" were supposed to perform. Women at New
Harmony thus were caught in a no-win situation: their
idealized domestic tasks were also not "creditable to their
sex." Likewise, Owen later editorializes in "Hints on Conversation":

> It is our wish to see the conversation of well-bred
> women rescued from the vapid commonplace; from
> uninteresting tattle, from trite and hackneyed

> communication, from frivolous earnestness, from
> false sensibility, from a warm interest about
> things of no moment, and an indifference to topics
> the most important....
> Ladies commonly bring into good company minds
> already too much relaxed by petty pursuits, rather
> than overstrained by intense application (March 7,
> 1827).

Although Owen admits later in the essay that the "uninterest-
ing tattle" that makes up women's conversations is an effect
of socialization and not weakmindedness, he believes that
his role as a liberal editor and as a male allows him to
lead women away from the "things of no moment" that occupy their minds filled with "petty pursuits."

Not only do the New Harmony Gazette editors advise
women either by their own essays or through those they re-
publish, but in this very advice-giving and selecting, they
prescribe an immutable "nature" for woman. It is not surprising that the New Harmony reformers depicted woman's
true nature as being a self-sacrificing influence--the same
conception so pervasive in the mainstream culture, the image so inimical to equal rights.

The disparity between the reformers' ideal of equality
and their unquestioning belief in the vastly different natures
of men and women is revealed in the hundreds of brief articles, aphorisms, notices, and poems that comprise the
last pages of the Gazette. Unlike the articles in the front
pages of the paper, these brief pieces include no pretense
that men and women are or could be equals in any sense.
Women are repeatedly depicted as "bright ornaments" whose
"delicacies and peculiarities unfold all their beauty and cap-
tivation." Also "peculiar to the female sex" is "tenderness
of feeling and charity of sentiment."[13] All these "feminine"
virtues led women to their most important quality:  self-
sacrifice.

The editors of the Gazette often chose poetry of well-
known women poets--most often Sarah Hale or Mrs. Stanley
Hemans--to conclude their paper "gracefully." The lessons
to be learned in this didactic doggerel are obvious. In an
anonymous poem entitled "Woman," reprinted from the
Philadelphia Album, woman's self-sacrificial nature is ro-
manticized in typical sing-song couplets:

Pain, peril, want she fearlessly will bear
To dash from man the cup of dark despair;
And only asks for all her tireless zeal,
To share his fate, whate're he feels to feel;
To breathe in his fond arms her latest breath,
And murmer out the lov'd one's name in death.
(August 20, 1827)

In a similar poem "woman's love" is extolled because it is
"unceasing" and "rich with humid springs of truth," but
most importantly because it "throbs for other's pleasure"
(May 31, 1826).   It comes as little surprise that woman's
amazing ability to "love with more truth and fervor than
men" (January 15, 1828) culminates in a brief aphorism
about woman's purpose for living:

> a thousand thoughts distract, a thousand passions
> are a substitute for the devotions of a man; but
> to love is the purpose--to be loved the consuma-
> tion--to be faithful the religion of a woman; it is
> her all in all (January 3, 1827).

Here is the nineteenth-century Cult of True Womanhood expressed in its clearest form.   As Barbara Welter has discovered, a True Woman had only two rights--to love and to
comfort.   All the proposed rights in the world could not
hold a candle to woman's "natural" rights--those springing
from her nurturing, loving, self-abnegating character.

Woman's unique duties derived from her self-
sacrificial, loving nature were also spelled out clearly in
the latter part of the New Harmony Gazette.   Woman's importance was forever depicted as coming from her salutary
(and passive) influence upon a man, or upon the society,
never from her own initiative, courage, or intelligence.
Women "smoothed" men's manners; when women conversed
with men those men, according to brief articles in the
Gazette, "lose their pedantic, rude, declamatory, or sullen
manner" (November 8, 1826), for "nothing serves so much
to polish man as the soft intercourse of refined female society" (January 25, 1826).   Without a woman's friendship
"our manners have not their proper softness, our morals
their purity and our souls feel an uncomfortable void" (November 22, 1826).   Not only did woman give an individual
man's morals "their purity," but her very existence purified
the whole culture.   But woman had to beware, for even if
she possessed a "well-cultivated mind" and was "industrious

and economial, " should she be "destitute of neatness and taste, she depresses rather than elevates the character of her sex, and poisons, instead of purifying the fountain of domestic and public happiness" (May 10, 1826). The "ideal" woman portrayed by the composite images found throughout the last pages of the New Harmony Gazette is aptly exemplified in the brief article "Woman" from the November 5, 1826 Gazette. Here, her nature and purposes are concisely summed up:

> She is the purest abstract of nature that can be found in all its works. She is the image of love, purity, and truth; and she lives and moves in all who possess virtuous innocence.
> Woman ever has been, still is, and always will be, the mainspring of every masculine achievement-- her influence is felt by ALL, from the hero to the clown, from the man to the stripling: and whether she fire a Troy or excite emulation at a game of marbles; whether she influence a court or rule in a dairy, the end, cause and effect are still the same. We may talk of patriotism--we may prate of fame--but who could feel the one, or seek the other, but for the sake of woman?
> Woman! Still more interesting when we contemplate her, night and day, watching by the pillow of a friend, administering the healing balm, sustaining the drooping head on her sympathizing bosom, and wiping the clammy dews of death from the sunken cheek--it is in such a scene lovely Woman shrines unrivaled and constrains man to pay homage due to angels of humanity.

The editors of the New Harmony Gazette, and some thousand members who flocked to New Harmony during its two-year existence, all carried with them some heavy cultural baggage. Clashing strongly (and silently) were the community's expectations of, and proclamations for, sexual equality with the subtle, yet all-pervasive imagery of "True Womanhood. " It is no surprise then, that this letter appeared in the March 7, 1827 Gazette, just as the community was dissolving:

> I will not undertake to controvert your position that females are, naturally, as capable of acquiring strength of mind and accuracy of perception and of reason as any other sex, but will content myself with suggesting that the physical difference

between the sexes admits that there is a corresponding degree of mental inequality, and, therefore, that it would not deteriorate the aggregate of happiness to retain the most rational parts of that system which was designed to educate them for their respective spheres.

Caroline

Caroline's request for a retention of separate educational systems is understandable. Her unquestioning assumption of men's and women's mental inequality, though disclaimed and verbally refuted in the main articles and editorial comment in the Gazette, is implied over and over again in the briefer articles, poems, and aphorisms in the closing pages of each issue. Certainly a woman who was depicted as a "delicate," "pure," and "self-sacrificing" creature, whose only thoughts centered on smoothing and comforting those around her, had little need for a "rational" education or for increased rights. If, indeed, a woman's goal was to "love and be loved," she certainly was a different being from one who used intelligence and creativity to forge ahead in the world. Caroline understood, as did Robert Owen and all his nineteenth-century colleagues, that woman's "nature"--her female character-- dictated different occupations (servile ones), different roles, different temperaments for the sexes.

In our rush to analyze the uniqueness of utopian communities we have too often failed to look for the unquestioned beliefs underlying the community. Perhaps one reason utopian experiments like New Harmony failed is that the reformers could not understand how their unconscious assumptions about the nature of woman could conflict with their glowing rhetoric for true equality between the sexes. By attacking only a superficial extension of the deeper problem, the reformers doomed their egalitarian proposals. Equal educational opportunities became mere frosting on the cake of woman's "true" nature.

Notes

[1]Books that emphasize those communities that attempted to change the marital and familial structures include: John Humphrey Noyes, History of American Socialisms (New York: Hillary House, 1961); Raymond Lee Muncy, Sex and Marriage in Utopian Communities (Bloomington: Indiana University Press, 1973); Mark Holloway, Heavens on

Earth: Utopian Communities in America 1680-1880 (New
York: Dover, 1966); and Rosabeth Kanter, Commitment and
Community (Cambridge, Mass.: Harvard University Press,
1972).

[2]Muncy, p. 9.

[3]George B. Lockwood, The New Harmony Movement
(1905; rpt. New York: Dover, 1971), p. 188. In all his
theoretical writing on the requisite assumptions underlying a
successful communal experiment, Robert Owen stressed the
primary importance of equality. Sexual equality particularly
captured the interest of Owen and many of the other reformers at New Harmony because they were interested in reme-
dying woman's unequal and "false and vicious" place in traditional families. See Robert Owen, Lectures on the Marriages of the Priesthood of the Old Immoral World (Leeds,
Eng.: J. Hobson, 1840), 20, 68; for other formulations of
Owen's egalitarian theories see Owen's May 1, 1825 "Address"
to the New Harmony community, published in the October 1,
1825 Gazette; see also all of Owen's serialized essay "Social
System," published in the January and February 1827 New
Harmony Gazette.

[4]Robert Owen's "parallelogram," his plan for a
closed village with living apartments around the four sides
and school, church, and communal dining across the center,
was never built. Although several boarding schools were
begun in New Harmony, participation in them appeared to be
optional. Owen's conception that all children were to be
taken from their parents at age two to live together in the
boarding school was not rigorously enforced. See, for example, New Harmony, An Adventure in Happiness: Papers
of Thomas and Sarah Pears, edited by Thomas Clinton
Pears, Jr. (Indianapolis: Indianapolis Historical Society,
1933).

[5]Muncy claimed that "in New Harmony no distinction
was made on the basis of sex in the enjoyment of rights and
privileges" (p. 218), while Mrs. Frederick Baly, the President of the New Harmony Memorial Commission, said at the
first meeting of the Owenite Forum: "We are memorializing
that first recognition, right here in New Harmony, of the
equality of women" (Proceedings of the First Memorial Owenite Forum, New Harmony Memorial Commission, 1942, p.
53). But women at New Harmony were not equal to the men.
For over a year wives of members were not considered to

be members of the community and thus could not vote on any issue. Although women did work in the community, they were also responsible for their family's domestic requirements--a situation that allowed the men considerable leisure. See Pears Papers; and Education and Reform at New Harmony: Correspondence of William Maclure and Marie Duclos Fretageot, edited by Arthur Bestor (Indianapolis: Indiana Historical Society, 1948).

[6]J. F. C. Harrison, in his scholarly book on Owenism, Quest for the New Moral World (New York: Scribner's, 1969), has also criticized the traditional liberal accounts of such movements as Owenism. Such renderings, says Harrison, "have been imprisoned within the confines of some implicit doctrine of progress and the reformer himself has been presented as simply a far-seeing man who responded to the problems of society more unselfishly and intelligently than his fellow man."

[7]Barbara Welter, "The Cult of True Womanhood: 1820-1860," American Quarterly, 18 (Summer 1966), 151-74. Welter's results follow an extensive survey of all the women's magazines published for more than three years during 1820-1860. She also analyzes gift books, sermons, diaries, journals, memoirs, and novels of the era. Though Welter specifically labels the four attributes of a True Woman as purity, submissiveness, domesticity, and piety, I have found "self-sacrifice" to be a more descriptive label than piety. See Kathryn Kish Sklar, Catharine Beecher, A Study in American Domesticity (New York: W. W. Norton, 1976) for an excellent discussion of this "self-sacrifice."

[8]Sidney Ditzion briefly refers to the "fill-ins" in the New Harmony Gazette, which described woman's softening and polishing effect on man. See Marriage, Morals and Sex in America (New York: Bookman Associates, 1953), p. 106.

[9]"Articles of Union and Cooperation," Article III, February 15, 1826, New Harmony Gazette.

[10]See both the July 12, 1826 "Declaration" oratory and the "Social System" in the February 28, 1827 NHG.

[11]Robert Owen, "Social System," in the February 28, 1827 NHG.

[12]See two such examples in the December 20, 1826

NHG.   One purported to be "authentic research" and classi-
fied 6112 couples who hate each other cordially; 5142 couples living at war with each other under the same roof;
4102 husbands who have fled to avoid their wives; 4012 couples living together with the most marked indifference; ...
and 2 faithful and happy couples.

[13] See December 7, 1825; May 3, 1826; and November
8, 1826 NHG.

## VI. JOHN WOOLMAN AND THE QUAKER UTOPIAN VISION

William L. Hedges

Published only two years before the Declaration of Independence, John Woolman's Journal carries what those who first published it called his "Life, Gospel Labours, and Christian Experiences" down to within a few days of his death from smallpox in York, England, in October of 1772.[1] Yet, although the debates and demonstrations that culminated in the American Revolution had begun almost a decade earlier, his record of those years makes no reference to the conflict. Had he lived a few years longer, he would undoubtedly have supported the general effort of American Quakers--because of their pacifism--to stay neutral in the Revolution, to refuse military service and avoid paying taxes in support of the war. In its early stages, however, the Anglo-American controversy seems not to have aroused him one way or the other, in spite of the fact that opposition to British "tyranny" at times led the colonists to techniques of protest (such as the boycott) with which he as a Friend was very familiar. Allegations that Britain sought to make slaves of the colonists may have rung somewhat false to a man as preoccupied as Woolman was with the brutal actuality of American chattel slavery.

But it is not only the America of the Patriot pamphleteers that the Journal ignores. Leaving out of the record most of his own personal and domestic life, he concentrates chiefly on the "Gospel Labours" that drew him away from home for weeks at a time. Out of these journeys, which in fact consumed a relatively small portion of his total life, the Journal creates an image of Woolman as a nearly perpetual pilgrim along colonial back roads, cowpaths, and Indian trails, from New England to North Carolina. Amazingly, however, the Quaker mystic seems for the most part not to see the new country or the countryside. The distances are there--the remoteness of far-flung settlements in danger

of slipping out of touch with one another. But the eye of
the frail and at times solitary traveler is on God or the
Truth--on slaves or the poor--not on the landscape.

The beauty of farmland and forest he takes almost
for granted. It is there to be felt when the conscience is
easy or clear. But as long as he must testify to human oppression, the land he traverses does not look like Eden,
Canaan, or Arcadia. What he observes is the fallen world:
"lying in the wilderness and looking at the stars" (mosquitoes
and damp ground have kept him awake), he is "led to con-
template the condition of our first parents when they were
sent forth from the garden." Their Father did not desert
them in spite of their disobedience. He "showed them what
was acceptable to him and tended to their felicity as intelligent creatures.... To provide things relative to our outward living in the way of true wisdom is good, and the gift
of improving in things useful is a good gift and comes from
the Father of Lights." But it is extremely difficult for
human beings in a fallen state to exercise this gift in the
pure "way of true wisdom"--that is, without being motivated,
at least to a degree, by "creaturely cunning" or "self-
exaltation" (pp. 72-73).

Woolman had recognized the weakness in himself.
The son of a New Jersey farmer, he went to work for a
storekeeper at an early age and soon saw opportunities for
prosperity in business opening before him. It was a path
that numerous American Quakers had already taken, particularly in expanding commercial centers like Philadelphia and
Newport. Even in the countryside, as pioneering waned,
people were demanding material comforts over and above
bare necessities, and some had the wherewithal to buy luxury items. Woolman's Journal shows the situation clearly.
His training as a Friend taught him that while "trading in
things useful is an honest employ," it was difficult to be in
trade and not be contaminated by the demand for "superfluities" (p. 55). He tried living for a while as a part-time
tailor and part-time shopkeeper. But

> I grew uneasy on account of my business growing
> too cumbersome. I began with selling trimmings
> for garments and from thence proceeded to sell
> clothes and linens, and at length having got a con-
> siderable shop of goods, my trade increased every
> year and the road to large business appeared open;
> but I felt a stop in my mind.

He recognized that his "natural inclination was toward mer-
chandise" (p. 53).    And he "felt at times a disposition" to
seek for "outward greatness. "    But

> I saw that an humble man with the blessing of the
> Lord might live on a little, and that where the
> heart was set on greatness, success in business
> did not satisfy the craving, but that in common
> with an increase of wealth the desire of wealth in-
> creased [p. 35].

Eventually, he gave up buying and selling altogether and, in
the interval between his ministerial journeys to other communities of Friends, supported himself by tailoring and light
farming.

If, as a modern commentator suggests, Woolman "regarded agriculture as the business most conducive to moral
and physical health, "[2] the significance of the view may lie
in the (perhaps inadvertent) identification of business and
agriculture.    For Woolman made no clear-cut distinction between the two.    If agriculture was more healthy than commerce or industry, he was under no illusion as to the innocence or simplicity of rural life in America--or anywhere
else.    On the farm, he knew, the hard work extolled for its
redemptive value by both Puritans and Quakers was too apt
to become back-breaking, soul-killing labor exacted of slaves,
indentured servants, tenants, or even of themselves by farmers or landowners not content to "live on a little" but "set
on greatness" and the accumulation of "superfluities. "    There
is in Woolman's Journal no celebration of America as a
pastoral or agrarian utopia.

His was a more severe idealism than that which under-
lay the general Revolutionary euphoria.    If he was blind to
the landscape, he was blind also to distinctions among
persons--to a far greater extent than were the signers of the
Declaration of Independence, whatever their understanding of
the allegedly self-evident proposition that "all men are created equal. "    Created equal Woolman knew them to be, in
the Quaker sense--all being possessed of the Christ within,
the inner light.    But the light did not shine forth equally.
Various inequalities of condition--most glaringly slavery and
poverty--helped obscure it.    And those miseries the American Revolution was not pledged to alleviate, even if one argued (and the argument was questionable) that in the long run
chattel and wage slaves would stand a better chance for free-

dom in an independent American republic than in British colonies.

The Society of Friends had been uneasy about slavery almost from its beginnings in the seventeenth century. Woolman is only the most famous of the colonial American Quaker anti-slavery advocates. Intellectually, he moved with comparative ease (whatever pain it cost him in personal dealings) from the doctrine of the inner light and the Quaker principles of tolerance and non-violence to the two contentions that were to become the foundation of the American abolitionist position three or four generations later: slavery is incompatible with the spirit of Christ's teachings and also with a natural-rights political philosophy--the latter having been early articulated for American Friends by William Penn. [3]  Long before the Declaration of Independence Woolman was saying, "liberty" is "the natural right of all men equally" (p. 61)--and meaning "all. "

The Quaker rank and file, however, were not so scrupulous when it came to slavery. Many owned slaves and justified themselves by rationalizations Woolman was adept at seeing through--the Biblical defense (blacks were the descendants of Cain or Ham and branded for bondage), the argument that slavery saved blacks from the violence of tribal warfare in Africa, or that Quakers made compassionate slave-owners. In the course of his itinerant ministry, then, as a sanctioned representative of the Burlington, New Jersey, Friends' Meeting, Woolman took it on himself to attempt to persuade Quakers to give up their slaves. The Journal records his success and the anguish it cost him to keep broaching this sensitive issue, often with venerable Friends of high standing whose lives were otherwise irreproachable. His method was an application of Quaker quietism, a gentle persistence that began with a respect for the views and feelings of the slave-owner being appealed to--as well as for the slave's. Speaking to Friends both in private and, when he felt the opening toward Truth, in open meeting, also publishing his views on slavery in pamphlet form, Woolman developed "undoubtedly the most influential single voice" in the movement that culminated in the abolition of slavery among American Quakers in the annus mirabilis 1776. [4]

Woolman was above conscious nationalism. He does not seem to have thought of himself as particularly American--or English. "There is a principle ... placed in the

human mind," he wrote in "On Keeping Negroes" (Part II),
that "is pure and proceeds from God. It is deep and inward, confined to no forms of religion nor excluded from
any, where the heart stands in perfect sincerity. In whom-
soever this takes root and grows, of what nation soever,
they become brethren in the best sense of the expression"
(p. 236). On one level he identified with the Society of
Friends, which was an international community, on another
with "all men," even with all "brute creatures," because
God made them (p. 28).

Yet he could not avoid consciousness of America as
the new country where Friends, like Pilgrims, Puritans,
and other religious groups, had found haven for a time from
the "wickedness" with which "the earth is so generally pol-
luted." In typical Biblical (and American) fashion he wrote,
"The God of our fathers ... furnished a table for us in the
wilderness, and made the deserts and solitary places to rejoice." The question was, could the spirit of the original
Quaker settlements in New Jersey and Pennsylvania be sustained? As long as Friends "were labouring for the neces-
saries of life, many of them were fervently engaged to promote piety and virtue in the earth"; they "were disposed to
work righteousness, and walk uprightly one towards another"
(p. 99). Subsequently, however, Friends had been "tried
with favour and prosperity" (p. 83), and their growing interest in what he called "outward greatness" (p. 35) made Woolman sorrowful. Like so many New England divines in the
so-called "declension" that succeeded the exalted first-
generation piety of the original Puritan settlements, Woolman
echoed Jeremiah in warning of the day of reckoning in store
for a complacent Quaker community.

Events in Pennsylvania and New Jersey in Woolman's
lifetime demonstrated that Friends could not exercise dominant political power in a society in which a large majority
did not share their scruples, particularly against war. In
Pennsylvania the intense nationalistic rivalry between England and France for the interior of the North American continent, together with the eagerness of settlers to push back
the frontier, created problems of colonial defense that finally made office-holding for Friends virtually impossible, except at a cost to conscience that few would pay. Woolman
encouraged Friends to resist paying taxes to support the
Seven Years' War and to give up offices in which they were
required to encourage a war effort. To him the loss of a
large measure of their political power by his co-religionists

during the 1750's may have seemed a blessing in disguise.
He undoubtedly felt that the consequent humbling of Quaker
pride was deserved.   In his mind there even seems to have
been a connection between Quaker power and affluence on
the one hand and war on the other:   wealth creates a power
that almost inevitably leads to oppression, exploitation,
jealousy, then conflict.   Not that he charged Friends with
consciously abandoning their anti-war principles.   But wealth
and security, the Journal suggests, may well have lulled
them into merely formal efforts, lacking forcefulness, on
behalf of peace.   The "Holy Experiment" of the Friends'
settlement in Pennsylvania had not been, for Woolman, a
total success.

   The society he looked forward to was one in which
people would be willing and able to "live on a little. "   He
seems to have cherished a vision of a non-political utopia,
an extended society of Friends, who would have no need for
police power or protection or for any government at all perhaps beyond the regulation of common concerns through consensus, as in the Quaker meeting.   But it was not in the
long run a separate community of the committed that he
hoped for, the righteous withdrawn from contamination by
the world at large.   Woolman's Quakerism would not let
him ignore injustice or oppression anywhere.   The ultimate
end was universal recognition and realization of the Christ
within.

   One comes to see that slavery was only the most
glaring form of the evil against which Woolman felt compelled to testify--at what the Journal suggests was an ever-
increasing cost to himself in discomfort and outright suffering.   The general evil was the willingness of human beings
to live at the expense of other human beings, profiteering
from their toil to lay up treasure that moth and rust will
corrupt.   Not only could he not accept the hospitality of a
slave-owner without leaving cash to be distributed among
the slaves, he developed scruples against eating sugar (a
slave-produced commodity), against wearing dyed clothes,
even against dining with Friends who used "silver vessels"
(p. 186).   Having, while a storekeeper, sold not only sugar
but also rum and molasses and thereby profited from the
outrageously harsh slavery of the West Indies, he felt compelled years later to spend money of his own to take his
ministry there.   Since he could make the voyage only in
ships employed in the West Indian trade, however, he feared
that his passage money would indirectly go to promote the

very oppression that he wanted to alleviate. The quandary was resolved only by his contracting pleurisy, which he apparently took for a sign that he should abandon the voyage.

Next he wanted to journey to England. Woolman still felt the pull of the old country, particularly of Yorkshire and the north country, the birthplace of Quakerism under George Fox. He desired also to attend the London Yearly Meeting--the Mecca of Quakerism. The costly appointments that cabin passengers on transatlantic ships had to pay for, however, offended him, and he insisted on going steerage--only to be afflicted there by the wretched conditions under which the sailors worked.

In the Yearly Meeting, to which he rushed on disembarking, his plain white, undyed (and probably untidy) clothes created consternation among the prosperous bourgeois English Friends. It was openly hinted that the American brother had discharged his obligation (though he had come three thousand miles) merely by putting in an appearance, and that he might now be excused. Almost overcome with humiliation, Woolman composed himself sufficiently to speak--and in such a way that the Londoners were brought to apologize; he stayed in the Meeting. The American provincial, a walking effigy of plainness and simplicity, had put metropolitan Quakerism to shame. 5

Beyond London, Woolman walked to the end. He had made walking journeys in America as a protest in heavily slave-owning districts. In the mild English summer of 1772 the journey toward York was not overly arduous. But this time he walked for the most part by himself. His protest now was against the callous treatment of the post-boys and the horses employed on the English stage-lines. Not only could Woolman not ride the stage-coaches, he felt he could not even send or receive letters by post. More and more his scruples hemmed him in. The purchase of virtually any product or service threatened to involve him in some form of exploitation.

A capacity for self-mortification that in some Friends went as far as a willingness to suffer martyrdom had been a prominent factor in what D. Elton Trueblood calls "the Quaker explosion," the dynamic expansion of the faith in the forty years after George Fox began preaching the inner light in England in the middle of the seventeenth century. 6 Only four Friends were actually executed, all in Boston, Massachusetts.

But, as the sect sought to implement their vision of con-
verting the world almost overnight to a religion of peace,
their attempts to propagate (or simply practice) their faith
in quarters where it was not welcome (which was almost
everywhere) brought fines, confiscation of property, corpor-
al punishment, or imprisonment to thousands of Friends.
Several hundred died in jail. Woolman was fully aware that
suffering was central to the Quaker testament. An affinity
for the discipline of suffering was a part of his mysticism.
It was a part also of the early Quaker inheritance from
German pietism, from the Anabaptist movement on the radical left of the reformation in the sixteenth century.

In the tradition of Christian mysticism the intense
longing for immediate spiritual union with God or Christ did
sometimes lead to the cultivation of something like a death-
wish for the body. This otherworldly pull is one half of the
tension or ambiguity in the Quaker perfectionism that Woolman's life so strikingly exemplifies. It is important, however, not to exaggerate this side of Quakerism, in Woolman
or anyone else, especially at the expense of its concern for
life in this world. Indeed, as the Journal shows, these two
themes of Quakerism are so closely intertwined as to be
virtually functions of each other.

Given his familiarity with significant biographies,
autobiographies, and journals in the literature of Christian
experience[7] (Friends were often great readers and, beginning with George Fox, prolific writers), it was virtually inevitable that Woolman's account of his life should be structured around the traditional drama of the spirit's struggle
to overcome unwilling flesh. But with the Quakers a significant change in the traditional Christian outlook on the material world was occurring or had occurred (one can see it
beginning in George Fox's Journal and coming much closer
to completion in Woolman's): the view that the body or
physical reality is evil recedes in favor of the conception
that what is truly evil is the mistreatment of human beings
by one another and their indifference to the sufferings of
their neighbors. It is for this inhumanity that the Quaker
suffers, unable in good conscience to participate in the wordly
(i. e. , discursive) activities that generate conflict, not peace.
The more sensitive the conscience, of course the more suffering the body must endure--to the point where death (conscience having prepared both flesh and spirit for it) must be
welcome. But such a world-weariness does not imply that
the world is not fundamentally a decent place in which to live.

The final months of the Journal show Woolman fully prepared for death as the only solution to the problems posed for him by mortal life.  He revised the Journal--as far as it then went--for publication before leaving for England.  In what he wrote subsequently the emphasis is on the increasing personal distress and suffering that he experienced through his almost unremitting consciousness of human oppression.  When in his last entry he actually mentions his final illness, it seems not a new disease (he doesn't describe it or identify it as smallpox) but a culmination of the afflictions he has endured all along.  One is almost tempted to believe that he willed his own death.  And we know from a record of his last days made by English Friends who attended him in the illness that he refused to take medicine that came "through defiled channels or oppressive hands. "[8]

The ending is latent in the Journal almost from its beginning.  Written retrospectively, the three opening chapters of the published version of his "experience of the goodness of God" (p. 23) give the first thirty-six years of his life a definite shape and establish a direction or manner for the remainder of it to move in. [9]  To "bear the cross" (p. 29), to live under "the power which crucifies to the world" (p. 98) had always been for some the deepest Quaker commitment.

For a spiritual autobiography Woolman's Journal records his youthful religious conversion somewhat routinely. The account has little of the passion of, for instance, Jonathan Edwards's Personal Narrative, written only a generation earlier.  But one gradually discovers that coming to an early realization of the nature of what he calls "true religion" (p. 28) was, for Woolman, only an initial step in a lifetime process, a mere theoretical apprehension of what had to be put to practice again and again.  To be fully converted, one must be entirely crucified to the world--and ready for death.  "No man can see God and live, " he wrote (echoing Exodus 33:20) near the end, aboard ship en route to England (p. 176).

On the surface his interpretation of God's words to Moses was, in the light of the understanding supposedly "opened" by Christ in the New Testament, serenely and reassuringly figurative.  Seeing God means the dying of the mortal will:  " 'Blessed are the pure in heart, for they shall see God. '  In purity of heart the mind is divinely opened to behold the nature of universal righteousness.... "  Paradoxi-

cally, then, to see God is to be reborn and live--even in
this world, "the desire for gain" being fully "subjected"
(pp. 176-77). Nonetheless, the terror of the literal meaning of the pronouncement in Exodus persists: mortal life is
irreconcilable with truly seeing God.

While ill with pleurisy before his trip to England,
Woolman had had a dream or vision in which he first forgot
his name, then felt himself "mixed" in a "mass" of "human
beings in as great misery as they could be and live," then
heard a voice saying "John Woolman is dead." Subsequently
he was "carried in spirit" to witness the oppression of poor
people forced to dig "rich treasures for those called Christians." Again Woolman chose the figurative interpretation.
The vision meant "the death of my own will." In the dream
he felt himself saying (after Galatians 2:20), "I am crucified
with Christ, nevertheless I live; yet not I, but Christ that
liveth in me" (pp. 185-86).

Woolman, however, records this vision in his Journal
not where it belongs chronologically but two and one-half
years later during his trek afoot through England when his
identification with the suffering of the poor is becoming so
intense that one wonders how much more mortification his
own frail body can stand. So placed, the dream seems a
conscious prognosis of imminent death. His conversion is
finally complete, the Christ within has risen, replacing his
own will. Though the path opens toward eternity, it must
bring him first, one cannot help feeling, to the end of mortal life--and sooner, not later.

But to posit an active cultivation of martyrdom as
the driving force in Woolman or in Quakerism is to ignore
the substance of their testimony and the social protest that
is central to it. Christian perfectionism, as John Passmore
has shown, has in various times and places taken contradictory forms, reflecting contradictory conceptions of the imperatives of the holy life. [10] In part, ambiguities in the
Sermon on the Mount itself and in other relevant New Testament passages (especially Matthew 22:37-39) account for the
contradictions. Loving God with all one's heart, for instance, has not always seemed to allow much room for loving one's neighbor. Not that the perfectionist has ever in
theory argued that uncharitable souls can be said to love
God. Indeed, charitable works have generally been a part
of the discipline of perfectionism--as, for instance in medieval monasticism. But until the Reformation contemplation

was apt to be valued over action as the highest form of reverence. Platonic and Neo-Platonic influences seem to have reinforced this tendency from an early time on. The perfect life often seemed best exemplified by the mystic cultivating a direct apprehension of the divine being through exercises in spiritual transcendence. And where perfection-sim was a less personal and more cooperative endeavor, the preparation of believers' souls for eternal life traditionally took precedence over attempts to alleviate human misery in the world at large. Thus, typically after the Reformation small groups of sectarians withdrew into separate commun-ities, tried to imitate the ways of Christians in the apostolic age, and waited, as sinlessly as possible, for the supposed-ly imminent Second Coming--instead of working, like the Quakers, to bring the millennium about.

Not that Friends were not themselves interested in reviving apostolic Christianity, but they believed that "the re-establishment of the true church on earth" would itself be, in the words of Sydney James, "the Second Coming, the founding of the kingdom of God which would embrace all man-kind" and "would renovate and purify" the world. [11] The "religious temper" of the Friends, Frederick Tolles has said, "was not mysticism in the classical sense, but rather what contemporaries in fear and scorn called 'enthusiasm.'" Basic to this was George Fox's conviction that men and women can "live in accordance with the injunction of the Sermon on the Mount, not in a future Kingdom of Heaven but here and now in this world of flesh and blood." Fox sought to regain for himself and humanity the "innocency" and "righteousness" of Adam, "before he fell."[12]

Fox's unabashed perfectionism, as it combined with his belief in the latency of the inner light in every human being, had far-reaching implications that Quakers themselves only gradually came to realize. Perfection was a possibility for everyone, since its source was submission to the guid-ance of the light of Christ within. Furthermore, perfection involved helping others to be perfect--helping not simply by exhortation and spiritual consolation but in more tangible form as well. Pacifism is a corollary to loving one's neigh-bor as oneself. And keeping the peace or promoting it, Friends gradually saw, meant not only refusing to bear arms but actively working to reduce human conflict and resentment.

"Basically," says James, quoting William Penn, "Friends regarded charity as an expression of 'the love of

God, which first made us love one another.'" Charity eventually had to be very broadly defined and its function seen in
more far-reaching ways. James notes, for instance, that
whereas Christians had traditionally felt obliged to give alms
to the poor because they "were the image of God," by the
early eighteenth century Friends were developing a practical
theory of charity, seeing it as essential to the promotion or
maintenance of social harmony. At first they largely confined their humanitarian efforts to fellow Friends in need,
but gradually came recognition that Quaker doctrine theoreti-
cally can draw no boundaries around the charitable commitment: one's neighbors are the world. [13]  It is thus not illog-
ical, though it is highly ironic, that a leading American
Quaker in the twentieth century should speak of "the dominant ideal" in Quakerism, the "vision of a world that ought
to be" in very pragmatic terms: "This group of people is
trying to demonstrate the fact that Christ's Galilean pro-
gramme is a way of life which 'works' better at least than
any other one does. "[14]

At certain points in their history, especially after
they were forced by loyalty oaths during the Revolution to
relinquish political power in Pennsylvania altogether, Friends
have emphasized their sense of themselves as a "peculiar
people. " And historians both sympathetic to and critical of
them often accept this conception as the essence of early
Quakerism. Frederick Tolles, for instance, a major authority on the Society, endorses the political abdication as consistent with Quaker principles. So does Daniel Boorstin,
who interprets the abdication as a refusal by Friends to accept their share of responsibility in the building of a viable
society. [15]  But it is important to note the limits of Quaker
peculiar-ness. The tendency toward separation from the
world and wordly involvements has been less pronounced
generally in Quakerism than among such pietistic and apostolic sects as the Moravians, Dunkers, Mennonites, and
Amish. The Quaker brand of perfectionism did not encourage extreme communitarian exclusiveness.

Accordingly, Friends are not much mentioned in accounts of American utopianism. This of course is as it
should be if "utopia" is defined primarily in terms of withdrawal from ordinary society rather than as the effort to
implement a vision of its radical transformation. Such a
conception (withdrawal) of course always carries latent within it the "no place" connotation in Thomas More's original
use of the term. Frivolous dreamers, vain players with

life--these are the charges typically leveled by self-styled
"realists" at those who go off to join communitarian experiments.  The charges imply an attitude toward utopians that
Hawthorne, as his The Blithedale Romance suggests, was
prone to apply to the residents of Brook Farm, himself included.  It is not easy to avoid having such thoughts about
the men and women who established the numerous early
American religious utopias that were primarily sectarian and
millennialist in conception--one thinks, for instance, of The
Society of the Woman of the Wilderness, of Conrad Beissel
at Ephrata, of the Shakers, of Jemima Wilkinson, or of the
Rappites--sublime escapists they often appeared, even when
they thought of themselves as forming a vanguard for the
world to follow.

True, a separatist tendency in Quakerism may be
suggested in the fact that the Shakers began as disaffected
Friends or that the mother of the Universal Friend, Jemima
Wilkinson, was also a Quaker.  But the tendency can easily
be overstated, as it is, for instance, in Michel Guillaume
Jean de Crèvecoeur's account of Quaker life on Nantucket in
Letters from an American Farmer (1782).  Reading
Crèvecoeur, one would think that Friends had actually come
close to producing their own sectarian utopia on Nantucket--
equipped even with certain slightly socialistic or communistic property arrangements.  But the settling of that island
was not originally a Quaker project.  And whatever social
harmony prevailed there, including the holding of much of
the land in common, was undoubtedly evidence rather of the
ability of Friends to cooperate with their neighbors than of
their exclusiveness.  For non-Quaker Puritans had always
made up a substantial proportion of the island's population.

While Penn's "Holy Experiment" was in one sense a
mass "coming out" from a corrupt world, it is worth remembering that it was at first viewed with suspicion by many
Friends in England as an escape from persecution, which
ought, they argued, to be (non-violently) resisted, not run
away from. 16  Moreover, the value that Friends placed on
religious freedom operated against their remaining separated
in Pennsylvania, which from the beginning was committed to
admitting and tolerating any and all non-Quakers who wanted
to settle there.  Friends rapidly became a minority in their
own colony.  Ultimately forced out of power, however, they
nonetheless held their ground there.  While reaffirming themselves a "peculiar people" in religious observances, dress,
speech, and manners, they continued to mix in the world

economically and, as far as was consistent with their principles, socially and politically.   They spoke out on unpopu-
lar causes and extended their outreach through increased
humanitarian effort.

        In the end Quakerism's ambivalence toward the ordin-
ary world is a large part of its significance.   Non-participa-
tion under certain circumstances is one of its faces, but not
total rejection or withdrawal to utopia.   Rather it lives on
the faith that the world itself can become utopia.   Tolles
helps clarify this outlook when, referring to Pennsylvania,
he asks, "Where else, outside of Utopian fiction, has a
government founded upon such idealistic principles survived
for as long a period as three quarters of a century?"[17]
Through their quiet or quietistic persistence and through the
commitment to pacifism, humanitarianism, and, when conscience dictates, civil disobedience, Quaker faith continues
to exert an influence far out of proportion to the size of the
actual membership in the Society of Friends.   Its substantial
impact, for instance, on the radical dissent in America since
the early 1960's can easily be documented.

        The moral republic that Woolman envisioned, vaguely
anarchistic or communistic, called for a far more radical
and extensive revolution than the one that American Patriots
were perpetrating when he died; his would be a revolution
against the excessive valuation of private property then developing in America.   Until that happened he had in a sense
no home but remained perhaps the most unsettled of all
Americans, endlessly seeking not the good life but the good.
Who else in eighteenth-century America worried as he did
about the poor?[18]   They were not supposed to exist in a
land with unlimited natural resources and an intense labor
shortage.   But Woolman could see that they are always with
us, even if not so visible in the new world as in the old.
Vaunting America was thus hardly called for.   At once the
most pessimistic and optimistic American of his age, he
saw the risk of complicity with evil at virtually every step;
nonetheless he sustained a literal faith in the final revolution to which he dedicated his life, the coming of the "pure
peaceable government of Christ" to "prevail amongst man-
kind"--"on earth as it is in Heaven" (p. 174).

## Notes

[1] The title of the first edition (Philadelphia, 1774) was
A Journal of the Life, Gospel Labours, and Christian

Experiences of that Faithful Minister of Jesus Christ, John Woolman, Late of Mount-Holly, in the Province of New-Jersey. The standard title today is The Journal of John Woolman. The edition cited in this article is that in The Journal and Major Essays of John Woolman, edited by Phillips P. Moulton (New York: Oxford University Press, 1971). Page numbers in parentheses in the text following quotations from Woolman refer to this book.

[2]Note by Frederick B. Tolles, ed., The Journal of John Woolman and A Plea for the Poor (New York: Corinth Books, 1961), p. 42.

[3]Frederick B. Tolles, Meeting House and Counting House: The Quaker Merchants of Colonial Philadelphia, 1682-1763 (Chapel Hill: University of North Carolina Press, 1948), pp. 12-14.

[4]D. Elton Trueblood, The People Called Quakers (New York: Harper & Row, 1966), p. 162.

[5]Although this story apparently lived only by word of mouth for many years after the occurrence, its authenticity is generally accepted. See Tolles, ed., The Journal of John Woolman and A Plea for the Poor, pp. 207-08, note.

[6]Trueblood, p. 1.

[7]See Frederick B. Tolles, "John Woolman's List of 'Books Lent,'" Bulletin of Friends Historical Association, 31 (August 1942), 72-81. On the relation of Woolman's Journal to similar works by colonial Puritans and Quakers, see Daniel B. Shea, Jr., Spiritual Autobiography in Early America (Princeton, N.J.: Princeton University Press, 1968).

[8]The Journal and Major Essays of John Woolman, pp. 283, 302.

[9]He had actually begun to keep diaristic notes earlier, but in 1756 or 1757 revised what he had recorded thus far into what (in contrast to the rest of the book) is more auto-biography than diary or journal (see ibid., p. 284).

[10]The Perfectibility of Man (New York: Scribner's, 1970), pp. 88-89 and chapters 4-7, passim.

[11]Sydney V. James, A People Among Peoples: Quaker

Benevolence in Eighteenth-Century America (Cambridge, Mass.: Harvard University Press, 1963), p. 20.

[12]Meeting House and Counting House, pp. 5-6.

[13]James, A People Among Peoples, pp. 32-33.

[14]Rufus M. Jones, The Faith and Practice of the Quakers (London, New York [1927]), p. 165.

[15]Tolles, Meeting House and Counting House, Chapter 10; Boorstin, The Americans: The Colonial Experience (New York: Random House, 1958), Part II, passim.

[16]Tolles, Meeting House and Counting House, pp. 34-35.

[17]Ibid., p. 240. Cf. Sydney E. Ahlstrom's characterization of Quaker faith as "reformed optimism" and his differentiation between the early Quakers and the Mennonites in regard to their attitude toward the world, in A Religious History of the American People (New Haven, Conn.: Yale University Press, 1972), p. 211. Quakers and Quaker faith are frequently referred to as "utopian," even though Friends have not tried to establish exclusive utopian communities.

[18]See his remarkable essay "A Plea for the Poor" (Journal and Major Essays, pp. 238-72), in which his implicit critique of capitalism is quite pronounced.

# VII. TOWN PLANNING FOR THE CITY OF GOD

Paul H. Douglas

Twenty miles north of Pittsburgh on the east bank of the
Ohio River and surrounded by huge industrial plants and the
sprawling, working-class town of Ambridge, Pennsylvania,
lies an orderly little block of buildings, vineyards, and gardens that were once parts of a thriving communitarian village.  Called Economy by its inhabitants, this town was the
third and last community that was built by the Harmonists,
a group of German pietists who came to America in the
first decade of the nineteenth century.  The Harmony Society
was prosperous and long-lived.  Only the Shakers have a
longer history.  For a hundred years these practical Ger-
mans were living proof of the possibility of a successful
communal society in an essentially capitalistic environment.

Unlike any other communal group in nineteenth-century
America, the Harmonists set up three successive villages,
reshaping them to meet their beliefs and needs.  As a result changes that appear in the philosophy of the group are
more evident in the town planning and material culture than
they would be if the Society had remained in the same location throughout its existence.  An examination of the town
planning of the three Harmonist villages--Harmony, Pennsylvania (1805-14); New Harmony, Indiana (1815-24); and Economy,
Pennsylvania (1825-1904)--reveals that the Harmonists were
not, as some historians have suggested, primarily conserva-
tive peasants with a reactionary conception of an ideal community pegged at a certain level in time.  Instead, they were
progressive and experimental, capable of changing to meet
the social, cultural, intellectual, and physical needs of the
members and of competing successfully with the outside
world in financial matters.  Far from being a static community, the Harmony Society was in many respects fluid and
flexible.  A good deal of its success resulted from the ability to balance religious ideals with the economic necessities
of time and place.

103

Without exception the visitors who came to the
Harmonist towns and left written records were favorably
impressed with their location, regularity of plan, and at-
tractiveness. John Melish, for example, who visited
Harmony in 1811, said that after coming from Pittsburgh
through country that was "rather rough and uncultivated" he
reached the top of a hill and saw, "at a little distance, the
town of Harmony, elegantly situated amid flourishing and
well cultivated fields." Melish then noted that the town was
"regularly laid out" with a village square, streets crossing
one another at right angles, and a quarter-acre lot provided
for each family. An English visitor to New Harmony in
1823 described that town as being "regularly laid out into
straight and spacious streets, crossing each other at right
angles, with neat and commodious brick and framed houses
which are extremely well built, the uniform redness of the
brick ... giving to the place a brightness of appearance
which the towns of England are quite destitute of." Finally,
Economy, the third home of the Harmonists, was described
by Charles Nordhoff in the 1870's:

> Economy has, in truth, one of the loveliest situa-
> tions on the Ohio River. It stands in the midst of
> a rich plain, with swelling hills behind, protecting
> it from cold winds in winter; a magnificent reach
> of the river in view below; and tall hills on the
> opposite shore to give a picturesque outlook....
> Streets proceed at right angles with the river's
> course; and each street is lined with neat frame
> or brick houses, surrounding a square in such a
> manner that within, each household has a sufficient
> garden.

While there was nothing revolutionary about the planning of the Harmonist villages, especially if one compares
them to the elaborate complexes proposed by such utopian
visionaries as Charles Fourier or Robert Owen, who en-
visioned an enclosed city resembling a combination medieval
bastide and an eighteenth-century London square, each was
a practical rather than a theoretical solution to the changing
needs and attitudes of the Society. As one visitor to Economy stated, one "should not imagine some fairy temple, but
merely a very common, clean, and tastefully built garden
city with factories, and at the edges of town the incidental
buildings needed for farming."

## The Locations of the Villages

The locations of the three villages built by the Harmonists reveal a gradual change that took place in the economic system of the community. The site for the first town was chosen by George Rapp, who with his son and two followers examined land in Pennsylvania, Virginia, and Ohio before the first large group of Harmonists arrived in America. Although Rapp wanted to purchase a large tract of land in Ohio, the down payment was more than the Society could afford. The site finally chosen was in Butler County, Pennsylvania, an area consisting of rolling hills and resembling the landscape of Iptingen in Germany where Rapp was born. Since the leader of the community was a vine cutter by trade, the land was bought with an eye towards the production of wine as a major economic factor in the Society. While it was true that the hillsides provided good drainage for the vines, Rapp underestimated the duration of the Pennsylvania winter. As a result the quality and production of wine at Harmony were never up to the expectations of the Society.

In addition to the supposed suitability of the Butler County site for the cultivation of the vine, the area was chosen for its general fertility, for the Connoquenessing Creek, which provided power for the mills, for the proximity of German-speaking neighbors, and probably for its isolation from major urban centers. At Harmony the Society planned to build a village with an economic base of agricultural production that would become a commercial center for the area. The Harmony Society, like other successful communal groups in the nineteenth century, including the Shakers, the Society of Separatists at Zoar, Ohio, and the Society of True Inspiration at Amana, Iowa, realized the necessity of interacting financially with the outside world in order to achieve prosperity. The Harmonists, for example, built an inn at each village to accommodate visitors who came to the community on business matters or merely out of curiosity, and at Economy they had a community store that both distributed goods to the members of the society and at the same time sold items to outsiders on a capitalistic basis. Thus, without compromising their communal or religious ideals, the Harmonists managed to get the hard cash necessary for financial stability. This lesson from the successful nineteenth-century communes may have been absorbed by the contemporary Twin Oaks community in Virginia, which sells hammocks to the outside world. On the other hand, the early 1970's saw the demise of a number of short-lived communes that attempted to isolate themselves completely from what they perceived as the decadence of the outside world.

By 1811 the Society had built grist, oil, hemp, and cloth processing mills and was providing the surrounding area with a variety of goods, including whiskey, shoes, and hats; by 1813 agents, through whom their manufactured goods could be sold, were established in Philadelphia, Lancaster, and Pittsburgh. However, although the Society was prospering, the Connoquenessing Creek, which was suitable for powering the mills, was not a navigable river and therefore could not be used to transport the increasing amount of goods that were being produced. For that purpose the Harmonists used the Ohio River, which was twelve miles distant. Moreover, by 1814 the leaders of the community were convinced that the growing economic market in the West could be served more efficiently and more profitably if a western location were used as a center of manufacturing and distribution.

When the Harmonists moved to New Harmony, Indiana, in 1815, they purchased over 20,000 acres of land and located their village on the Wabash, a river substantially larger than the Connoquenessing and one that was both navigable and easily accessible by steamboats from the Ohio River, the main route of transportation from the East to the West. The Wabash also provided a route to the Mississippi and thus to the important port of New Orleans. The increasing use of steam engines to power Harmonist mills freed them from the seasonal changes in the Wabash, which was essentially unsuitable for continuous mill operation at New Harmony, and allowed them to locate their manufacturing structures where they could be used most efficiently, that is, in relationship to the landings, the homes of the workers, and the roads.

The Indiana site was chosen also because of the milder and shorter winters there as compared to those in Pennsylvania. The area was not as hilly as that in Pennsylvania, but the climate was better suited to the cultivation of grape vines and therefore to the subsequent production of salable wine. Even though the Harmonists were not in the vicinity of as many friendly German neighbors as they were in Pennsylvania, they were less than fifty miles from the Shaker community of West Union, which flourished between 1810 and

1827. The Shakers and the Harmonists, in agreement on a number of religious tenets, were on friendly terms. Gertrude Rapp, George's granddaughter, even stayed with the Shakers at West Union for a short time to learn English. And there was some correspondence between Shaker and Harmonist leaders about the possibility of a merger.

The frontier, however, appears to have been an unsatisfactory environment for communitarian societies. The Shakers at West Union lasted for a short seventeen years, and the Harmonists stayed at New Harmony for only ten. Rather than being conducive to the spread of communitarianism, the frontier seems to have had the opposite effect. John Humphrey Noyes, the leader of the Oneida community, assessed the failures and successes of a number of American communes in his History of American Socialisms (1870) and concluded that the

> fondness for land, which has been the habit of Socialists, had much to do with their failures. Farming ... is the kind of labor in which there is ... the largest chance for disputes and discords in such complex bodies as Associations. Moreover the lust for land leads off into the wilderness, "out west," or into by-places, far away from railroads and markets; whereas Socialism if it is really ahead of civilization, ought to keep near the centers of business, and at the front of the general march of improvement.

Although there is no evidence to indicate that the frontier had a negative effect on the social unity of the Harmony Society, there were positive economic benefits to be gained by relocating in a more settled and industrialized area of the country. For this reason the Harmonists made their third and final home at Economy, Pennsylvania, only fifteen miles southwest of their first village and twenty miles north of Pittsburgh. There were significant differences in the location of Economy and those of the previous villages. First of all, unlike Harmony, Economy was located on the banks of a major trade route, the Ohio River, rather than on a relatively small creek. By the 1820's the Harmonists were not content to be a commercial center for the surrounding area only, but instead had intentions of becoming a major commercial center for the Ohio River valley, certainly not on the scale of Pittsburgh, but taking advantage of the trade that Pittsburgh created. Second, the Harmonists purchased only

3000 acres of land at Economy as compared to the 20,000 acres they owned at New Harmony. While they were to continue with their farming and viticulture at Economy, their economic base would consist of woolen and cotton manufacturing and the production of shoes, hats, and whiskey. The name of this third village, Economy, derived from the German Oekonomie, signified to the Harmonists what they termed "The Economy" and referred to the combination of their method of communal living, their social life, and their beliefs. It also connoted a well-balanced and profitable form of agricultural and manufacturing production.

Thus, the three villages of the Harmonists were situated for considerations of agriculture, of trade, and of the changing concept of the communal good, which by the 1820's included substantial economic interaction with the outside world and the introduction of manufacturing on a large scale. The combination of an efficient communal system of production and an expanding economic market in America gradually increased the Society's economic interaction with the outside world and significantly influenced its choice of location. In addition, the adaptability and the economically progressive nature of the Society were revealed in its willingness twice to abandon a settled village for a new one. Unlike the Shakers, whose increasing numbers allowed them to create new, and quite similar, villages in different locations while maintaining the old ones, the relatively stable population of the Harmony Society (approximately nine hundred members) dictated the abandonment of the old with the creation of the new.

Street Patterns of the Harmonist Villages

In each village built by the Harmonists the streets were laid out in a rectilinear, or grid, pattern with the major streets on a north-south and east-west axis. In choosing the rectilinear plan the Harmonists broke away from the irregular street pattern that was common in Germany. George Rapp's birthplace of Iptingen, for example, consisted of just such an irregular pattern (which was characteristic of most medieval villages). For the Harmonists the rectilinear plan provided several advantages. As the name of the Society and of their first town indicates, the Harmonists conceived of their community as a unified and orderly entity in which all elements-- spiritual, economic, social, and physical--were in harmonious proportion to one another. The geometric precision of the rectilinear plan was therefore desirable. Whereas the irregular plan is appropriate for and characterizes villages in which growth is gradual and haphazard and in which each structure is considered separately rather than as an integral part of the whole, the rectilinear plan is especially suitable where the village is seen as an entity, though capable of expansion. Second, the rectilinear plan is the logical one if an equitable distribution of property is required, as it was in the communal philosophy of the Harmonists. By using this pattern the Harmonists could apportion rectangular plots, which fitted neatly into the predetermined pattern.

The irregular street pattern that characterized most medieval European villages often resulted from a competition between private and public interests for property fronting the street, with the stronger interest appropriating as much space as possible and thereby encroaching into the area of the other. Since there was no such competition at Harmony and at the other villages, the irregular plan would have been an unlikely development. Under the forceful leadership of George Rapp, the Harmonists created villages that were far from random and haphazard in their planning, but instead were concrete embodiments of a vision of a harmonious society.

Even though there are a number of theoretical reasons for a communal group such as the Harmony Society to choose the rectilinear pattern, more than likely those who proposed this pattern were influenced by similar plans in Germany and in Pennsylvania. By the time the Harmonists came to America there were a number of towns and cities in Germany laid out in an orderly and unified fashion that reflected the classical influence, which reached its peak in the eighteenth century. One of the most famous of the books describing the ideal city plan was De Architectura, by Vitruvius, the first-century B.C. architect and engineer. By the eighteenth century in Germany a number of renaissance princes had absorbed the ideas of Vitruvius and his disciples and had laid out towns with a rectilinear pattern. These systematized towns that evolved from the renaissance were centered mainly in Württemberg, the area from which the Harmonists emigrated. Ludwigsburg, a town to the north of Stuttgart and only fifteen miles east of Iptingen, may have been the model for those who planned the Harmonist towns. It seems reasonable to assume that George Rapp, or Frederick, his adopted son and the man usually considered responsible for much of the town planning and architecture of

(continued on page 114)

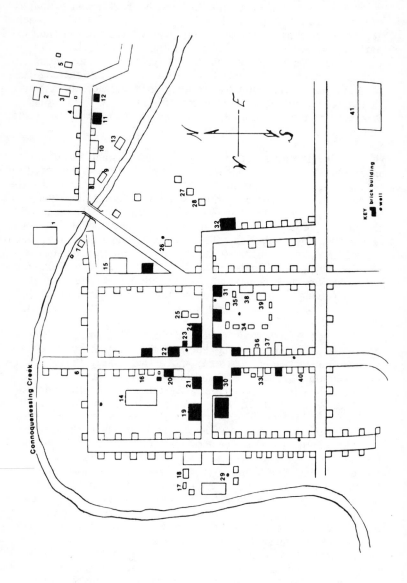

Harmony, Pennsylvania

Key

1. Doctor's Garden
2. Sheep Stable
3. Hay House
4. Cider Press
5. Sheep Stable
6. School
7. Soapmaker
8. Wine Press
9. Old Distillery
10. Bark House
11. Slaughter House
12. Dyer's Shop
13. Tannery
14. Granary
15. Barn
16. Carpenter's Shop
17. Lime Storage
18. Stable
19. Weaver's Shop and School
20. George Rapp's Residence
21. Store
22. Frederick Rapp's Residence
23. Community Kitchen
24. Hotel
25. Stable
26. Hatmaker's Shop
27. Ropemaker's Shop
28. Cooper's Shop
29. Barns
30. Shoemaker, Tailor, and Warehouse
31. Machine Shop
32. Distillery
33. Blacksmith's Shop
34. Small Barns
35. Hay House
36. Wagon Shop
37. Infirmary and Apothecary Shop
38. Barn
39. Stable
40. Cabinetmaker's Shop
41. Grave Yard

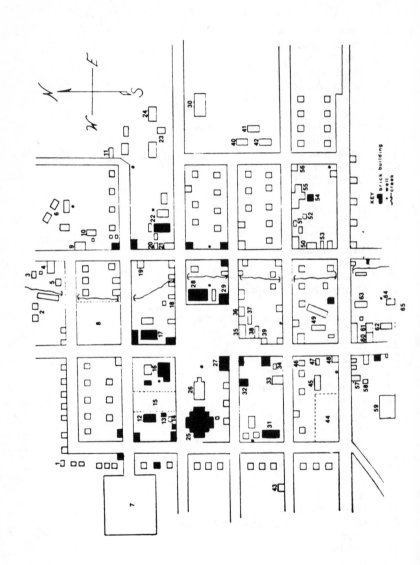

New Harmony, Indiana

Key

| | | | |
|---|---|---|---|
| 1. | Pottery Ovens | 33. | Blacksmith's Shop |
| 2. | Corn Yard | 34. | Wagon Shop |
| 3. | Malt House | 35. | Store |
| 4. | Brewery | 36. | Tailor's Shop |
| 5. | Wash House | 37. | Slaughter House |
| 6. | Pig Sties | 38. | Apothecary |
| 7. | Grave Yard | 39. | Hospital |
| 8. | Orchard | 40. | Machinery Barn |
| 9. | Distillery | 41. | Food House |
| 10. | Corn Cribs | 42. | Granary |
| 11. | Stables | 43. | Ropemaker's Shop |
| 12. | Granary and Fort | 44. | Garden |
| 13. | Greenhouse | 45. | Stable |
| 14. | Wine and Cider Press | 46. | Hatmaker's Shop |
| 15. | Garden | 47. | Hatmaker's Shop |
| 16. | George Rapp's Residence | 48. | Wash House |
| 17. | Bruderhaus No. 2 | 49. | Corn Yard |
| | (Dormitory) | 50. | Granary |
| 18. | Saddler's Shop | 51. | Weaver's Shop |
| 19. | Carpenter's Shop | 52. | Steam House |
| 20. | Cooper's Shop | 53. | Lime Storage |
| 21. | Carpenter's Shop | 54. | Dyer's Shop |
| 22. | Bruderhaus No. 4 | 55. | Grist Mill |
| 23. | Barns | 56. | Wash House |
| 24. | Hay Shed | 57. | Soapmaker's Shop |
| 25. | Church | 58. | Tannery |
| 26. | Old Church | 59. | Nursery (horticulture) |
| 27. | Hotel and Tavern | 60. | Stable |
| 28. | Bruderhaus No. 3 | 61. | Barn |
| 29. | Shoemaker's Shop | 62. | Corn Yard |
| 30. | Cotton Gin | 63. | Sheep Stable |
| 31. | Bruderhaus No. 1 | 64. | Sheep Stable |
| 32. | School | 65. | Brick Yard |

the Harmonist communities, was familiar with Ludwigsburg,
for not only is the street pattern there rectilinear, but the
architecture and the formal gardens of Ludwig IV show
marked similarities to features at Economy.

If the Harmonists were not influenced by the rectilinear plan in Germany, they must have been aware of its
existence in Pennsylvania. The influence of Philadelphia's
street pattern on other American cities in the nineteenth
century was substantial. As John Reps observed in Town
Planning in Frontier America (1969), "For many of the
towns that sprang up later during the westward march of
urbanization, Philadelphia served as the model. The regular pattern of streets and one or more public squares were
features that became widely imitated. "

In addition to the classical revival in Europe and
America the Penn proprietorship, which laid out Philadelphia
in 1682, was directly or indirectly responsible for the introduction of the rectilinear street pattern throughout Pennsylvania. When the Harmonists came to America in 1804 there
were almost one hundred towns in Pennsylvania using this
pattern. If they were not influenced by the street pattern
they saw when they arrived in Philadelphia, they may well
have been by those towns they saw in Pennsylvania on their
way to Harmony.


The Village Square and Garden

The Harmonist villages, centered on a square at Harmony
and New Harmony and on a community garden at Economy,
reflected changing economic and social patterns in the society. The earlier use of the square by the Harmonists indicated that the Society was originally based on the idea of
limited trade within the village and its environs. Like the
market square in Germany the squares at Economy and New
Harmony were gathering places for members of the community and for those from the outside world who bought the
products of the Society or lodged at its inn. The town
square was central to the community both visually and economically. It allowed for an architectural enclosure of
space within the village and it funneled traffic to that space.
As Tunnard and Reed have noted in American Skyline (1956),
"the strong medieval strain of the early settlements, to be
seen in the half-timbering, the use of thatch and the over-
hanging second story, rarely produced the enclosed arcaded

market square found in Europe. Part and parcel of the
walled town, the architectural enclosure could not be expected in open towns where the individual rather than the
community consented. "

When the Harmonists moved to Economy the abandonment of the village square marked a change in the economic
orientation of the community. By the 1820's the Harmonist
economy had passed out of the village handicraft stage and
into manufacturing on a large scale, which depended on the
markets in the Ohio Valley. At Harmony, which was somewhat isolated from the major trade routes in Pennsylvania,
the streets that led from and into the square were the major
sources of economic communication with the outside world.
At Economy, on the other hand, the Ohio River provided the
Harmonists with a major regional and national transportation
route and made the streets leading into a square less important for their economic growth than they were at Harmony.
Since much of the economic activity and movement was from
the means of production in the village to the river, the main
street in Economy (Store Street), was perpendicular to the
river and provided access to the boat landing. Along this
street were located a number of small shops, the post office, the store, and the doctor's office; this constituted the
commercial center of the village.

The Ohio River, then, functioned as another major
"street" at Economy, allowing the Harmonists to receive
raw materials from the outside and send out finished goods,
and also brought travelers to the community, where they
could purchase at the store items that would be used when
they settled in the West. Therefore, by the time the Harmonists moved to Economy they recognized that the village
square, which had served them well in Germany and in their
two previous villages, was no longer necessary. The economic focal point of the community, by the 1820's, had
moved from the square to the river. In moving into the
economic mainstream of America, the Harmony Society
abandoned an element which did not serve their communal
needs at a particular time and place.

At Economy the village square was replaced as the
visual center of the town by a garden facing the Ohio River
and taking up an entire village block. Although the Harmonists had botanical and pleasure gardens at their other towns,
judging from the reports of travelers none had the visual
significance of the garden at Economy. These reports
(continued on page 118)

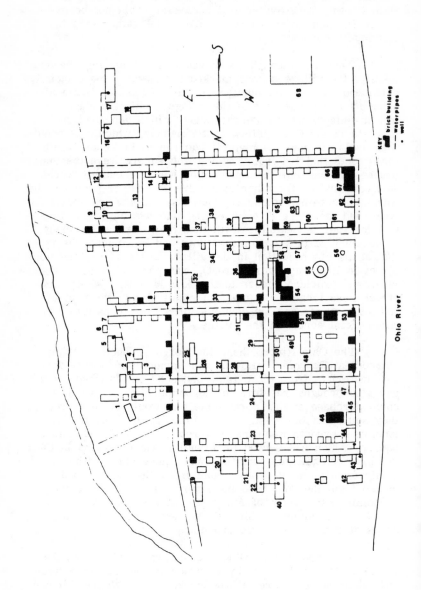

Economy, Pennsylvania

Key

| | | | |
|---|---|---|---|
| 1. | Hogs | 37. | Saddler's Shop |
| 2. | Wash House | 38. | Dormitory |
| 3. | Distillery | 39. | Dormitory |
| 4. | Older House | 40. | Granary |
| 5. | Soapmaker's Shop | 41. | Potter's Shop |
| 6. | Slaughter House | 42. | Bark House |
| 7. | Silk Factory | 43. | Tannery |
| 8. | Tavern Stable | 44. | Granary |
| 9. | Hay House | 45. | Flour Mill |
| 10. | Ox Stable | 46. | Cotton Mill |
| 11. | Dray Horse Stable | 47. | Brewery |
| 12. | Stable | 48. | Granary |
| 13. | Wagon Shed | 49. | Community Kitchen |
| 14. | Calf Stable | 50. | Cabinetmaker's Shop |
| 15. | Horse Stables | 51. | Music Hall |
| 16. | Barn | 52. | Tailor's and Shoemaker's Shop |
| 17. | Sheep Stable | | |
| 18. | Straw Shed | 53. | Store and Apothecary |
| 19. | Hay House | 54. | The Great House, Residence of George and Frederick Rapp |
| 20. | Barn | | |
| 21. | Stable | | |
| 22. | Calf Stable | 55. | Garden Pool |
| 23. | Cooper's Shop | 56. | Meditation Grotto |
| 24. | School | 57. | Bakery |
| 25. | Blacksmith's Shop | 58. | Greenhouse |
| 26. | Wagon Shop | 59. | Wheelwright's Shop |
| 27. | Dormitory | 60. | Drying House (Woolen Mill) |
| 28. | Old Church | | |
| 29. | Hatter's Shop | 61. | Wool Storage |
| 30. | Dormitory | 62. | Dyer's Shop |
| 31. | Hospital | 63. | Paint Shop |
| 32. | Hotel and Tavern | 64. | Weaver's Shop |
| 33. | Dormitory | 65. | Old Wine Press |
| 34. | Dormitory | 66. | Wool Storage |
| 35. | Dormitory | 67. | Woolen Mill |
| 36. | Church | 68. | Grave Yard |

indicated that the garden changed from time to time, but usually consisted of flowers, fruit trees, vegetables, and hedges.  Friedrich List, who visited Economy in 1825, noted that there were even cotton and tobacco plants.  The garden also included a classical pavilion surrounded by a moat, a grotto, a greenhouse, and a small, fan-shaped grape arbor.  The Grotto, with its rough bark exterior and elegant interior, represented the debased body and the beauty of the soul.  The Pavilion, a variation of the classical rotunda and similar to those pavilions that graced many Renaissance and English landscape gardens, had at its center a life-sized, carved figure of Harmonia, who, by the Economy period at least, was a symbol of the Society.  The existence of the classical pavilion at Economy indicated the growing prosperity of the community by the 1830's.  As a focal point for the garden and as a platform for the Harmonist musicians who periodically gave concerts to the members of the Society, and occasionally to outsiders, the Pavilion served the social and aesthetic needs of the Harmonists.  At neither Harmony nor New Harmony did the community have the time to indulge its aesthetic sensibilities with such a structure. And in no other communitarian village in nineteenth-century America is there a structure that so obviously reflects the high European culture of the Renaissance and Enlightenment. If the essentially ascetic nature of the Shakers is revealed in their unadorned furniture and architecture, the strong classical strain in the Harmony Society as well as its indulgence of aesthetic needs was made manifest in the Pavilion.

The location of the garden behind the George Rapp house reveals that the Harmonists recognized and honored the role of their patriarchal leader.  Even though the garden was accessible to the average members when they had the time, and as such was a communal garden similar to that provided by the aristocracy in some German towns, it was also a private garden similar to those of the German nobility or to the simpler ones that graced the homes of important figures in German villages.  From the piazza on the back of his house, George Rapp, who might be considered as a combination German noble and minister, could admire his garden and could see the members of his community enjoying themselves during periods of leisure.

The garden may have also served a symbolic purpose in representing the community as a garden of beauty in the wilderness.  The garden, like the town itself, was somewhat

isolated from the everyday activities of the world.    In the
words of George Rapp,

> There is no stopping nor retrograding in the King-
> dom of Heaven, but a pressing forward to the goal
> where a temple of God is erected in a green and
> tranquil, and delightful valley, that those who are
> susceptible of light may find consolation and re-
> pose, and worship in the holy Tabernacle, in uni-
> son, in order and in harmony.

Throughout Rapp's Thoughts on the Destiny of Man are images comparing the Society with a garden.   For example,
the cooperation of the Society "is the production of our time,
and will certainly blossom and bear fruit"; the existence of
luxury and pride in the outside world "could not destroy the
germ and fruitful tree, the branches of which are destined
to overspread the earth and spontaneously unite and flourish
in perpetual bloom"; and in such a Society, "where the great
design is mutual prosperity, and the indissoluble friendship,
the exertions of all, in the useful employment of arts or
science, for the common happiness, is a pleasing exercise
for the members in a pure and delightful climate, and on
the green and flourishing plains of peace."


## Harmonist Buildings

The existence and location of the structures at Economy reveal that the Harmonists provided, to an extent unusual in
western Pennsylvania in the second quarter of the nineteenth
century, for the religious, social, educational, cultural,
physical, and economic necessities of the inhabitants.    At
all three communities there was a core area at the center
of town that provided basic services for the Harmonist and
for the outsider.    At Harmony the core area surrounding
the village square included the community kitchen, the store,
the church, the hotel, the homes of George and Frederick
Rapp, a warehouse, and the doctor's office.    At New Harmony two of the four community dormitories, in addition to
the above structures, were also located in the village core.
At Economy the core area included the George and Frederick
Rapp houses, the garden, the church, the feast hall, the
granary, the store, the post office, the doctor's office, and
some shops.    Surrounding this core area at all three villages was a ring of family dwellings and shops, and beyond
this the fields and buildings related to agriculture.

The changes in the locations of structures from village to village and the adoption or abandonment of particular buildings were determined by a number of factors, all of which indicate that the Harmonists had no fixed conception of the physical nature of a village but rather modified their towns to meet their changing needs.

The dwellings at the Harmonist villages show changes in the social structure of the community. Like most successful communitarian societies in nineteenth-century America, the Harmonists modified the traditional nuclear family for social and religious reasons. Some communitarians, like the Perfectionists at Oneida, created a system of "complex marriage" that allowed members to have sexual intercourse with a number of other members. Other communitarians, such as the Shakers, practiced celibacy and lived in dormitories that housed approximately fifty members of both sexes. The Harmonists were similar to the Shakers in their advocacy of celibacy. However, since celibacy was adopted as a tenet rather than an absolute rule after the Harmony Society was formed by a large number of married people, the ultimate form that the Harmonist "family" took emerged gradually over a period of years.

Most of the houses at the first Harmonist village were modest one- or two-story structures similar to those that the members had lived in as a nuclear family in Germany. The exceptions were the few larger houses occupied by the leaders and by those who had brought a substantial amount of money into the community. At New Harmony, however, only the house of George Rapp was larger than the others, indicating a consolidation of his power and a waning of the influence of others. A significant change in the social system is evident in the remaining dormitory at New Harmony, one of four built for the large number of young, unmarried members during the Indiana period. These were, for the most part, the children born before the adoption of celibacy. The experiment with the dormitory system at New Harmony was apparently unsuccessful, however, for it was abandoned at Economy. Rapp may have seen the dormitories as practical solutions for housing the young people who were reaching adulthood and for those who came to the Society unmarried during the New Harmony period. Why, then, were no dormitories erected at the final home of the Harmonists in Economy? The answer seems to be that Rapp saw the beginnings of discontent among the dormitory dwellers and decided that the "household" system was better suited to the needs of the individual and to those of the community as a whole.

This problem of maintaining the communal dedication after the challenge of creating a new society has been met is not unique to the Harmonists; the Israelis in the kibbutzim, the Chinese, the Amish, all must face the difficulty of making important for the second or third generation what was so vital to the first. At Economy in 1832 there was a major schism precipitated by Count Leon, a visitor to the community who advocated an end to celibacy. Of the 215 members whose names appeared in the Pittsburgh Gazette denouncing the Rapp leadership, 169 were forty years old or younger and 112 were less than thirty years old. These figures suggest that the individuals who left the community were those who were young enough to have children and were dissatisfied with the policy of celibacy.

At Economy all of the members (except the Rapps) lived in two-story houses of virtually identical dimensions. In these dwellings some four to eleven members, both male and female, and often married but celibate couples, lived together. Thus, by the Economy period the nuclear family had been transformed into a small household after the experimentation with the dormitory system. For the Harmonist, unlike the Shaker, a measure of freedom was available within the limits of the household group. Although he was a member of a communitarian society in which each individual identity was submerged, the Harmonist was also a member of an intimate group of people who lived in a semi-private dwelling with its own garden. The institution of the household eliminated the exclusiveness engendered by the nuclear family, and it provided a sense of belonging to a group smaller than the community as a whole.

The location of a number of houses at the Harmonist villages shows that even though the Harmonists were a communal society, there existed a certain degree of social stratification. The most obvious example was the centrally located, large, and relatively elegant house built for George Rapp. When the Reverend William Passavant visited Economy in 1840 he noted that not only was Rapp's house the most elegant in town, but that those houses located near to Rapp's were inhabited by "the most influential members, and those who originally invested the largest capital," and that "those ... whose interest was little or nothing, inhabit the squares most distant from the center."

A similar arrangement existed at Harmony and at New Harmony. The Bentels, the Wagners, Dr. J. Christoph Mueller, and Joseph Neff, all of whom brought money or important services to the community, had homes close to the village square. Similarly, at New Harmony many of the homes in the blocks near the square were inhabited by the "important" members. On the other hand, of the four couples who had large families in this essentially celibate community, two of them, the Ralls and the Vogts, had houses on the perimeters of New Harmony. Was this a form of community disapproval for the failure of these couples to practice celibacy?

A balance of personal and economic elements within the Society by the time the group settled in their third village is seen in the fact that at Economy no one block was completely residential or commercial. At both Harmony and New Harmony some village blocks consisted entirely of dwellings. At New Harmony, for example, six blocks consisted of family houses only. At Economy, however, although some blocks were predominantly residential, all had at least one, and usually three or four, buildings that were important in the economic system of the village. This mixture of commercial and residential buildings is certainly an issue of concern for town planners today, who are interested in combining work, domestic, and leisure-time structures in a community so that there will be a diversity of activities throughout the day and night. Although the "new towns" of Ruxton in Virginia and Columbia in Maryland are primarily bedroom communities for Washington and Baltimore, there have been some attempts to encourage economic development so that a larger number of the inhabitants are working in, rather than outside, the community.

One of the major buildings that the Harmonists built only at Economy was the Feast Hall. Located at the center of town and the largest structure in the core area, the Feast Hall was used by the Harmonists for social, religious, educational, and cultural purposes. It was a nineteenth-century version of a civic center. Here the Society had its feast room, or saal, where the Harmonists gathered during various community celebrations; a museum that was open to the Harmonists and to the general public; a school; and a library. At the previous villages the Harmonists used the church for social and religious gatherings, but by the 1820's the leaders saw the need for a separate building that would serve a number of non-religious, or semi-religious, functions

FRONT ELEVATION

SIDE ELEVATION

Feast Hall at Economy

in the community. The size and the central location of the
Feast Hall was a practical response to the changing needs
of the members, who by the Economy period seem to have
had more leisure time than they had at the previous settlements; it was also a focal point that indicated to the Harmonists and to outsiders the opportunities available in a religiously oriented society.

## Conclusion

The three villages of the Harmony Society were situated for considerations of agriculture, of trade, and for the changing concept of the communal good, which by the 1820's included a substantial amount of economic interaction with the outside world. The adaptability and the practical nature of the Society are revealed in its willingness to abandon a settled village for a new one, to alter or discard some of the elements of the previous village, and to create new elements in the new village.

All three towns show that the Harmonists abandoned the typical street pattern of the rural German village, but that they may well have been influenced by the rectilinear plan that existed in both Germany and Pennsylvania as a result of the classical movement.

The Harmonist villages centered around a square at Harmony and New Harmony and around a community garden at Economy. The earlier use of the square was appropriate for a society based on the idea of limited trade within the village and its environs; with the gradual expansion of the economy and its growing interaction with outside markets, the square was abandoned as unnecessary and the garden was created as the focal point of the village. By the time the Harmonists settled at Economy their economic system had passed out of the village matrix and into the world at large. The abandonment of the square also indicated that the Harmonists were practical communitarians who could reject an element of their German heritage when it did not serve their American needs.

The existence of certain structures at the Harmonist villages shows that the Society experimented with particular forms in order to provide for the religious, social, educational, economic, and cultural needs of the inhabitants during different periods. At New Harmony the Harmonists built four dormitories to house the young celibates, and they built a large church that was used for social functions as well as for purely religious purposes. At Economy the dormitory system was abandoned, and a separate building, the Feast Hall, was built as a community center.

The locations of some of the dwellings indicate that there was a degree of social stratification within the community: those who were in positions of authority were often located near the center of the village, while some of those who continued to have children had houses at the outskirts.

There is no doubt that the Harmonists were aware of the values of a planned community. None of the three communities occupied by the Society was settled in a haphazard fashion; since the size of the Society remained relatively stable, the leaders were able to visualize the ultimate shape of the community and to improve each subsequent village. As such, the three Harmonist villages are noteworthy and significant contributions to town planning in America.

## Bibliography

Arndt, Karl J. R. George Rapp's Harmony Society, 1785-1847 (Philadelphia: University of Pennsylvania Press, 1965).

Bole, John A. The Harmony Society (Philadelphia: Americana Germanica Press, 1904).

Hiorns, Frederick. Town-Building in History (London: Harrap, 1956).

Larner, John. "Nails and Sundrie Medicines: Town Planning and Public Health in the Harmony Society, 1805-1840," Western Pennsylvania Historical Magazine, 45, No. 2 (June 1962), 115-38, and No. 3 (September 1962), 209-27.

Nordhoff, Charles. Communal Societies of the United States, from Personal Visit and Observation (New York: Harper & Bros., 1875).

Noyes, John Humphrey. History of American Socialisms (Philadelphia: J. P. Lippincott, 1870).

Pillsbury, Richard. "The Urban Street Pattern as a Cultural Indicator: Pennsylvania, 1682-1815," Annals of the Association of American Geographers, 60 (September 1970), 428-46.

Reps, John. Town Planning in Frontier America (Princeton, N.J.: Princeton University Press, 1969).

# VIII.  THE SPIRITUAL IMPETUS TO COMMUNITY

## John V.  Chamberlain

To speak of the American experimental communities as
"utopias" is immediately to place them into a category anal-
ogous to western religious tradition.   The universe is to be
trusted as benevolent; history moves under transcendent purpose; present society suffers from the blight of its own re-
sistance to that purpose, but the perfection of society lies
just ahead in the reconciliation to that purpose effected by
an inspired leader and his or her faithful followers.

Rosabeth Kanter holds that the impetus for American
utopias and communes has come from three successive critiques of contemporary society; first a religious criticism of
worldly society, then economic and political dissatisfaction
with industrialized society, and finally psychological and
sociological disaffection with mass, uniform society.   It is
the thesis of the present essay that the religious, the politico-
economic, and the psycho-social critiques all proceed from
one spiritual wellspring:   the biblical perception of history.

## Symbol and the Human Struggle for a Just Order

The "reconciliation of society to transcendent purpose" is an
abstraction, which must be made concrete to persons by vital
symbols in order to have immediate meaning in their lives
and decision making.   It is also profoundly ethical, requiring
both a Vision and a Way, to use the title of Jacob Agus's
book on Jewish ethics.   How do persons proceed to such a
Vision?   By what symbols are persons moved to seek to effect such a reconciliation?

One of the functions of religion, I believe, is to supply symbols by which persons may acquire at least a working
comprehension of the world in which they live, and at best

may perceive meaning or purpose for their lives and for
society. The need for such symbols, or keys of comprehension, is deeply human and universal. We "struggle to
achieve integrity," says Yale University ethicist James
Gustafson. "The personal situation of the moral man always involves an effort to come to wholeness and orderli-
ness in life." The world is huge and filled with a near-
infinity of encounters that seem to be meaningless. We
must learn to find and apply meaning that relates one en-
counter or encountered object to another. Life is immense-
ly complex, and we are called upon to act in innumerable
ways. Each action is detached from every other unless we
discover patterns that tend toward that wholeness and order-
liness. Thus, symbols are essential to meaning.

We start life with no comprehension or perception
and gradually become acculturated to those of our heritage.
The occasional genius among us will develop new perceptions
and the symbols by which they may be communicated.
Martin Buber's image of a baby glancing about in a crib is
instructive:

> Before any particulars can be perceived, dull
> glances push into the unclear space toward the
> indefinite; ... soft projections of the hands reach,
> aimlessly to all appearances, into the empty air
> toward the indefinite.... [P]recisely these glances
> will eventually, after many trials, come to rest on
> a red wallpaper arabesque and not leave it until the
> soul of red has opened to them. [1]

So, in the western religious tradition meaning is inherent in
the universe, waiting to be discovered.

Those mature people for whom not only "the soul of
red" has opened, but for whom the whole of life itself has
opened through a set of symbols that express such meaning,
may have such strength of spirit as to reshape the world to
fit their symbols. Or to implant their image in other persons so that they too see life through their symbols. James
W. McClendon, Jr., has interpreted Martin Luther King,
Jr., in this way, saying, "... we will not understand his
dream or his achievement if we neglect the role of Martin
King's religion, which happened to be the religion of a Black
Baptist from the South." That black Baptist-ism (King was not
a "Southern Baptist," of course) provided King with his
"call," the hortatory preaching, the singing, the clapping,

the power of prayer, the prophetic vision of justice, the image of Moses at the mountaintop, and Jesus's "creative weapon of love. " "Martin really believed those 'redneck' Southern sheriffs and politicians were human beings, sheep who had strayed from the fold, men who could be redeemed by love. " So, in the western religious tradition inspired persons who have discovered meaning in life can move society toward reconciliation to that transcendent purpose. Such persons were the founders of the utopias.

Not only individuals like King or groups like the Freedom Movement that was so dependent on him, but also whole peoples may perceive and transmit a sense of purpose in their corporate existence through religious symbols. Here our symbols have become myths--stories about God(s) by which a people's values and perceptions of reality are conveyed. Thus, the escape of a few Israelites from Egypt in 1290 B. C. E. was only the tick of a clock. Pharoah never even noticed. But Israel perceived the hand of God, and said, "That's the way things really are! God chooses whom He will; God is the deliverer of the oppressed. God, by His covenant is the creator of the just society. " Three thousand years later, at Passover, Jews still say, "God delivered us by a mighty arm and an outstretched hand, " and leave the door open for Elijah, who will bring the just society. So, in the western religious tradition societies, as well as individuals, may discover purpose in existence, and may press toward that purpose.

In this way symbols derived from religion press themselves into cultures and become parts of heritages that are transmitted from generation to generation. Once there, the meanings they symbolize may be held, consciously or unconsciously, even by the irreligious people of a society who have cut loose from the symbols themselves. Thus, a people's spiritual self-understanding may be secularized but still retain its power to move the society. One thinks of Robert N. Bellah's oft-reprinted article, "Civil Religion in America, " which maintains that in addition to the institutional religions in this country there exists an unofficial "civil religion" by which we celebrate our American spirituality.

> In [Bellah's] work we ... see that civil religion
> in America is a fairly well-formulated set of be-
> liefs, values, symbols, and institutions in which
> our society expresses its sense of meaning and
> destiny and to which it demands assent and loyalty

as a condition of citizenship. It articulates the
transcendent foundations upon which our society
exists and finds its unity. [2]

Similarly, many of the experimental communities were (or
are) secular, even anti-religious, yet retained religiously
derived symbols by which they understood and guided themselves.

Many observers have seen in American spiritual self-
understanding a strong strain of biblical-Christian covenant
theology. The New World is the Promised Land to which the
pilgrims and the immigrants have been delivered and which
they have been charged to remake into a faithful and just society. Ernest Lee Tuveson writes of America's historic
self-image as a "Redeemer Nation," an image that includes
elements of "chosen race, chosen nation; millennial-utopian
destiny for mankind; a continuing war between good (progress) and evil (reaction) in which the United States is to
play a starring role as world redeemer...."[3] Tuveson seeks
to derive these elements of American self-understanding,
which he documents from the writings of American politicians and thinkers, from Protestant interpretations of biblical
apocalypticism--especially the book of Revelation. The Protestant Reformers had rejected the Augustinian eternal distinction between the City of God and the City of Man in
order to argue that God had allowed the Church to become
utterly corrupt--the "Babylon the great, mother of harlots"
of Revelation 17:5 and elsewhere. But, by making Babylon
historical, the Reformers also made the expected millennium
(the expectation of the imminent irruption of God's Kingdom)
of Revelation 20 historical, as Augustine had not. Then,
under the influence of Enlightenment and Romantic-Idealist
thought, the western understanding of this millennium became the golden age at the fulfillment of evolving history,
and "was to be dominant, especially in the United States,
and to form a cornerstone of the popular philosophy of history." As we shall see, the American utopians often considered the millennium to have arrived with their communities.

Utopian Paradigms for Just Orders

Tuveson is concerned with the whole of American spiritual
self-understanding. We are here concerned with the utopian
experiments as American phenomena. More specifically,

my concern is to seek a common spiritual impetus that has moved persons to make the radical breaks from the societies around them into their own microcosmic societies. Although, as I will seek to show with my own analysis below, I think Tuveson is correct to say that the American spiritual self-understanding is biblically derived (though more broadly than just from apocalypticism, as he supposes), the word "spiritual" here will not have a specifically religious meaning. It will refer, with Webster, to that which is "immaterial, intelligent or sentient" about a person, "providing personality with its inward structure, dynamic drive and creative response...." We may note that St. Paul contrasts spirit with flesh as the higher call to transcend mere appetite and instinct, as well as the human willful response to that call (Galatians 5:16-25). "Spiritual impetus" here, then, will intend a sensed higher possibility for human society, not focused on material values, which evoked creative, dynamic efforts to structure such societies.

In the first wave of American utopias, according to Kanter, the goal was creation of a purified religious society in which members would be enabled to live their shared ideals with fellow believers. Such groups often emerged from European separatist or pietist denominations and frequently coalesced around some charismatic leader who persuaded them that such a society was required and assured by God. These people were deeply troubled by the evil of surrounding society, and they stressed doctrines and practices of perfectionism (the belief that men and women can be morally perfected in this life), celibacy, and millennialism. Sometimes they understood their communities as actually ushering in the millennium. Communal ownership of property was often adopted as an economic necessity and defended on grounds of its practice in the primitive Christian church (cf. Acts 4:32ff).

We may take the Shakers as illustrative of this first wave of utopias. Properly called the United Society of Believers in Christ's Second Appearing, they had their origin in a split from English Quakerism in about 1760. "Second Appearing" and Quaker origins illustrate the millennialist and separatist characteristics of the Society. It reached the height of its development about 1830 when it comprised eighteen communities with over 5000 members, spread over several states in America. 4 Soon after their beginning the Shakers coalesced around the figure of Ann Lee, a serious, thoughtful person whose obsession was the sinfulness of sexual union and whose charismatic leadership rested on her heavenly visions and pentecostal gift of tongues, as well as her intelligent sincerity. After a vision in 1770 her followers became celibate. She brought her followers to America in 1774, where their pacifism during the American Revolution made them suspect. After Mother Ann's death in 1784, her second successor, Joseph Meacham, organized the Shakers into communistic communities and codified their rules and theology. Their perfectionism is shown in the prohibition of any "amusement": no literature, art, plays, games, musical instruments, or tobacco; vigorous efforts at mortification of the flesh through strict discipline, and the characteristic dancing ("shaking") by which, apparently, sexual tensions and energies were released. [5]  God was now perceived as bisexual, with Mother Ann the second incarnation of Christ. The millennium, therefore, had begun with the appearance of Mother Ann. Mark Holloway cites examples of Shaker community life by which he justifies this observation about their conception of the millennium:  "These wrongs the Shakers put right within the boundaries of their societies: ... anti-semitism, slavery, racial prejudice, war, and the subordination of women. "

In Kanter's analysis the social criticism of the second wave of utopias was rooted in the dislocations that came in the wake of the Industrial Revolution. Communism was embraced not as a necessity, but as a welcome refuge from the unregulated factory system. The moral complaint was not "worldliness" but excessive labor of many for the benefit of few. It was not a question of more moral persons creating a better society, but a perfect society producing more moral persons. New groups coalesced around the ideas of inspirational and radical thinkers, rather than around the personalities of charismatic leaders.

As illustrative of this second wave of utopias we may take Robert Owen's grandiose failure at New Harmony, Indiana. Although his social scheme failed for reasons that seem obvious in retrospect, some of Owen's ideas and those of some of his distinguished associates have had powerful effect on American social and educational development. Owen, a wealthy British industrialist who had drawn international attention to the social and economic reforms he instituted for the workers and their families at his factories, also lectured widely in continental Europe on the need for reform. He was, moreover, willing to devote his wealth and energy to the creation of a new and just society.

> In the present system ... strife and contention
> are unavoidable. The man who does not prefer
> his own interest necessarily falls into poverty....
> In this state of the world, it is impossible to es-
> tablish the love and good will which are necessary
> to the comfort and happiness of the human race.
> Hence we have the evidence that some other and
> different course is imperiously called for and must
> be adopted. 6

When Owen came to America with a flourish in 1825,
he was heard by President John Quincy Adams and many
other distinguished persons. He promised to rid the human
race of evil by changing the environment in which people
lived. Evidently a deist, in his program he attacked both
religion as it was then understood and practiced and the institution of private property:

> ... [M]an up to this hour has been in all parts of
> the earth a slave to a trinity of the most monstrous
> evils that could be combined to inflict mental and
> physical evil upon the whole race. I refer to pri-
> vate or individual property, absurd and irrational
> systems of religion, and marriage founded upon
> individual property, combined with some of these
> irrational systems of religion. 7

Owen's utopian experiment began with the purchase of
the Harmony community in Indiana from the religious Rappites who had founded it, and who were now moving back to
their former area in western Pennsylvania. Renamed New
Harmony, the community consisted originally of eight hundred
recruits and a plan for the construction of a vast communal
building with all necessary rooms and offices for integrated,
friction-free, cooperative work and living. But it was never
built. Within two years New Harmony had disintegrated
under the stress of bickering, secession, and lawsuits.
Kanter's assessment seems justified, that the failure is
traceable to the absence of commitment to Owen's ideals on
the part of the members of New Harmony, as well as to
Owen's own unrealistic planning. He had advertised for recruits "industrious and well-disposed of all nations," and
the response was large and motley. His son, Robert Dale
Owen, observed that New Harmony "found favor with that
heterogeneous collection of radicals, enthusiastic devotees
to principle, honest latitudinarians, and lazy theorists, with
a sprinkling of unprincipled sharpers thrown in." Given the

diversity of membership, a sense of community simply did not develop.

The modern commune movement--Kanter's third wave--was a response to the social complaint that modern society with its rapid pace, impersonalism, and stress on achievement puts people out of touch with each other and their own fundamental natures, thus producing social isolation, alienation, loneliness, and inner fragmentation. The goal, then, is to create small communities, or "families," conducive to intimacy and psychological health, and leading to healthy, natural lives. The perfectionism of the earlier utopias is not usually an aspiration of the communes. The intention is a more modest one of abandoning many of the customs and mores ("hang-ups") of the larger society outside, which are perceived as divisive or depersonalizing. Communism is adopted as a reconciling or bonding structure.

Since communes exist in very large numbers and in myriad forms, and since they are a present, evolving phenomenon, they are not so easily examined as the utopias of the past. Generalizations about the communes are risky. Kanter distinguishes between "retreat" and "service" communes. The former have no ideology or scheme for the future. Rather, they are past-oriented, romantic turnings from progress back to the land and nature. In Judson Jerome's words, they seek Eden rather than Utopia. Having more of a "drop out" mentality than a teleological vision, they tend to be shifting, changing, and impermanent. The "service" communes, in Kanter's view, are more like their nineteenth-century counterparts in that they have ideological focus, stricter discipline, concern for future human society, and considerably more commitment and endurance. Twin Oaks, Virginia, may serve to illustrate this latter type. [8]

Twin Oaks was founded in 1967 by eight like-minded people who bought a 123-acre farm for their venture. It soon developed into a community of thirty-six members, with about ten resident visitors at any one time. Predominantly white, middle-class, and in their twenties, with a few older members, they raise their own food and earn needed cash by the sale of crafted items and by working at short-term routine jobs away from the community. The property is jointly owned by the members and equal access to goods is carefully protected. Labor is distributed by a credit system giving the most credit to the least desirable jobs. To minimize the buildup of animosity, meetings are held for the

airing of mutual criticism and feedback. Although members
pragmatically accept many of larger society's customs (for
example, regular medical care by outside physicians), other
practices that are felt to divide or categorize people are
eliminated. Thus, while there are singles and couples in
the community, there is also a trio and a homosexual couple. Distinctions between male and female or higher and
lower status are minimized. A trained computer engineer
in the community does not employ his skill in outside work,
but takes the same routine jobs as untrained members.
There is no leading personality; the community is governed
by three "planners" appointed to staggered terms. Long
hair, beards, tattered jeans, long flowered dresses, and
other counter-culture indications are there. "The U. S. is
a crummy place, but I don't have to go there often," reads
a sign. Equality and social justice are the reigning values,
says Kanter, quoting the following from Twin Oaks' behavioral code:

> We will not use titles of any kind among us. All
> members are "equal" in the sense that all are en-
> titled to the same privileges, advantages and re-
> spect. This is the reason we shun honorifics of
> any kind, including "Mrs.," "Dr.," "Mother,"
> "Dad," etc....

> All members are required to explain their work to
> any other member who desires to learn it....
> Observing this rule makes it impossible for any
> member to exert pressure on the community by
> having a monopoly on any certain skill....

> Seniority is never discussed among us. This is
> because we wish to avoid the emergence of pres-
> tige groups of any kind....

> We will not boast of individual accomplishments.
> We are trying to create a society without heroes.
> We are all expected to do our best, so making a
> big fuss about some accomplishment is out of
> place.

Note that the stated goal of creating a society without heroes
bespeaks their concern for future human society. Warmth
and affection are shown all around by hugging and teasing.
Genuine--and successful--effort is made to keep good relations with neighbors outside the community.

## The Biblical Vision Beneath the Paradigms

Underlying all three motives to community noted by Kanter
(religious, economic-political, psycho-social) is, I think, a
single spiritual thrust: a romantic version of the biblical
vision of a perfect society at the fulfillment of history. The
vision was there in literal form in the first wave, in secularized form in the second wave, and in non-symbolized,
existential form in the third wave. [9] Several analytical observations must be made about that biblical vision itself in
order to see its place in the utopias.

Time, in the biblical understanding, is lineal. It
proceeds from creation to fulfillment, not in a programmed
way, but nevertheless under the direction of God. Biblical
man and woman find themselves between memory and hope.
Events in time are irrepeatable. There is no return to beginnings. The paradigm for understanding what is happening
is not the cycle of nature--birth, growth, maturity, decay,
death, and rebirth--but the orderly movement of history
from an open-ended past toward an open-ended future. Events
are not only irrepeatable, they are revelatory. God, to the
biblical writers, is known by what He does in the irrepeatable events of history--not that God causes all of the events
of history, but that He is at work in whatever happens. His
work may be perceived, and thereby His very nature and
will may be known. History, or time, is both past and future, and, therefore, memory and hope are the keys to
understanding. Israel remembered that in the event of her
escape from Egypt God was at work, and so perceived that
God is redemptive of His people. Therefore, God's redemp-
tiveness was the hope for future history, the Kingdom of
God that would be history's fulfillment.

It is important to note that the Kingdom of God in
biblical understanding is a social concept. It is neither a
geographical place nor a one-to-one relationship between a
believer and the believer's Savior, but a community of people and God, in which God's sovereignty is acknowledged.
As a result of that acknowledgement, in the biblical vision,
all of the consequences of human sin (sin understood as the
wilful alienation of people from God and from each other)
are gone. Ignorance, suffering, disease, hunger, enmity,
loneliness, finally even death itself, as the ultimate loneliness, disappear. The wolf lies down with the lamb, the
sowers overtake the reapers, the mountains drip sweet wine,
men do not say to their brothers, "thou fool!" nor look at a

woman to lust after her, and they do not hurt nor destroy
in all God's holy mountain. 10

     Efforts to realize this eschatological hope are as old
as late biblical times themselves.  The so-called Dead Sea
Scrolls, discovered only in 1947, tell the story of a pious
and casuistic sect of Jews who in the first century before
the common era became disillusioned with the lax Judaism
of Jerusalem and withdrew to Qumran in the Judean desert
to form their self-supporting community.  They were determined to "prepare the way of the Lord" (Isaiah 40:3), that
is, to keep God's Torah so perfectly as to invite--induce?--
Him to bring in His kingdom then and there.  The characteristics of utopian communities that we discussed above (communism, perfectionism, celibacy, and millennialism) were
all marks of the Qumran community.  Jobs were assigned
to members according to the needs of the community, and
proselytes were admitted only by stages, as they proved
their faithfulness and endurance.

     It seems to me that the biblical understanding of his-
tory is inherently romantic, the story of men and women
grounded in their memory and questing for the fulfillment of
their hope.  Be that as it may, romanticism was certainly
the dominant mode of philosophy in the nineteenth century,
spilling over into all of the fields of intellectual endeavor,
including theology and biblical interpretation.  While I was
preparing this essay a student gave me the following quotation from Walter Rauschenbusch, the great Social Gospeler
whose work spanned the end of the nineteenth and the beginning of the twentieth centuries:

> I can imagine the sad smile on the lips of the
> wise as they watch one more bark hoisting purple
> sails and laying its course for Utopia:
>
> > A thousand creeds and battle cries,
> > A thousand warring social schemes,
> > A thousand new moralities,
> > And twenty thousand thousand dreams.
>
> Let them smile.  I would rather meet God in a
> dream than not meet him at all.  I would rather
> join in the Exodus and lay my bones to bleach on
> the way to the Promised Land than to make bricks
> for Pharoah forever, even if I could become an
> overseer over other slaves, and get big spoonfuls
> from the garlicked fleshpots of Egypt. 11

Rauschenbusch was not a utopian, of course.  He was a committed reformer of society at large.  Though a theologian and a Baptist minister, his complaints against human society were the economic-political complaints of Kanter's second wave of utopias, with which Rauschenbusch was contemporary.  His targets were child labor, unsafe working conditions, and long working hours at low pay in the factories of America's new industrial revolution.  His sympathies, as the quotation shows, were romantically with the New Harmonys of his day.

Thus, it seems to me that the utopians of nineteenth- and twentieth-century America owe their hope for a radically better society either directly or indirectly, knowingly or unknowingly, to assumptions about the nature of history that are derived from the biblical tradition.  The Shakers, like the Qumran Essenes of biblical times, sought simply to make the biblical vision concrete in their society.  Robert Owen saw religion as a hindrance to human community and so let go of the biblical symbols.  But New Harmony was to have been a secular Kingdom of God where the physical needs of humanity would be met in equality.  Twin Oaks seeks to minister to the human spirit by overcoming the alienation of person from person, also without the symbols of religion.  None of these utopian hopes were without basis, nor even truly radical; they were based on remembered and interpreted experience of the past.  Not that there had ever been a perfect society, but there were canons for the values of such a society, and there were the remembered sufferings for the past violations of those canons.

> Thus says the Lord:
> 'For three transgressions of Israel, and for four,
>     I will not revoke the punishment;
> because they ... trample the head of the poor
>     into the dust of the earth,
>     and turn aside the way of the afflicted.'
>
> (Amos 2:6ff., Revised
> Standard Version)

But history is open to the future, it is not bound to endless rounds to beginnings.  "A new heaven and a new earth" (Revelation 21:1) were the certain hope of a hundred generations in that biblical tradition.  The Shaker communities and New Harmony, and Twin Oaks today, were not radical departures from that tradition.  They were believers whose hope was so imminent that they sought to force the hand of God--even if they demythologized God Himself!

## Notes

[1] Martin Buber, I and Thou, trans. by Walter Kaufman (New York: Chas. Scribner's Sons, 1970), p. 77ff.

[2] George C. Bedell, et al., Religion in America (New York: Macmillan, 1975), p. 22ff.

[3] Ernest Lee Tuveson, Redeemer Nation: The Idea of America's Millennial Role (Chicago and London: University of Chicago Press, 1968), p. viiff.

[4] Mark Holloway, Heavens on Earth (New York: Dover, 1966), p. 69ff. Most of my information about the Shakers is taken from Holloway's chapter on them.

[5] Holloway quotes a shout that sometimes accompanied a dance: "Shake! Shake! Shake!! There's a great spirit on you--shake him off! off! off!! Christ says shake him off!!!" (p. 76).

[6] Preamble to the Constitution of the Friendly Association for Mutual Interests at Kendal, Ohio. Quoted by Kanter, p. 6. Information about Owen and New Harmony is drawn from Kanter and, especially, from Holloway.

[7] From Owen's Declaration of Mental Independence. Quoted by Holloway, p. 110.

[8] The illustrative material about Twin Oaks is excerpted from Kanter, pp. 18-31.

[9] The Shakers believed that with the coming of Mother Ann Lee the biblical vision of the perfect society at the end of history had literally been fulfilled. Robert Owen tried to build a material, non-religious eschatological society by human economic effort. Twin Oaks keeps the spiritual rather than material goal of the biblical vision, but without the forms of religion.

[10] This biblical hope may be sensed in its passionate yearning by consecutively reading Isaiah 11, Amos 9:11-15, Jeremiah 31:31-34, Matthew 5-7, and Revelation 21.

[11]Walter Rauschenbusch, Christianizing the Social Order (New York: Macmillan, 1914), p. 325ff. The quotation was called to my attention by Helen McLean.

## Bibliography

Bellah, Robert N. "Civil Religion in America," Daedalus, 96, No. 1 (Winter 1967).

Dupont-Sommer, A. The Essene Writings from Qumran, translated by G. Vermes (Cleveland: World, 1973).

Kanter, Rosabeth. Commitment and Community (Cambridge, Mass.: Harvard University Press, 1972).

McClendon, James Wm., Jr. Biography as Theology (Nashville and New York: Abingdon, 1974).

Neusner, Jacob. The Way of Torah: An Introduction to Judaism (Belmont, Calif.: Dickenson, 1970).

Thrupp, Sylvia L., ed. Millennial Dreams in Action (New York: Schocken, 1970).

Wright, G. Ernest, and Reginald H. Fuller. The Book of the Acts of God (New York: Doubleday, 1957).

## IX. IMAGININGS AND DREAMS FOR THE FUTURE: A PSYCHOLOGIST LOOKS AT POSSIBILITIES FOR COMMUNAL CONSCIOUSNESS AND COMMUNES

Jean Bradford

> To venture causes anxiety, but not to venture is
> to lose one's self.  And to venture in the highest
> sense is precisely to be conscious of one's self.
> --Kierkegaard

The theme of this chapter is that to "know oneself" and to help build the "Good Society" are not polar opposites, but in fact are essential complements of one another.  In America, especially, it has been my observation that we have categorized individuality and collectivity so rigidly that we no longer see the interrelatedness of inner and outer, of self-growth and communal consciousness.  I must make a clear distinction at the outset that when I use the term "individuality" I am not referring to the so-called "New Narcissism" or solipsistic ego tripping.  On the contrary, I am using this term more in the framework of Jungian psychology, where what Jung calls the "process of individuation" (which involves intense exploration of all facets of one's psyche) leads not to the ego or egotism, but to the opposite; to a transcendence of the ego and a realization of the oneness of all life.  We are both unique and universal, and this process of individuation would lead to a heightened sensitivity to ourselves, to others, and to the cosmos.

I am not a professional futurologist and would feel very uncomfortable in that role.  Instead of making predictions for the year 2000 and beyond I would like to make some suggestions and examine some of the alternative ways of being and loving one another and all other living creatures.  The concept of Utopia is too abstract for me.  The future is now, and how we realize (in the sense of making it real) in our own personal daily lives what we want for others in the future is for me far more relevant and alive than a prescription for a Utopia. I am sure there are many positive paths, many possibilities to tap, many new and creative forms that can only be glimpsed by us now.

I do not have much in common with those "experts" who do feel comfortable about setting forth a blueprint for the future. In the past several years there have been a rash of books, conferences, and symposia devoted to what life will look like in the year 2000. I am sure it is natural to be curious about life on our planet in the future and to try to make some plans for the years to come. What is depressingly shocking to me, at least, is that a good proportion of this literature on the future is purely technological in nature, with a science-fiction ring. It is not concerned with ethics and morals, to say nothing about human choice, will, and decision to intervene in this technological growth. It is almost as if we are seen as being lemmings drawn to the sea by a force outside of ourselves, or worse yet, as becoming like machines or robots bowing down to the power of our new mythology--technology. We do not have to wait for 1984 to see the profound effects of dehumanization, depersonalization, and the crisis of love and will, about which Rollo May has spoken so urgently. [1]

I am reminded here of a recent incident at the college, where a young student working with computers was in all seriousness commenting upon how sad it was that people were not machines! From her point of view they would be ever so much more efficient and predictable. I hope that some of our "great minds on the future" will examine possibilities for changing this direction, or at least acknowledge that human beings have it within their knowledge and power to determine the shape of their destinies. I am reminded here of a quote by the physicist/philosopher Michael Polanyi who in his book Personal Knowledge says:

> In the days when an idea could be silenced by showing that it was contrary to religion, theology was the greatest single source of fallacy. Today, when any human thought can be discredited by branding it as unscientific, the power previously exercised by theology has passed over to science; hence science has become in its turn the greatest single source of error. [2]

We need, I think, more thought and planning that is

truly imaginative in the sense of not assuming that the future will be an extension of the past and present; we need human and not machine models for future interpersonal relationships and most of all a sense that we can be masters of our fate, and that we must look at questions of human relationships, questions of closeness, intimacy, and love. These are crucial for any vision of communal living in the future. In effect, then, we need some real visionary prophetic thinkers, not doomsayers and technocrats!

Before turning my attention toward what lies in the future in terms of human consciousness and communes, I would like to examine the communal movement of the 1960's. There are some essential and good reasons for starting there, as well as some lessons to be learned concerning what went wrong in many of these experiments. I realize that there is a long history of intentional communities in this country and that there are some similarities between nineteenth- and early twentieth-century communitarian thinking and goals and those of the 1960's. But I want to focus on the period from 1965 to 1972 for the reason that by 1968 we saw more communal experiments in this country than had existed at any time before.

It seems almost passé by now to remind readers what motivated the setting up of these communes. (By "commune" or "community" I am referring not to group living for sheer economic expedience, but to those groups that had a goal, a dream, whether it was religious, political, or personal. ) Many of these reasons seem clichéd in the so-called "realistic" 1970's, but I think we need to be reminded of some of them, such as:

(a) feelings of dehumanization and alienation;

(b) a profound sense of the destruction and killing in the war in Vietnam coupled with a desperate search for closeness and community;

(c) the slogan found in so many communes, "Make Love, Not War";

(d) a feeling that technology was taking over our lives and that we needed to "get back to the land";

(e) a sense of spiritual loss and lack of meaning that could be alleviated by communal living;

(f) a protest against capitalistic materialism and colonialism;

(g) the effort to effect radical change through small communal experiments.

I realize this list is incomplete and does not include the specifically religious or drug-oriented communes, but it will suffice to make us aware of three major points. First, that these problems exist today (with the exception of the actual war, which I do not feel we have come to grips with psychologically or in terms of "man's inhumanity to man" and our own spiritual and moral bankruptcy). Second, that young people did venture and did gain something. And third, that the dreams of the 1960's have not become a reality-- why?

I do not pretend to have all the answers to this last question. I do have some reflections that bear on my major theme--that one needs to look, to venture, inwardly to have a sense of self, before being able to commit oneself to a group, a commune, or a community. We need an individual strength, we need to plant the seeds of new creative growth in ourselves in order to give birth to others. It seems to me, on the question of alienation, for example, that the generation of the 1960's saw this in terms of external causes--which surely were and still are there (poverty, racism and sexism, ecological violence, crime, etc.). There was, however, an imbalance in only looking at outward signs of alienation and neglecting the vast issue of personal alienation, such as a separation of mind and feelings. Much of our own sense of self and self-worth had been destroyed, as well. That has to be recognized for the future. We have to turn to ourselves as a creative piece of work--for the re-creation of our lives. I firmly believe that personal growth is related to human compassion and understanding. As in the saying, "Physician heal thyself," only then can we help, inspire, heal, and love others in a more communal sense. Individuality, then, is not egotism but its very opposite, the prerequisite for living together. I can speak from personal experience here: the more aspects of my psyche that I confront (positive and negative), the more sensitive and attuned I am to the feelings of others and the more able I am to be helpful to others. I have also become, in both my personal life and as a teacher, more tolerant of many points of view and to the necessity of allowing others to grow and develop their own creative talents.

If one senses a divine spark in oneself, one simply cannot ignore the reality that others are also divine, that divine flame cannot be destroyed. The journey inward has also caused a recognition of my own hostilities, jealousies, and anger, so that I no longer need to project these feelings onto others, to blame them, but to work on these emotions in my own life and to take responsibility for my own actions. I am suggesting that by and large this lack of intense self-examination was not deepened in the 1960's because most people were out fighting the good fight and did not realize that the war might be within themselves. An exception would be some of the more drug-oriented communes, many of which showed a concern with inward growth and the heightening of consciousness. Again, I would say that for the most part this concern was too superficial, and that for many a thrilling turn-on was an end and not the beginning of psychic exploration. But many who did feel that the new Utopia was connected with drug use, now realize that a major problem was the lack of synthesis of the "opening of the doors of perception" by drugs and one's daily life and consciousness. For many it was good while it lasted, but it seemed not to last, and one then had to search in other directions.

The 1960's slogan "Make Love, Not War" is still appropriate if one is clear about the many meanings of love. I think that love, like almost all other emotions, has been technologized and reduced to a physical act only. We can talk ad infinitum about sex, but we are still unable to let ourselves love ourselves and to allow our "loved ones" to love themselves. Universal love has been trivialized, and many men and women are cynical about the possibilities of genuine lovingness between people. That to me is the ultimate in hopelessness. I feel that in the 1960's there were several problems in the sphere of loving--a narrow physical interpretation, and the vast exploitation in love relationships, especially for women. This may not have been true for all communes, but in many there was a stated or underlying assumption that women were communal property.

Other aspects of the 1960's communes that caused many to falter, if not to fail, was an inability to share "mundane" responsibilities, household chores, for example. In some instances responsibilities were parceled out, but often a couple of people did most of the work. There was often no long-term sense of sharing, and discouragement and disillusionment often set in. It seems to me that a

give-and-take attitude toward others, as any effort or movement, requires a strong sense of self and self-worth.   Of
course, this lack of sharing is often found in the so-called
nuclear family as well.   (I say "so-called" because statistics
show that few families consist of mother, father, and two-
to-three children.   The high divorce and separation rates
mean that more and more families are headed by a single
parent. )

   Moreover, if one expects that a person, a group, or
a commune will solve personal and collective problems, one
is in for a rude awakening.   The resulting disillusionment
and backlash cause people to give up and become hostile to
the dream they embarked upon.   That did happen because
many lacked the personal strength, roots, and reserves to
understand that patience and long-term commitments were
necessary, especially in view of our culture's general hostility to communal experiments--on one level there were
media hype and fascination, but on another great distrust
and fear of those who formed alternatives.

   The lessons I would draw from these communal experiences in the 1960's are mixed.   I applaud the attempt to
do things differently, to create a sense of brotherhood (I
wish there had been more of an awareness of sisterhood), and
to rejuvenate spiritual values.   I see the greatest flaw in the
ideology that opposed individual and collective growth, and in
the attempt to launch a full-scale war on alienation, fragmentation, and the inability to relate, without a true center, a
source of strength and personal roots.   As Martin Buber
said, "The real essence of community is to be found in the
fact that it has a center. "[3]   To sum up, the individual's and
the group's sense of "centeredness" have to synthesize and
harmonize to create a balance.

   The question to be posed now is:   How will we live,
love, and create in the future?   I would remind the reader
of two points made earlier--that I have no blueprint and am
merely suggesting alternatives, and that the future is now.
No ultimate salvation, whether religious or scientific, will
spring forth in the year 2000 or later, outside of ourselves.
We must sow the seeds of change now and live out a new
reality to the best of our capabilities.   Searching for the
possible now will determine who we are and what we shape
for the future.   We must learn, feel, sense, intuit, and especially love and embrace life.   We are just beginning to
glimpse the fact that we are standing on shaky, new, exciting,

and bewildering ground, full of dangers and possibilities.
We cannot retreat into the past; which ways might we go?
I would like to discuss four particular areas of human concern for the future.  These are:  our attitudes toward children; the role of women; family relationships; and the life
of the spirit.

I will attempt to discuss these questions in terms of
both personal and communal growth.

## New Attitudes Toward Children

It seems to me that for several centuries now we have
treated children as if they were our property, as if "Father
knew best" what was in "their own best interest," (but mothers were always to blame if anything went wrong).  My observation is that, despite all the concern over permissive-
ness and the so-called coddling of the young, the opposite is
the case.  Children are still treated (or mistreated) in a very
openly authoritarian manner as no other group in our society.
They are told what to eat and when to sleep, they have no
economic, political, or legal clout.  Their dreams and imaginations are destroyed beyond belief, and yet we expect
them to be "creative" (by whose definition, one has to wonder).  If the future is to hold out more freedom, then we
must begin by allowing children to grow to be themselves.
This does not mean a lack of love, protection, or concern,
as many so often think.  It means we will have children out
of love, not accident.  Children will be wanted and cared
for, whether by a single parent, a group, a family, or a
commune.  The form makes little difference; the attitude of
what Carl Rogers terms "unconditional love" does.  I hope
there will be more of a respect for the uniqueness, beauty,
and ingenuity of the young.  Perhaps initially we will need
more laws to protect children, especially in the areas of
physical and mental abuse.  My hope is that gradually laws
will be unnecessary and that all children will be born into a
world that loves, protects, and honors them.

One issue that needs to be raised here is that of the
development of children who have been raised communally in
this country.  Since communes differ in so many ways, it
would be hard to make solid conclusions about these children.
Only several authors have studied this area; among their im-
pressions are the following:

(1) Communally raised children are unpredictable in

their behavior.  One can see this as positive or negative.
I clearly see it as positive, in the sense that no one pattern
of socialization or homogenization is imposed upon them and
that many unique patterns of behavior emerge.

(2) The children were treated as human first, and as
children second.  It was observed that much love and respect for the young were present, but not necessarily continual supervision or "parenting" (to use the current jar-
gon).  Children were not raised in the image of their parents, and their parents were not threatened by these differences.  For me, as a child psychologist, this means a great
deal; children should not have to be like or please their parents or live up to someone else's expectations, never even
knowing who they are and what they expect for themselves.
I am sure this can happen in a nuclear-family situation, but
it is rare.  So many of the problems that a child clinician
sees in children and families are related to being different,
growing, and going one's own way.  This need not lead to
friction and turmoil in a family, but may indeed lessen the
"generation gap" so that a real respect and love for family,
based on real feelings and not on a sense of obligation, duty,
or guilt, may finally emerge.

(3) Rothchild and Wolf, in their major 1976 study of
children growing up in American communes, [4] see somewhat
the same patterns as Berger describes, for example, less
traditional parenting and an atmosphere that gave much more
freedom to the children.  They also observed much less concern about materialistic "things," saying, "It was the first
living room we had seen where one worried more about what
the things might do to the children than what the children
might do to the things."

They also found that children could vent feelings of
anger and frustration with parents or adults and had more
emotional rights than one normally sees in a regular family
unit.  Needless to say these children were more independent
and were able to see their parents or adults as people, with
all their flaws and fine points.  Rothchild and Wolf observed
that some children were able to choose their own parents
(which is reminiscent of Aldous Huxley's utopian novel Island
and is also a part of what both John Holt, in Escape from
Childhood, and Richard Farson, in Birthrights, advocate).

Rothchild and Wolf did not see everything as positive,
however.  They point out that often communal life "tore
every one of the families apart" and that the sexual rela-

tionships and jealousies were very difficult for the children
to handle. They found people trying to cope with the problems that beset many nuclear families today, reaching no
easy solutions, but at least exploring alternatives for the
future.

Probably the central requirement in either communal
or more traditional family relationships is that the adults
must be emotionally stable and have a faith in themselves as
persons and a faith in the future for their children. All
parents say they love their children, but the real test of
that love is, can they let their child be, be different, be
unique and grow in her or his own way? Pablo Casals in
his autobiography Joys and Sorrows: Reflections, says:

> Each second we live is a new and unique moment
> of the universe, a moment that never was before
> and will never be again. And what do we teach
> our children in school? We teach them that two
> and two make four, and that Paris is the capital
> of France. When will be also teach them what
> they are? We should say to each one of them:
> Do you know what you are? You are a marvel.
> You are unique. In all of the world there is no
> other child like you. And look at your body--
> what a wonder it is! Your legs, your arms, your
> cunning fingers, the way you move! You have the
> capacity for anything. Yes, you are a marvel.
> And when you grow up, can you then harm another
> who is, like you a marvel? You must cherish one
> another. You must work--we all must work--to
> make this world worthy of its children. 5

At the present time we are a nation afraid of its
young people. Such a nation is, it seems to me, in deep
trouble. We need to start anew to prevent the anger, frustration, and suspicion on both sides--and we can if we decide to cherish and trust the young and not let our own childhood die in us.

## The Role of Women in the Future

Some women in the present generation do realize that the
future is now, and with heightened consciousness and active
efforts are changing the stereotypic picture of woman as the
passive, submissive helpmate of man. Women want what

everyone wants, freedom to be creative as well as procrea-
tive, to be independent as well as aware of the interconnectedness with all of life. I hope that in the future women will
not sell themselves short, but instead will play a predomi-
nant role in all aspects of benevolent social change, of public life and endeavor.

Women, like children, have been abused in physical
and mental ways, and initially there will need to be legisla-
tion to protect their basic human rights. But again, the
legal question will be put aside in a society that says, "but
of course, be you." The more one grows as a person, the
more one has to give and share with others. "What about
the children?" one always hears people asking. There will
be many possibilities open to people. The role of men,
many of whom now feel that they are deprived of being with
their children during their growing years, would be central
here. Perhaps women will choose to raise children in some
type of communal living situation with other women or with
men and women. We need not decide these questions, but
the choice must be there. It is crucial to all of us that we
grow from children into adulthood and our later years, with
love, a sense of fulfillment and contribution to society. We
can all be a little more honest and acknowledge that need
for love. Women are often said to be love addicts or to
need too much love. I think this is nonsense. Each person
needs a sense of security and belonging, and only other people can affirm that. These are the seeds of self-growth,
which women, men, and children can help spread throughout
the land.

## The Role of the Family in the Future

The two preceding sections are integrally related to the
issue of the family and its future. Obviously, if the roles
and rights of children and women are taken seriously, major
changes will occur (and are already occurring) in the family.
I can envision many different formats, ranging from two
parents with children to communal living, with variations in
between. Many contemporary writers have focused on the
changing family, and there is soon to be a White House Conference on this question as well. People are worried about
the breakup of the traditional family. But this has already
happened, and the questions for the future revolve around
such issues as whether people can live together in a loving,
creative, life-enhancing way. I think we can. Divorce may

not be the tragedy so many people envision. Pain, anger,
and suffering are always involved in separations, but perhaps
holding onto a sterile relationship eats away at the soul and
prevents anyone from growing and feeling fully human.

Undoubtedly, many people will opt to live together and
not have children (with no stigma attached to being child-
free). They will have to work out the same problems of
sharing, giving, loving, and working at a relationship as before. These couples may be heterosexual or homosexual;
the sexual choice is a side issue. For people who do want
children the problems of responsibility and care are obviously more complex. No child should be born who is not wanted
and where care and facilities for children are not available.
In the case of working women it seems clear that planning
must be done, and now. This planning can take many forms,
including a real commitment to child-care facilities supported
by people who love and respect children and not necessarily
by an "expert" in child development. We do not want "perfect models"; we want happy, creative, loving individuals.
In the future we may see extended families or, more likely,
extended groups of people who live together because they like
each other and not necessarily because of a blood relationship. We may also see support groups spring up to give aid
and support to children and adults, without people actually
living together. The future will bring novel changes in family living, and, once again, I think that from a personal
sense of centeredness one can develop communal consciousness so that it is understood that we do have the opportunity
to share with others, not out of guilt, but out of love.


Spiritual Growth and Communion

It is clear to me that the United States is a country lacking
a life of the spirit. I prefer to use this term rather than
"religion," feeling that organized, dogmatized religions are
equally bereft of a living spiritual sense. "Spiritual" for me
connotes an awareness of human and cosmic unity; of the
interrelationship of all things to the whole, and of a deep and
responsive caring for all living things. Simply put, life is
sacred. I do not feel that people presently live with this
reality and sense. They do not "love their neighbors as
themselves" (probably because they have lost a sense of love
for self and an ability to love others). "Spiritual" also connotes for me a deep sense of awe and mystery in the world.
I am reminded here of a phrase from the Diary of Anaïs Nin:

"What kills life is the absence of mystery. " Our culture
has been so concerned with mastery that we have overlooked
the mysterious in life.

I respect the young people of the 1960's and 1970's
who are searching through various systems, be it astrology,
oriental religions, mystic paths, or communal attempts.
These are not ways of dropping out or escaping, but are
searches for human and spiritual alternatives. I am hopeful that in the future people will see that beyond computers,
space exploration, and technological advances, we need to
look for ethics and values that are not externally imposed
but flow from the heart. Rollo May reminds us that "communicate" is related to "commune" and to a sense of communion and community.

I am exceedingly skeptical about religious leaders in
any guise, any type of guru who promises salvation. Psychology is filled with such; the trend is dangerous in that it
leads people out of themselves to follow yet another secular
system or leader. We all must live a life on earth that is
related to the mind, the body, and the spirit. The Native
Americans knew this and had a great reverence for the earth
and the world of the spirit. That message should not be
buried. It is simple, really--it involves an openness to
universal love and an ability to manifest this essence in whatever one undertakes in daily existence.

I began this chapter by linking individuality and communal consciousness as a starting point for a re-vision for
the future. The person who has touched my own soul so
deeply and has really transformed my life is one who lived
out her dreams for the future; she lived out the dream of an
expanded life, of love, of genuine human intimacy and creation. That person is Anaïs Nin. I purposely say is even
though Anaïs died in 1977 (shortly after I had met her in
August of 1976). Her spirit will always live with me, and
it was her wisdom and deep psychological insights that
showed me the possibility that, as she phrased it, "the personal life if lived deeply enough becomes universal. " In a
1973 interview Anaïs Nin said:

> The only utopia I believe in is the one I hope some-
> day we can have when we have recognized the im-
> portance of assuming personal responsibility. A
> day when we will tackle our prejudices, hostilities,
> and angers in such a way that they will not be

projected onto to the collective.  To me the war
is an aggregate of all our individual hostilities and
prejudices, and I still see the majority as a lot of
individuals who have projected the destructive part
of themselves.  My only utopia is the hope that if
we have prejudices, we find out what it means and
convert it to something else, convert it to energy.
Then we might have a more humane society.  There
is a possibility of that.  But it will depend on our
quality. [6]

The quality will depend on our ability to transform
ourselves and society.  We must put the self at the center
of collective life and then we have a chance!

Utopia is always a personal concept, a dream; one
that can never be forced upon another.  Utopian thinking
serves as an inspiration for all, an inspiration that says,
"There Must Be More To Life Than This," an inspiration
that keeps the flame of love and life illuminated for ourselves and for generations to come.


## Notes

[1]Rollo May, Love and Will (New York:  Norton,
1969).

[2]Michael Polanyi, in Rollo May, Psychology and the
Human Dilemma (Princeton, N.J.:  Van Nostrand, 1967),
p. 182.

[3]Martin Buber, in Keith Melville, Communes in the
Counter Culture (New York:  Morrow, 1972), p. 184.

[4]John Rothchild and Susan Berns Wolf, Children of
the Commune, 1976.  Excerpt reprinted in Mother Jones,
April 1976, Vol. 1, No. 11, p. 18.

[5]Pablo Casals and Albert E. Kahn, Joys and Sorrows
(New York:  Simon and Schuster, 1970).

[6]Anaïs Nin, A Woman Speaks (Chicago:  The Swallow
Press, 1975), p. 25-26.

## X. EXTREMES OF THE CONTEMPORARY COMMUNAL FRONTIER

Mary Isabelle Kilchenstein

As most people know by now, there has been a great revival of experimental utopian communalism in the United States over the last ten to fifteen years. It has grown primarily out of the radical dissent of the 1960's. By 1971 it was estimated by the National Institutes of Health that there were over 3000 communities in existence,[1] and the movement does not yet show signs of diminishing significantly.

The new communalism has been widely written about, and numerous experiments in communal living have been described. The purpose of this paper is to characterize two contemporary communities, which, though they radically contrast with each other, together reveal a great deal about the current phase in communal history.

The first community, The Farm, located in Summertown, Tennessee, is a 1700-acre, 1200-person venture that operates under the charismatic "teachership" of Stephen Gaskin. The second is the Philadelphia Life Center, a collective of 130 people living in twenty houses in West Philadelphia, who operate on a decentralized, democratic, socialist political model.

Instantly apparent are the more obvious ways in which these two communities are different; rural vs. urban, authoritarian vs. democratic. Upon close examination it will be discovered that there are many more points of conflict between the philosophies of the two communities--issues of religion, sexuality, child-rearing practices, to name a few. However, both communities have a sense of history with regard to American (and non-American) utopian communalism and share in this tradition in a rather conscious way. Furthermore, both are aware of how modernization has affected the world, forcing intentional communities to re-examine their purposes and strategies if they are to survive for any length of time and have a meaningful existence.

As representatives of the present movement toward community in the United States, The Farm and the Life Center can hardly be defined as "typical." It is not my purpose to present typical communities. These two experiments are among the "cream of the crop" in a way. They represent a small number of communities that have evolved well-articulated goals and appear fairly stable. For this reason they offer us a better teaching model than the so-called typical utopian commune.

In order to prepare the reader for what are obvious differences in the presentation of the Life Center and The Farm--and for possible biases in the presentation--I should explain my relationship to the two communities. All of the information in this paper concerning The Farm was obtained from The Farm's own published literature, articles published about The Farm, and conversations with Farm visitors and past members. I have never been there myself. On the other hand, I have been familiar with the Life Center for about five years, have stayed in different houses there many times, and know most of the residents personally. Written sources of information about the Life Center have been much less important to me than first-hand experience. Nonetheless, I have tried to convey information free from personal judgments about both communities' life-styles and philosophies.

## Stephen and The Farm

> We came down from Nashville to Lewis County
> which is just the boondocks of Tennessee, and
> drove in off the main road--off the interstate, off
> the four-lane, off the two-lane onto the dirt, off
> the dirt across the back of this farmer's cornfield,
> down through the woods into a little one-acre
> clearing ... and we found that a neighboring farm
> was for sale.... And it was exactly what we
> wanted. It was just perfect ... a thousand and
> fourteen acres in all ... and we bought it for
> seventy dollars an acre. You can't get a kiln for
> seventy dollars can you? You can still get an
> acre of dirt for that. And you can live on an
> acre of dirt. [2]

It all started in San Francisco, as the Haight-Ashbury era was entering its decline. Hundreds of young people were looking around for some new involvement, many of them disillusioned by the disintegration of their short-lived "flower-power" movement--the drug-oriented hippie cult that was so popular in the mid-sixties. It was around this time that thirty-five-year-old, Colorado-born Stephen Gaskin, who had left the Marine Corps and gotten his Master's in creative writing, in his own search for something meaningful to do began teaching a course at San Francisco State's Experimental College. The students in the course set about the task of reading almost every major piece of religious philosophy that they could uncover. Stephen had also been "uncovering" things for himself by taking LSD "once or twice a week for two years." He says that he "dynamited [his] personality ... and the part that ain't to shambles seems to be the real part." Shortly after his twenty-sixth trip he began holding meetings on Monday night with his experimental class. [3] Others joined them, and they discussed different metaphysical questions from the point of view of Buddhism, Hinduism, astrology, Christianity, Judaism, literary fantasy, science fiction, Zen, and the Tarot.

Over the course of a few years, the class grew from only a few people to five hundred; they moved twice and finally relocated in a rock hall on the Pacific Ocean. Their numbers soon exceeded two thousand. That was 1970. Still guiding the discussion was the charismatic presence of Stephen Gaskin. Each week he filled the place in order to, as he puts it, "talk and argue and hassle about enlightenment and about truth.... Monday Night Class was like a forum that met for four years in San Francisco--a meeting that was dedicated to Spirit and religion ... we were--a society of co-trippers dedicated to the idea of helping each other out." [4]

Understandably, the word got around to colleges and churches that "something" was happening in this forum. Stephen started getting invitations to come to speak; when he announced to his "class" that he was going to go traveling for awhile, about two hundred of them decided it was a fine idea, bought school buses, and joined him. Seven months later they had gone through forty cities, had added about two hundred people to their sixty-school-bus caravan (including several infants born along the way), and had made a lot of friends. Arriving back in San Francisco in February of 1971, Stephen was asked in an interview, "And what was the purpose of the trip?" He replied, "The purpose of the trip was to go out and put the word on folks." [5]

In the course of the journey--indeed, the pilgrimage--
a transformation had taken place that was not anticipated.
They had come back but were unwilling to part from each
other. The decision to buy a farm and live together was a
rapid one. As Stephen puts it,

> When we got back to San Francisco we'd become a
> new thing--and we weren't the same as we were
> before, and we couldn't quit what we were doing,
> because we'd become a community from working
> together, and we knew we could do heavy stuff
> from working together. The next Sunday we met
> and I said, 'Man we can't separate like this, be-
> cause we've become a thing. We're something.
> We've shared so much Karma and so much heavy
> stuff has come down and we've done so much heavier
> stuff than we ever thought we could do together....'
> I said, 'Let's go to Tennessee and get a farm,'
> and everybody dug it. We packed up the buses
> and took off that afternoon for Tennessee. 6

That was 1971. Since that time they have managed to convert 1050 city-raised, mostly college-educated, rather
middle-class young people into very efficient farmers, in
true pioneering fashion. They've made mistakes, lost crops,
spent time in jail, had babies die and survived bouts with
hepatitis--in their short life span as a community they've
come through quite a few hard times. They've done it,
primarily, through outright hard work--the dirt-digging,
hammer-and-saw kind; and they've done it under the firm
and direct guidance of their "teacher"--Stephen.

It is, at first, a bit disconcerting to pick up one of
the published books that contain Stephen's (and The Farm's)
religious philosophy and find ancient, mystical religious concepts being taught in the rhetoric of the drug culture. The jux-
taposition of Buddha, an acid-rock band, and a cornfield is really quite impressive. And The Farm has all those things. But
perhaps the best way of getting to know about "life on the farm"
is to look at the community's main activity--farming.

As one might expect, the farming crew take their
work as a spiritual discipline. The attitude is that in farming "it's just you and the dirt and God." Their goal is to
"have a stoned connection with the dirt and the plant force
and at the same time have a sane enough use of the technology that we can feed ourselves."7 When viewing The Farm's

agricultural achievements one is reminded of the sometimes forgotten fact that America has always been an amazingly agricultural nation. Here are one thousand people out to make a living, as they say, the "clean way." And they seem to be doing it. The job of the farming crew is to plan the year's crops to feed everybody for an entire year. It then takes one-fifth of the men (women are not found in the fields for the most part, although they are not forbidden to be there) to keep the ploughing, planting, and upkeep of the crops efficient.

This crew system supports the entire community. Each separate job, e.g., farming, making soymilk in the dairy, and midwifery, has a separate crew. Each crew has a chief who belongs to a general decision-making committee.

At first the farming crew tried doing all their work with horses. This did not last long, and they bought tractors. Their first attempts were often rather abortive. They made nearly every mistake imaginable--waiting too late to plant, or not waiting long enough, or planting things that have never grown in Tennessee. But they have now progressed to being able to feed all the community members.

The farming crew has learned much from their neighbors (who have watched with curiosity and amusement while the "young beatniks" planted crops that they knew would never grow in Tennessee). And apparently there is much sharing and cooperation now among farms in Summertown. The Farm is partners with one other farmer in a sawmill, for instance. The Farm has had very little trouble with its neighbors. In fact the relationships are quite good. The impression one gets is that the surrounding farmers looked on for a while without making any friendly advances. And one of the first things that happened was that some members of The Farm planted their marijuana in a rather obvious place; subsequently the sheriff paid them a visit. The community appealed the case up to the State Supreme Court, maintaining that marijuana was a "material sacrament" of their religion. They lost the appeal, but in the meantime had won over their neighbors who helped them petition and were quite upset when Stephen and three other men had to spend a year in the Nashville State Penitentiary (February 1974 through February 1975). [8]

Reports are that there is still a sizable amount of grass smoked. The community also uses an organic hallucinogen called "magic mushroom," as well as peyote. Stephen put a stop to all other "inorganic" hallucinogens (e. g. , LSD). The Farm has never used speed or barbit- uates. Their guideline is never to use any laboratory- produced drug. Stephen was on probation for a year and during that time promised the sheriff, named Homer, that he wouldn't use any drug at all; reports are that in fact, he did abstain during that time.

The Farm also has its own dairy, which produces sixty gallons of soymilk per day at a cost of about $.30 per gallon. Since the community is strictly vegetarian--they eat no meat or animal products, including milk or eggs-- they rely solely on soymilk for their milk protein. Soy beans are, generally, a widely used staple; it would seem that a day does not go by that a person doesn't find them in some form on the table.

Work of all kinds is viewed by the community as a material expression of love. And love is, as they put it, being able to "find it in your heart to get off your tail for [somebody]." They seek to integrate their religious beliefs in their daily lives--here again are echoes of past communal societies, though the language is very different.

> We don't quit being spiritual to go do our material plane. We think being spiritual at the motor pool, for instance, is being sure that the car is well blocked up so it ain't going to fall on anybody ... we say that work is a yoga ... you ought to be consciously mediating when you're hoeing a row of corn. 9

There are many areas of work to which people on The Farm go about applying this philosophy. There are crews that take care of horses, build the houses and meet- ing places and outhouses on the land, repair tractors and cars, as well as performing a variety of other tasks. Most of the division of labor on The Farm is done in a way that places men and women in traditional sex roles. Although the claim is that anyone can do the work that he or she chooses to learn, a glance over the work crews shows that the "choices" have been those that segregate men and wom- en in work, with some exceptions in the areas of the dairy, the flour mill, and menu-crop planning. 10 Conversations with some people who have lived there indicate that sexism is not a political issue at The Farm but a spiritual one; and

so there is no deliberate effort to contradict cultural stereotyping.

As one might suspect, given the traditional orientation of sex roles in work, The Farm community places a
great deal of value on the family; Farm members make
marriage contracts "forever," as they say; and, of course,
marriage is considered a very spiritual state--a sacrament.
Most people are involved in monogamous marriages. Sexual
relations outside the marriage are thought of as irresponsible--
in fact, sinful. Stephen performs all the marriages. These
take place on Sunday morning after the regular service,
which he presides over; he has secured a license to perform
marriages on the basis that the community is a Church.

Married people live together either in their own
homes or in tents or in sections of a communal dwelling.
Their children live with them, and often brothers and sisters or other relatives are in the family circle. Married
people are not encouraged to live separately as couples. A
strong emphasis on kinship is pervasive throughout the community.

Having children is also a very important part of the
family life for these people. Birth control is frowned upon;
the only kind even permitted by their religion is a rhythm
or temperature method. Parents are taught by Stephen that
it is their sacred duty to raise "sane" kids. He teaches
that

> if you're a parent, you have accepted the karma of
> another human being who is too young to fend for
> himself for many years, and for whom you must
> be responsible until he is able to fend for himself.
> If you don't come up with everything you've got to
> give him a fair shake, which is an upbringing that
> gives him a reliable, accurate idea of the Universe,
> then you've short-changed him. [11]

In theory, at least, it would appear that the children at The
Farm are being well thought about, but recent reports raise
some doubts. There are visitors who have reported that
children are often ignored by their parents. This could be
because the religious philosophy at The Farm sees any show
of emotion, for instance, crying or temper tantrums, as unacceptable and best handled by isolating the child--or adult,
for that matter--until the individual has stopped any outward

display of negative feelings. The underlying strategy in dealing with children rests on the assumption that children are as intelligent as adults--maybe even more so--and that they can understand exactly what is expected of them.

The treatment of childbirth illustrates the importance that the community attaches to the family unit. All babies are delivered by the community midwives. And unless there is a very good reason for it being otherwise, all fathers are present when their children are being born. The father is the only male allowed in the room with the mother, except Stephen, who sometimes drops by to offer words of encouragement. (Stephen once saved a baby's life by administering mouth-to-mouth resuscitation when the newborn didn't start breathing.) The woman having the baby and the father are encouraged to be physically, emotionally, and spiritually close with one another during the entire process.

It is considered very important to allow the mother and child to have an intensely close relationship for the first year of the baby's life. When these people say "close" they don't mean it in quite the usual way. They put a great deal of emphasis on telepathic communication--they think that this is the way all people would communicate if they were not "hung up on material planes of spirituality." Thus, within the family unit it is important for them that the relationships remain clear, wholesome, and have no backlog of bad feelings in order for this kind of communication to be nurtured. In child rearing this is especially important.

The community has its own school. A number of Farm members had the right degree-status to get teacher accreditation in Tennessee. The philosophy of education at The Farm has a rather unintellectual tone. Young people are taught enough math, reading, and history to pass an eighth-grade exam. The rest of their time is spent in apprenticeship-type tasks. Stephen says, "The school's more to introduce them into our life and not to educate them to some abstract standard."[12] It will certainly be interesting to see whether these children grow up to follow the path that children in past communal societies traveled when they were shut off from the pursuit of a more academic life. They left.

The community takes childbirth so seriously that they have delivered a call to all women who care to take them up on their offer. "Hey Ladies! Don't have an abortion, come to the Farm and we'll deliver your baby and take care of it, and if you ever decide you want it back, you can have it." If a woman were to take them up on the offer, and many do, she would discover that the community views not just giving birth, but delivering babies as a sacrament. Their religious teachings tell them that every birth is the birth of the Christ child. "Every time a baby is born it means that another being capable of free will has been added to the Universe, and the Universe has to move over and shift a little bit...."[13]

To supervise and facilitate these sacred moments there is a midwife crew that is on call day and night. The first member of the crew was Ina May. She began delivering babies when the community was in caravan (ironically and sadly, the child she had during that time--her first-- died). Occasionally, a woman may go to the local hospital, but only in cases of very serious complications--either anticipated or emergent (the community has two ambulances). Ina May and the crew are in close touch with the local doctors and enjoy good rapport with the hospital. In fact, the hospital staff have reached the point of allowing the midwife to participate in the delivery even when it is being done in their facility.

There are a number of very definite ideas upon which the crew operates. Ina May writes,

> The midwife's gig is to do her best to bring both the mother and child through their passage alive and stoned and to see that the sacrament of birth is kept Holy. The Vow of the Midwife has to be that she will put out one hundred per cent of her energy to the mother and the child that she is delivering until she is certain they have safely made the passage. This means that she must put the welfare of the mother and child first before that of herself and her own family, if it comes to a place where she has to make a choice of that kind ... it will be necessary for you to get spiritual if you're going to be handling life and death karma ... you ought to have had a child yourself and you ought to have a good, solid, loving relationship with your husband and children so that you can be a standard for what a good wife and mother is.[14]

Reports from recent visitors are that there have been at

least six hundred babies born at The Farm; about two-thirds
live there, the others have been born to women who have
come specifically to have their children at The Farm's midwife clinic.

Being born into the community is, however, not the
only way of entering. The Farm has a gate; consequently,
another important function to be filled is that of gatekeeper.
The gate is much like their front door--or perhaps even
more like the guard post at the entrance to an army base.
Stephen says,

> The gate ain't to keep the monkeys in. That's
> one thing about it is that it swings out really
> easily.... Getting in may be a little harder.
> But everybody on The Farm came through it at
> one time or another. The man at the gate came
> through it once.... To get through the gate you've
> got to work it out with the gate man. The gate
> man believes in telling the truth. [15]

And so the gatekeeper's job is not only that of gatekeeper
but of preliminary screener--a sort of director of admis-
sions. He keeps a written record of all who enter and
leave, what the reason for coming and going is, and when
the person or persons plan to leave or come back. Reports
are that people have come to The Farm and spent as much
as twelve hours at the gate talking to the gate man--and,
after a certain point, Stephen--trying to gain entrance.
When emotionally distraught people arrive (and they do)
Stephen spends time with them, offers them advice and
guidance, and sends them off, firmly.

Once people get past the gate they are, if planning
to stay, required to turn everything they own over to the
community. Like many of its predecessors, The Farm
"holds all things in common." When people come to live
there, for instance, they turn all their money over to the
community bank. If they need to buy something, and if
there is money in the bank, they can withdraw funds for
the necessity. But all of their basic needs for food, clothing, and shelter are taken care of by the community.

The next thing that will probably confront the new
members is how, politically, the community is run. The
Farm appears to be a theocratic society subject to Stephen's
absolute influence. But one shouldn't get the impression

that Stephen walks around overseeing everything. In the
first place the community is too large; and, too, Stephen is
often not there. It seems to be more the <u>idea</u> of Stephen
that has power over the community members. Stephen has
said he sees himself as a "teacher," not as a "leader."

> I'm a teacher, not a leader. If you lose your
> leader you're leaderless and lost, but if you lose
> your teacher there's a chance that he taught you
> something and you can navigate on your own....
> The Farm ought to run for generations without me.
> It's like building a machine ... I feel like a hun-
> dred people could handle themselves without a
> teacher. I think it would be a severe limitation
> to say you'd have to have something like that. On
> the other hand, I think that you have to be able to
> delegate some authority to somebody.... [16]

The community has had to manage without Stephen for
a number of prolonged periods of time. He was in jail for
a year, and at other times he has traveled to other Farms
in the United States and to similar communities abroad; he
also goes on tour with the Farm Band. [17] One thing that
has been very helpful in maintaining continuity while he has
been away is the ham radio set up at The Farm. There is,
of course, a radio crew; they operate three stations to stay
in contact with other Farms and with Stephen.

In matters of internal politics, according to Stephen,
there is no need to take votes or have a substantial political
structure. The assertion is that at The Farm, everyone
agrees. There is, in other words, consensus, though members of traditional Quaker groups who have developed the
concept of consensus over centuries would cringe at his use
of the word. What specific issue or issues The Farm has
reached consensus upon is rather vague. If--or when--there
are difficulties that arise regarding any aspect of Farm life,
meetings are called at which people can discuss openly their
feelings and criticisms. It is rather hard to imagine one
thousand people having meaningful discussion about a problem with no structure at all for dealing with the issue, but
apparently it works--at least for now. And one should remember that the community began out of just such discus-
sions, which, at that time, involved close to two thousand
participants.

My informants tell me that essentially things function

without the benefit of Stephen's opinions most of the time.
He may be involved in some issues of importance, but
crews make their own decisions. Apparently, the most influential group on The Farm are the midwives, whose opinions and judgments often sway the community. This seems
to make sense in light of their function and the philosophy
of the community regarding birth and spirituality.

In matters of external politics there is no doubt that
Stephen and his followers agree. They have a lot to say
about American culture and the United States' relationship
to the world. Stephen thinks that Americans sold out religion for technology and thus "cut loose the life force, they
cut loose of the energy, they pulled the plug." In making
this statement he is reiterating the views of many observers
of American culture. Stephen has this to say about American society:

> Compared to many ages in the past, we're a
> bunch of heathens. This is The Dark Ages--
> religious knowledge in the United States is just at
> an amazing standstill, has been for many years,
> because we've been taught to be materialists....
> If the culture teaches people to be materialistic,
> the culture will then find itself in the position of
> supplying everyone with materialistic needs and
> wants, and people's materialistic needs and wants
> cannot be satisfied. The only kind that can be
> satisfied is spiritual. 18

He also says this about the source of the underlying problem
in American society and The Farm's role in that society:

> The thing about the pilgrims is that they were an
> ice crystal and they flavored the country, but un-
> fortunately they were carrying guns, and this
> country was based in violence. It was conceptually
> based in justice, but it was materially based in
> violence. That's where it's at now, conceptually
> just and materially violent. So we're reaffirming.
> This is the Second American Revolution, the revo-
> lution of the soul. They said that you couldn't en-
> slave a man's body, but they left it open that you
> could enslave his soul. And you've got to say you
> can't enslave his body or his soul. So we try to
> be a good-shaped crystal like the pilgrims, but not
> carrying guns. 19

Stephen believes that he and the people at The Farm (and other religious communities) are only one step ahead of the rest of the country. He teaches that out of all the drug taking and social upheaval during the 1960's and early '70's, the most important consequences have been spiritual. Put in another way, the civil rights movement and the peace movement were "trees" in the forest--the real theme running through all of the liberation movements in progress right now is that of a spiritual liberation.

The role that The Farm as a community is playing in this movement is clearly stated. It is not interested in "fixing" the established institutions. The idea is that to direct attention toward American political institutions is to give acknowledgment to whatever particular institution is the recipient of the attention. The Farm's attitude is that the structures of the American government and of most social institutions simply do not deserve attention or recognition and in fact will crumble of their own accord much faster than if people waste their energy trying to patch them together. In short, the strategy is to "sit and wait" while being as harmless as possible. In their own lives they are trying to create a "sane" way of life for themselves that they would like to share with as many others as would care to join them. The emphasis is on close human relations; they do not wish to relate to external institutions at all.

This position with regard to politics is in keeping with their religious beliefs. A true example of ecumenical thinking, the religion of The Farm is, in some ways, unorganized and tends to elude a final label. Stephen does, however, openly claim some affinity with a few formal doctrines. One of the most influential of these for Farm philosophy is Mahayana Buddhism. This development of the original (or Hinayana) Buddhist thought stresses the "Great Path" where all people can--and must--be enlightened. (Hinayana is more exclusive, being the Small Path.) Stephen uses the analogy of a lifeboat, saying,

> ... we're going to have to have all hands on board. You can't say the boat will float better if you throw somebody over the side ... there's no final and perfect enlightenment until everybody is enlightened. And the closest you can get to it is to figure that out. And when you figure that out, there ain't nothing to do but hustle until we get everybody off. [20]

This philosophy tends to be borne out in the community's social attitudes--it certainly seems as though their thoughts and actions are, on the whole, consistent. A prime example of their creed in practice can be seen in their efforts in behalf of recent earthquake victims. The Farm and its offshoots have sent much of their surplus food abroad to aid such people in their crisis.

And, yes, The Farm does have offshoots. In light of this "save the world" attitude, it is not surprising that the community is also quite "serious about trying to get together a whole bunch of farms all over the country that would be really good places, that would have healthy kids and hard-working people, and that would make good enough friends with their neighbors that they didn't get busted all the time and didn't get run out." The book that The Farm has published called Hey Beatnik: This Is the Farm Book is, in fact, a "how to do it" book, describing exactly the way a group could go about starting a farm--including everything from how to tie umbilical cords to the best way to make soymilk and the most efficient manner in which to build an outhouse. "I think we ought to colonize the United States and colonize the planet," Stephen states. "And I think that a spiritual way of doing it is really necessary--not just on my opinion, but on things I've managed to discover--like that secular communites average making it about five years and religiously based communities average making it about fifty years."[21] It would seem that Stephen has a sense of history with regard to utopian communities.

One of the most interesting ways in which The Farm is trying to "spread the word" is through its band. The Farm Band travels around the country playing spiritual--naturally--rock music. This is one of the ways that Stephen and The Farm look for "converts." And they are quite open about it; as Stephen says,

> I'm the recruiting officer for reality, and I go around the campuses, and I'm trying to recruit people to join into reality.... You see, we don't just come out to rock out for you--we come to change your life. You could get stoned. You could make it work right. You could make it so it was a groove. You could make it so you know why you're here. You could make it so you're enough of an adult that you could get married and mean it. See, this is a trap. We trap you with

our rock and roll. When you get right down to it, we're a Salvation Army Band, and what we're out for is your gourd. [22]

## The Movement for a New Society--the Philadelphia Life Center

Walking down the tree-lined streets, looking up at the old three-story homes of West Philadelphia, one comes upon a house with a shingle over its porch that is painted with a rainbow--or a sunflower--or it may simply bear a name: The Gathering, Trollheim. These are the houses of the Life Center. Describing this community is a difficult task. Unlike The Farm or typical utopian communities of the past, there is no single person whose eyes we can look through-- and no formal doctrine to present. The Philadelphia Life Center is anything but ritualized or regimented. The minute one makes a statement about the way of life found in one house, there are nineteen others to contradict it. This diversity extends to all areas of living: religious practice, child rearing, sexual behavior, and financial arrangements. It does not mean, however, that there is no agreement with regard to life-style. Rather, it does mean that the Center is experimenting with a wide range of alternatives to the "average American" way of life. In general, the residents are all trying to simplify their lives, use fewer natural resources, operate on a consensus decision-making basis, and concern themselves with how well and clearly people relate to each other.

The Movement for a New Society/Philadelphia Life Center began in 1971 as an outgrowth of the thinking of thirty activists who had been working together for a long period of time on issues of social change. They were part of a radical Quaker Action Group that in the 1950's worked to oppose nuclear testing and armament and then in the sixties became active in the civil rights and anti-Vietnam War movements. By the early seventies these people were acutely aware of the need for a more integrated analysis-- showing how separate societal concerns, for example, ecology and economics, are interrelated. They decided that in order for them to work effectively together, maintain momentum, offer each other support, and live cheaply (to free up "job time" for movement work) they would need to live in community. Thus, in 1971 the Philadelphia Life Center became the living context for those people who began calling themselves the builders of the Movement for a New Society.

The founders chose to locate in the city knowing that they would have a wide range of problems not experienced by rural or even suburban communities. Their reasoning was that to really meet the needs of those people toward whom the present system (i. e. , social-political structure) is most unjust, they needed to be in contact with them, and that meant living in the city. Removal to the "safety" of the country meant isolation from the problems they sought to change. There was talk, however, of maintaining a rural sector; and there are groups of Life Center people now exploring this possibility.

The community sees itself as a training center where people from other places all over the world can come to train "for long term social change organizing and struggle. "[23] The idea is that these people will then take their new skills and knowledge to a different area and begin work organizing in the new community, wherever that may be.

Before proceeding further it is necessary to explain that the Movement for a New Society and the Life Center are two separate entities, even though they are interlaced in many ways; one quickly discovers that a complete distinction is nearly impossible, even for those living there.[24] Briefly, the Center is a collective of about twenty houses spread over a ten-block area of West Philadelphia. These are the homes of approximately 140 people (120 adults and twenty children as of February 1977). The Movement for a New Society is the structure through which these people work--through which they seek to realize their vision of a new society.

And it is essential to an understanding of the Center to recognize that the people living in it see their work, either within the Movement or in the arena of social change they choose outside the MNS structure, as their main activity (or activities, as most of them also tend to be extremely busy). There is, in general, a political thrust or implication to nearly everything they do, either collectively or individually-- inside or outside the Center. I am not going to attempt a discussion of MNS politics. In spite of the fact that PLC members live together as a community primarily for political reasons, I am interested here in the cultural aspects (i. e. , life-style) of the community. They, of course, involve political activity, but I will not go into a theoretical explanation--any more than I attempted to analyze completely Stephen Gaskin's theology.

Since the emphasis in the Life Center is on activity

for political-social change, members most often earn money
to support themselves by holding various kinds of part-time
jobs: house repair, child care, teaching, typing. The term
"bread labor" is used to describe work that offers financial
support but that is not intended to involve the individual
emotionally or take many hours each week. Of far more
importance are the hours spent in MNS/PLC activities.

As one soon discovers in spending any amount of time
in the Life Center, there is validity or logic behind the community's statement that, while it encourages self-examination
and personal growth as an integral part of social change--
and offers support for this--it seeks mainly to be an outward
community and is not a place for people to come who are in
poor emotional condition and in need of inordinate amounts of
support. It would be hard to remain even a day without being made aware of nearly all of the world's major injustices.
Here are two people discussing a meeting on war-tax resis-
tance; here is a group off to a meeting of the Namibia Action Group; and here one encounters a collective of radical
feminists leading a weekend workshop for Life Center wom-
en. Looking for a place to hide from all of this, you might
turn to find two adults with six or seven "active" children
engaged in play of some (loud) sort; and if by some luck you
think you've found a quiet niche, someone comes in to ask
if you'd like to take a walk from the Philadelphia Electric
Company to the Limerick, New Jersey nuclear power plant
site (fifteen miles) to demonstrate against U. S. development
and use of nuclear power--and on the way, would you write
a letter to your Congressperson to protest U. S. economic
involvement in some third-world country. The point of it
all is that there simply seems to be no end to the number
of involvements that the PLC's members commit themselves
to wholeheartedly. Indeed, a person might easily become
"burnt out" by the pace; and, although the number is minimal, some do. It is also clear that this type of involvement
and intensity could never develop in a peaceful and isolated
country setting.

For those who do not get "burnt out," there are any
number of ways in which to become involved in the community's activities; the approach that most people take is to join
an "MNS collective." This is a group of people (from two
to ten) who come together to think and take action around a
particular concern that they all share. There are about
fifteen MNS collectives currently active at the Philadelphia
Life Center. These break down into at least two types:
service and action-oriented. The service collectives help to

maintain the community's functioning and promote MNS
ideas. They are generally the "stable" and ongoing element
in the community's work. One such collective is the Training Organizing Collective. Its job is to organize the program that begins every fall for a group of about fifteen people who come to live in the Life Center to learn tools for
"social change organizing." The people in the collective take
applications, interview people, see to it that all the newcomers have goals in mind that are consistent with the
training program (that they plan to make use of the tools
and skills they acquire) and that everyone is taken care of
with regard to such things as housing--although, ultimate
responsibility for joining a house rests on the individual and
the house or houses they choose to explore. In 1977 two
such groups of people began a "long-term" training program
where previous years have seen only one. This is some
indication of the growth the community has undergone.

Another service collective that is essential in many
ways to the community is the Orientation Weekend Coordinating Collective. During the first weekend of every month a
group of about thirty people come to the Life Center to find
out about what the community does. The Center discovered
early that it was going to have to organize this event in
order to avoid having people pass through continually with
questions that can be very time consuming. This weekend
event involves the participation of many people in the PLC
who volunteer each month for specific jobs (from cooking
meals to doing training sessions); but the Orientation Collective is responsible for finding people to coordinate the
weekend, seeing to it that all goes well, and taking applications each month.

The second type of collective is the action-oriented
one. One with which I have been familiar and which is no
longer active (which makes it somewhat easier to make
statements about it!) is the Churchmouse Collective. People met for about three years in this group to plan cam-
paigns addressed primarily toward the Church and people
who identify with Christianity, emphasizing a simple life-
style in keeping with Christian principles, such as sharing
wealth with the world's poor. In 1976, during the
Eucharistic Congress in Philadelphia, the Churchmouse had
a week-long campaign outside the conference center, which
ended with a petition containing over 35,000 signatures being
sent to Congress in protest against U.S. support of dictatorships that practice the torture of political prisoners. And in

1977, during Easter week, the Churchmouse joined a group called Liberty to the Captives in a campaign in Washington, D. C., also protesting torture of political prisoners in third world countries to which the United States offers economic support.

The Feminist Collective, another action collective, began as a support group in the early days of the Life Center. When the community began, with high ideals of equality among its members, it soon discovered that, in fact, the men were still the ones who were doing all the speaking, leading workshops, demonstrating, etc. A core of women founded this collective to support each other in changing this situation. The collective now leads workshops for women in the community; helps organize women's support groups just forming; articulates, through community circulated papers, the feminist perspective consistent with MNS philosophy; and performs other supportive actions for women inside and outside of the community.

Aside from formal collective activities, there are general areas of action and thinking in which most--if not all--Life Center/MNS people involve themselves. Feminism is one of these. It is considered a prerequisite for joining the community in most houses (probably all of them, implicitly) that the individual be aware of his or her own sexist behavior and be taking active steps to end it. The "politics of sex" are thought about very deliberately when houses decide on such issues as house jobs and child care; women are encouraged to not automatically volunteer for stereotypic "women's tasks" and to do only an equal share of child care. Many men in the community are involving themselves in atypical male activity by, for instance, volunteering to do extra child care. Even when they live in a house with no children, they may offer time to houses where young people do live.

There is also an alternative catering service food collective called the Fatted Sprout that caters for group functions (not only in Philadelphia, but recently in Iowa, New York, and Toronto) and talks (on a sliding fee scale-- according to the ability of the catered group to pay) about the politics of agribusiness, the need for a vegetarian lifestyle and for serving well-prepared food. This collective is composed of six men and one woman at present, though it was not planned that way; Fatted Sprout may be a sign that women in the PLC are trying to move away from traditional role functions while men are discovering areas of creativity, such as cooking, previously not in their own experience.

Men's support groups are forming with much encouragement from the women in the community. The men are realizing how shut off they've been from their feelings and how the culture's patterns and values of competition, unilateral decision making, and success-orientation have made it nearly impossible for them to form lasting and deep relationships with other men. Now, instead of turning to a woman for nurturing and emotional support, they are often seeking other men to fill these same needs.

In close conjunction with this movement against sexism and patriarchy, many, though by no means all, of the Life Center people are exploring gay relationships. They are all committed politically to ending oppression of gay people through both legislative and attitudinal change. There is a rather large gay community in Philadelphia, and communication is maintained between it and the Life Center.

In view of the information given above it's not surprising to discover that interpersonal relationships often don't look like anything that most people identify with. There are almost no actual marriages in the community--some people have ended their marriages after having arrived at the PLC in couples, although both people involved may still live in the Life Center. There is a lot of painful growth occurring in PLC people's lives in their efforts to forge new models of behavior between two people. Although there are certainly those who want some kind of ongoing committed relationship with another person, and a number have this sort of arrangement, they are by far in the minority. The problems seem to arise around the tension between "us" and "self." That is, people are placing a higher degree of importance in the Life Center on making decisions about their lives that don't relate them closely to another person; and this often means relationships are secondary to self-oriented choices. This manner of decision making, which may be perceived as self-centered and could become inconsiderate of others' feelings and needs, often puts individuals in conflict with the "norm" of social interaction. To sum up, Life Center people often find that not "sticking to the rules" of society in forming relationships is difficult (that is, not buying stereotyped sex-role models), but more often than not they also find it inconsistent politically to follow traditional models--in other words, a sexist marriage is far worse than no marriage at all.

One consequence of this sort of interaction and lack of ongoing commitment is that there has been a total of <u>one</u> child born in the community since 1971. This is quite a stark comparison to The Farm's five-hundred-plus, in the same time span. Another consequence is that people have, it seems, more time for political or group activity at the PLC. I do not, however, want to leave the impression that relationships don't form; for in fact the average PLC member has many relationships, some more intense than others-- relationships with housemates, for instance, collective members, or friends. There are simply more places where a person at PLC can get his or her needs met than there seem to be for most people involved in ordinary nuclear families. This is probably true in most communal groups; however, it is a more striking feature of life at the PLC because of the deliberateness with which people go about involving themselves with many other people.

With such a diverse and large number of sometimes unrelated activities, there are some emergent problems that seem inherent to the nature of the community itself. One of the biggest is the degree of transience. Although there is no definite figure available, the turnover rate within households, collectives, and the community as a whole is high and raises a generally felt need in the community that calls for attention. On the one hand, MNS in Philadelphia (i.e., the Life Center) is trying its best to decentralize from its original roots and help form other training communities so that those who want to learn skills for social change organizing don't have to come to Philadelphia. MNS/PLC <u>wants</u> people to leave, often as a group, to go organize other areas. There is even a collective, the Network Service Collective, whose job it is to put interested people in various regions of the United States in touch with each other and in touch with other MNS people in their particular region--the goal: to organize themselves out of a job.

On the other hand, in order to accomplish their own goals with regard to having a supportive community to work for social change, there is a need for some stable environment. The people involved closely with children in the community especially feel that a more consistent home life is a priority that the community has not faced. Finding the balance between these two opposing desires--to have a stable community and to branch out to other places--is one of the most important and most discussed issues in the PLC and within the separate MNS groups at the present time.

In their search for new ways of thinking and more appropriate attitudes toward their own community, the Center has changed internally a great deal in its seven years of existence--and hopes to continue to do so. In the process of change the members have gathered a wealth of experience in community building that they can offer to other groups. And, much like communities of the past, they have discovered a need to have a context in which to deal with feelings, complaints, and conflicts. The most widely accepted model in the Life Center is one presented by Re-evaluation Counseling (RC). [25] This is a form of peer counseling that seeks to identify present "bad feelings" with their original source of distress in an individual's or group's past and, through a process called "discharge," free a person to respond to present realities accurately. Its focus is positive, stressing validation of the person, not "criticism," as most of us recognize and use the term.

Looking at the Life Center and at the Movement for a New Society as a whole, it seems at once ironic and quite appropriate that such an organization should have had its beginnings in Philadelphia. The Movement is now a loosely associated network of various kinds of groups all over the United States and abroad. It is coordinated into a system that resembles its Quaker roots. The autonomous groups (such as the one in Philadelphia) meet monthly on the local level, semiannually on the regional level, and have one yearly continental meeting. Thus, the members of MNS who are in the PLC and surrounding area of Philadelphia meet once a month to discuss Movement news and business and hear from each collective about its activities that month. Some of these groups, like the PLC, are residential communities, others are not. All MNS groups do, however, share a vision of a radically new society. The words and labels used to express this vision may vary greatly; however, there is general agreement that a rational world should be internationally oriented, decentralized, democratic, non-violent, and committed to the eradication of racism, sexism, ageism, [26] anti-semitism, and any other "ism" that spells oppression for any group of human beings. Along with this is an ecological concern for present and future generations. Indeed, there appears to be no important social problem that the people working with MNS are not actively seeking to solve.

In conclusion, I might say that it is very difficult to make a summary statement about the MNS/PLC, as one

might gather from the preceding pages.   One interesting
note is that, in a conversation I had with one of the original organizers of MNS/PLC, the question was raised as to
whether the Life Center is a utopian community.   The man
I was speaking to took a somewhat defensive manner and
"denied the accusation"--such was his tone.   His reasoning,
he said, was that thinking about utopia was not helping people eat, not making practical headway in any area.   I found
the response somewhat confusing in light of the enthusiastic,
seemingly unquenchable drive this handful of people pours
into solving problems that would, perhaps, paralyze a less
optimistic group five times its size.   I have come to the
conclusion that, given that these people do have an excellent
sense of their revolutionary tradition in America--and the
world--they do not want to be identified with any movement
that they feel was "stuck" in a theoretical discussion about
utopia; they want to live the Revolution--not just talk about
it.   Ironically, this may indicate the degree to which they
are, indeed quite utopian.


Conclusion

The Farm and the Philadelphia Life Center are illustrative
of the way in which present-day communities are based in
the American utopian tradition.   The Farm clearly has its
roots planted in the same soil as Amana, New Harmony,
and other rural utopian experiments.   The Life Center has
taken an assortment of Quaker ideas, particularly nonvio-
lence, together with ideas from other sources, and has
used them in molding an urban communal life-style to support an active political philosophy.   There is, however, one
major indication that both communities have grown past their
roots in a way unlike today's "typical commune. "   Because
of the improvements in transportation and communication
since the nineteenth century, both The Farm and the MNS/
PLC have been able to develop a network--other individuals,
groups, and communities who share a common vision about
the way society should be and who are planning together to
realize this vision.   It would probably have been impossible
in pre-industrial American society for utopian communalists
to have proceeded in this way, although the Shakers came
close and provide at least some model, with their twenty-
three villages and 6000 members at their peak.

    Whether the ability to create such a network will
have any great effect upon American culture remains to be

seen. And it also remains to be seen whether an extensive network of communities supporting the same belief system will add to The Farm's and the Life Center's individual "success." The point may be, however, not to maintain "the community," but, as Stephen says, to "spread the word." And as the network grows it will be interesting to discover how the "word" changes to suit other people's needs and visions of utopia.

## Notes

[1] Rosabeth Moss Kanter, Commitment and Community: Communes and Utopias in Sociological Perspective (Cambridge: Harvard University Press, 1972), p. 33.

[2] Stephen and The Farm, Hey Beatnik: This Is The Farm Book (Summertown, Tenn.: Book Publishing Co., 1974). Most information relating to life on The Farm can be found in this book (which, like all others published by Stephen's community, is not paginated).

[3] "Down on The Farm," in Robert Greenfield, The Spiritual Supermarket: An Account of Gurus Gone Public in America (New York: Saturday Review, 1975), pp. 107-08.

[4] Stephen, Monday Night Class (Summertown, Tenn.: Book Publishing Co., n. d.). This book is not paginated, nor is there a copyright date. However, Robert Greenfield (author of the Spiritual Supermarket) states that the book was published in 1970; the money made from sales was used to put a downpayment on the land that the community bought in Tennessee and is still being used to make land payments.

[5] Stephen, Caravan (New York: Random House, 1972).

[6] Stephen, Hey Beatnik.

[7] Greenfield, "Down on The Farm," p. 125.

[8] Stephen, Hey Beatnik.

[9] Ibid.

[10] The strange thing about the sort of sexism that operates at The Farm is that, in many ways, residents are making great efforts to not be sexist. In conversation, members do not use the pronouns "he" or "she." Instead, the

word "co" is substituted. While not trying to occlude the ways in which there is obvious sex-role stereotyping on The Farm, I must also add that there is an effort being made to maintain peer (i. e. , equal) relationships.

[11]Stephen, Hey Beatnik.

[12]Ibid.

[13]Ibid.

[14]Ibid.

[15]Ibid.

[16]Ibid.

[17]Ibid.

[18]Ibid.

[19]Ibid.

[20]Ibid.

[21]Ibid.

[22]Ibid.

[23]Susanne Gowan, et al. , Moving Toward a New Society (Philadelphia: New Society Press, 1976), p. 287.

[24]Cynthia Arvio, "Take Heart--All Those in the Struggle, " in Communities: A Journal in Cooperative Living, No. 18 (March/April 1976) 10.

[25]For an explanation of the basic theory of Re-evaluation Counseling see Harvey Jackins, The Human Side of Human Beings (Seattle: Rational Island Publishers, 1965). For an explanation of the way in which this theory is practiced see Harvey Jackins, The Human Situation (Seattle: Rational Island, 1971), especially "The Postulates of Re-evaluation Counseling, " pp. 1-8.

[26]"Ageism" is defined as the oppression of older members of society by younger members. This would be the opposite of "adultism, " which would indicate the oppression

of young people by adults. Both terms are gaining in popularity among people who are concerned with these issues and involved in work dealing with them.

## XI. AMBIGUITIES OF COMMUNITY: A KOINONIA EXPERIENCE

### Clifford J. Green

In the summer of 1973 I moved with my family to live for two years in the Koinonia community of Baltimore's Greenspring Valley. We were relative newcomers to the city, most recently being displaced New Englanders. In the previous year we had lived in the house of a colleague who was on leave, and now we needed more "permanent" housing. More importantly, we wanted to make an experiment in community living. Although we had not lived in a community before, my wife and I had studied and visited a number of religious communities in Europe in the 1950's: Iona in Scotland, Taizé in France, and Agapé, the Waldensian community in Italy.

In addition to this somewhat theoretical interest in communities from our own history, there was a more existential impetus. During our later years in Boston we had experienced a sort of informal community with a network of close friends who lived nearby. This had included the sharing of child care, cars, and other equipment. The women were involved in groups pursuing feminist concerns on both a personal level and in terms of their developing professional careers. Issues of the changing nature of the family and marital problems were regularly on our agenda. Several of the group were heavily involved in the peace movement. Also important was the fact that this informal community constituted a network of emotional support, and some of its members possessed considerable psychological expertise. We were available to each other literally at any hour of the day or night. Our move to Baltimore cut us off from this stimulating and supportive group, and we felt a deep sense of loss. Moving to Koinonia was partly an effort to find a community like the one we had lost, one that was certainly not to be found in the wilderness of suburban north Baltimore.

This chapter is an attempt to reflect on and analyze our experience during those two years at Koinonia. As such it is somewhat subjective. It is a personal account of how the experience looked to one person, not an "authorized" interpretation and history of the community during the period of our stay. Yet the issues I will discuss are not purely idiosyncratic; rather, they involve challenges that many communities must face. Issues of community identity, the relation between the community and families and individuals within it, the economic basis of the community and the status of work, the relation of the community to the larger society and culture, political and religious dimensions of community life, the nature of education within the community--these are fundamental questions which other communities can hardly avoid.

## Koinonia's Early History

The name Koinonia derives from the New Testament, where its basic meaning, in a quite profound sense, is "community."[1] (Incidentally, the Koinonia Foundation--the official name--in Baltimore should not be confused with the better-known Koinonia Farms in Georgia; there is no historical or organizational connection, though they derive their names from the same source. A comparison of the two could be instructive.) Its name thus witnesses to the Christian origins of the community nearly thirty years ago.

Physically, Koinonia is a place of compelling beauty. Located in the idyllic Greenspring Valley about ten miles north of downtown Baltimore, its estate comprises forty-five acres of woods, fields, streams, gardens, and orchards. Stately trees fill the woods and line the driveway, which winds up the hillside to overlook the valley from Gramercy, the turn-of-the-century building that is the heart of community life. In addition to Gramercy--which contains living rooms, kitchen and dining room, library, offices, and some accommodation--there are a number of other buildings on the campus: several houses, an eight-unit apartment building, and a former mews now converted into meeting rooms, accommodation, and a print shop. There is an irony in Koinonia's magnificent estate--formerly the home of a wealthy family--for economically the community lives at a subsistence level, while its neighbors are stud farms for horses, expensive private schools, and the expansive homes of some of Baltimore's wealthiest families.

Before I turn to the life of the community in recent

years it is necessary to look briefly at its earlier history, not only because some of the first-generation of Koinonians are still active staff but also because the contrast of past and present helps to highlight and interpret more recent developments. In the following paragraphs I am drawing on the experience and notes of one who was Director during the first stage of Koinonia's history from 1951 to 1968. [2]

When it began in 1951 Koinonia was described as "a Christian training center" preparing "technically equipped personnel to serve as Christian ambassadors in meeting the human world need." A large part of this purpose was inspired by Dr. Frank Laubach, known for his literacy work. In the years immediately after World War II Laubach was moved by what he called "the silent billion," the people across the world oppressed by poverty, hunger, disease, and illiteracy. He and his friends hoped that church mission boards, with their thousands of missionaries in the field, might respond to this need; but the churches lacked the funds to undertake the necessary technical training--in agriculture, health care, and so on. Laubach and his friends also approached President Truman, appealing for a government program of technical aid to impoverished and war-ravaged nations; Truman was sympathetic, but felt that the religious aspect of their proposal prevented government partnership and support. Nevertheless, they were heartened with Point Four of Truman's Inaugural Address in January 1949, which proclaimed a "bold new program" of technical aid for underdeveloped countries. [3] Even though the congressional appropriation of $20 million the following summer was meager, Laubach, Starr Daily, and other Christian leaders (who had met for almost a decade in Washington each New Year's Day as the "Twelve Men of Prayer") decided "to set up a training center to prepare Christian ambassadors to go out under the Point Four Program and all other possible channels to minister to human need in all the world." The founders and those who made donations for the new center acted in the strong consciousness that they were led in this venture by divine guidance.

And so Koinonia was born. Potential trainees who possessed technical skills were sought out and brought to the new community for training. In the following fifteen years over three hundred trainees went out to serve in more than fifty countries. The center itself did not provide technical training, but rather cultural and religious training and experience in community life. While trainees did not come seeking the community experience, it was found to be excellent preparation for living in other cultures with people of different races, religions, and life-styles. All trainees, however, were taught Laubach's method of literacy teaching and also the skills of organic gardening in case of future need overseas.

When the Peace Corps was organized by the Kennedy Administration the Koinonia staff was asked to advise in the planning. Indeed, they drew up a formal proposal to help train the volunteers; but, as with the first overture to Truman, this again met the constraints imposed by the doctrine of separation of church and state. The Peace Corps, however, did become an avenue of overseas service for many Koinonia trainees.

Effort was also devoted to raising consciousness among Americans about the urgent need of people overseas. A directory of overseas service agencies was published, conferences were held, a radio program on two hundred stations was produced for a time, a magazine and booklets were published in the Koinonia print shop--all with the goal of "educating our provincial nation." In the early 1960's the program also included seminars for several days on such world issues as peace, race, hunger, literacy, and education, often in cooperation with other concerned groups and with the assistance of outside experts.

A variety of reasons called for an evaluation of the Koinonia program in the mid-sixties and suggested the need for a new direction. Among these were the continued growth of government technical aid programs and universities contracting with the government to undertake overseas projects and training the personnel for them. In short, the field of overseas service in which Koinonia had pioneered now had many agencies working in it, the Peace Corps being the most prominent example. Accordingly, a new program under a new director was begun in the late sixties; this new program had been in effect for several years when we moved to Koinonia in 1973.

Before considering this new stage, one more general historical observation is necessary. This concerns the identity, self-definition, and sense of purpose that had characterized Koinonia for almost twenty years in the first stage of its history. During this period Koinonia had a clear sense of identity: it was a Christian training center for world service. The common religious commitment of its founders,

staff, and virtually all of its trainees had never been ex-
clusivist. People of other faiths--Buddhist, Hindu, Moslem--
had occasionally trained at Koinonia, and the fact that they
added an international, interracial and inter-religious dimension to the community was welcomed. There was no proselytizing. Nevertheless, the Christian basis of the center
was explicit and unmistakable. "Christ was our leader,"
wrote the original director; "His presence was sought for
wisdom, guidance and strength." Koinonians were committed to the goal of "service to others in need in the spirit of
love and sacrifice ... as exemplified by Christ." Christian
faith and world service, then, were the twin foundations of
Koinonia's life in the first stage of its history.

I emphasize this to highlight the problem of identity
with which the community grappled during our stay, and to
which I will return shortly. I am not suggesting that a
community can only exist on a religious basis, still less
that it can only have a Christian foundation; clearly, there
are a variety of shared commitments and goals that can
give unity, meaning, and purpose to a community.
But whatever the focus, the shared allegiance, it is extremely difficult for a community to thrive if it is unclear
about its unifying center. Erik Erikson has argued that
identity diffusion is a psychological liability; it is also a
sociological liability for a community that is unsure of its
raison d'être.

## Daily Life at Koinonia

Now I wish to describe and analyze the life of the community during the time of our direct experience. The resident
community numbered on average thirty to thirty-five people.
Some of these were staff, who were more or less permanent: the director, cook, organic gardener, one or two
maintenance people, a printer and photographer, secretary,
bookkeeper, nurse, people who worked with the mail, phones,
and fundraising, and a recruiter. Tasks were not rigidly
divided, and many people assisted with work that was the
primary responsibility of others. Several of the staff also
taught courses. Some of the staff were married, others
were single. The other main group of residents were the
"participants." Many of these were students who were on
leave from their colleges and taking an alternative semester
at Koinonia; others were at an interval in their education.
Most of the participants were young--in their late teens or

early twenties--though occasionally an older person who was
taking several months or a year off from ordinary life would
be among their number.

Besides the staff and participants there was usually a
family like ourselves: people who resided in the community
and participated to a large degree in its life, but whose
primary work was in some ordinary occupation rather than
in the Koinonia community itself. In our case I taught at a
Baltimore college, while my wife was a musician; our three
children, ranging in age at the time from six to fourteen,
attended nearby schools. Previously, a young doctor and
his family lived at Koinonia under the same arrangement.

In age the community ranged from a couple of infants
to people in their seventies. The median age of the new
staff group would have been about thirty. But more important than age was the generational difference between the
older and younger people on the staff. By generational difference I refer specifically to the fact that the younger staff
were relatively new to the community--having been there at
most for a few years--while the older people were original
Koinonians, and felt committed to the tradition and original
ideals of Koinonia in its first stage.

Daily life followed a regular pattern. All meals were
eaten together in Gramercy, and all members of the community (including children as soon as they were old enough)
belonged to teams that helped with meal preparation and
cleaning up, and general care and cleaning of the main
buildings and grounds. Each Wednesday afternoon several
hours of work were devoted to such tasks as tending the
organic garden, painting, gathering firewood, mowing and
raking, and so forth. During most mornings and afternoons
the participants attended classes and undertook private study
and other projects (e.g., pottery, weaving, journal writing),
while the staff engaged in their various duties. On Sunday
evenings a Christian communion service was held according
to a very flexible "liturgy," and other meetings for meditation were held with some regularity; attendance at these
gatherings for worship was voluntary, and some of the community participated regularly, others occasionally or rarely.
Thursday night was the time for community meeting, and
everyone was expected to attend. This was an opportunity
to review community life and problems, discuss policy and
coming events, and often have some program--a visit from
Scott and Helen Nearing or people from other communities

in the United States or Europe, a film made by a community member, or play at some homemade entertainment.

The basic concept informing the second stage of Koinonia's history was alternative education in the context of a spiritual community. In the late 1960's this was a timely vision, for many students across the land were both criticizing the traditional education in universities and colleges and also seeking for new forms of community life and personal commitments. In a mobile and rootless society towns and neighborhoods no longer provided a strong sense of community; the anonymity of suburbia or the city apartment was more typical. Nor were the nuclear family and traditional institutions like the churches filling this need. With its considerable experience of community life, and accreditation by the Maryland State Board of Education, Koinonia appeared to have the prerequisites for its new direction.

## Critical Issues

Let me now turn to several issues on which our two years of community life stimulated reflection and discuss first the relation between our family and the community. It is a commonplace that the nuclear family is in trouble on a number of fronts. Compared with its former setting in an extended family it pays for its freedom and mobility with isolation and the capacity to generate emotional conflicts that its own internal resources often cannot resolve. What difference did living in a community make? On one front the Koinonia community provided an unusual opportunity, namely for our two teenage daughters to experience considerable independence (while staying in touch with their parents) and to develop diverse relations with peers, as well as relate regularly to adults other than their parents. Since we lived in two adjacent apartments some independence was already built in. At mealtimes our daughters would normally sit with their friends rather than with their parents and younger brother. They also usually served on different work teams. In the evenings they could visit friends easily and safely have the run of the whole estate. Of course, there was plenty of time for joint family activities, too, so the independence they enjoyed did not fragment family life. Considerable tension in the relation between teenagers and their parents, then, was replaced by a comfortable independence on the part of our daughters.

Our young son, however, did not find the arrangement

so congenial. Although he played happily with the several
other young children, he was not so enthusiastic about communal eating. Partly this was because of the food, which
could broadly be labeled as a "health food" diet. More importantly, he seemed to miss the regular gatherings of the
whole family for evening and weekend meals; and at the common meals he always sat with his parents. To compensate
for this we arranged in our second year for the whole family
to eat the main weekend meals together in the apartment.

In one important respect communal living was a boon
for my wife. She was energetically developing her musical
career and wished to give most of her time to practice,
study, and performing. The division of labor in the community was ideal for her purposes. No shopping to speak
of, no regular meal preparation (after a while she began to
miss the opportunity to cook herself), and minimal house
care--the whole family helped to clean our apartments. Of
course, she was in a team for meal preparation, etc., but
that was on duty only about once a week. So most of the
time was her own. One minor problem arose here when
some community members felt that since she was on the
spot (whereas I was away at my college) she ought to be
more involved. But she quickly got across the message
that she was concentrating on serious work, and she was
able to devote herself to her music with a very convenient
schedule. Her experience demonstrates that community life
can have high potential, through new household arrangements,
for the liberation of women.

Another issue highlighted by our community experience is the economic question of productive work. Finances
were a chronic problem at Koinonia. Like the monks who
take a vow of poverty, the staff had accepted a fairly subsistence life-style and received minimal allowances. Still,
there were mortgage and insurance payments to make, bills
for some food, supplies and utilities, and maintenance ex-
penses. Sources of income were fees paid by student participants for tuition, room, and board; tuition for courses
paid by people from the Baltimore area who attended as
"commuters"; rent paid by community members like ourselves; rental of space and provision of services to weekend
conference groups who used the facilities; and donations from
friends of Koinonia. The latter group was chiefly made up
of people who had been associated with Koinonia during its
earlier history. Generally speaking, and as one might expect, they were Christians of a fairly evangelical-liberal

persuasion, and as the spirituality of the community took a more diffuse character their contributions shrunk according- ly. While newsletters, often with handwritten notes from staff members, went out regularly to the old Koinonians, one might ask whether a former constituency ought to be asked to support a new enterprise.

Indeed, a more fundamental issue is whether it is psychologically healthy for a community to depend on dona- tions from others. For there is a dignity that comes with supporting oneself and the community through productive labor, whereas self-respect and morale suffer when a com- munity is not economically viable through its own labor and resources. Resentment among many community members was evident toward paying groups that came for weekend conferences--they required more work, and in a real sense were intruders. And I believe there was a little resentment among some of the staff towards "temporary" community members, the participants and families like ourselves. For the element of financial necessity was involved in these re- lationships, and I think that was a contributing factor in generating resentment. (Perhaps, too, the fact that our family had a normal income compared to the staff's small allowances also generated a little low-level resentment. )

The basic economic fact is that Koinonia was not a viable income-producing community. Few educational enter- prises pay for themselves on the basis of tuition and fees, and in any case Koinonia did not have enough participants-- these ranged in number from about five to fifteen per semes- ter, whereas the facilities could have carried thirty or more. To be sure, the community contributed a great deal to its own support through the enormous amount of food produced by the garden, and by doing most of its own maintenance and repairs. But that still left a chronic cash shortage. Other communities have addressed this problem in various ways: some by having internal income-producing work like farming or the toy making of the Bruderhof; others have had sufficient members with paying jobs in the "outside" world (the Iona Community is a variant of this arrangement). The point here is not simply that the economic problem is ines- capable. My basic contention is that a healthy community needs the psychological well-being and sense of achievement that comes with productive and self-supporting labor. Per- haps there was an ideological (or class? or religious?) bias that prevented many people at Koinonia from being realistic about this. Perhaps economic productivity was not seriously considered in accepting people into community membership.

A crucial issue for Koinonia at the time of our stay was <u>community identity</u>. This was evident in many ways: from the difficulty members had in answering the question "what is Koinonia?" to the many meetings and hours devoted to clarifying "goals," to the questions about the religious dimension of its life, and so on. We have seen that the identity of the original Koinonia was rooted in Christian faith and world service. Now, service to world need had been replaced by a program of alternative education that was directed to students who brought plenty of their own personal identity questions to complicate the community issue. Christian faith was not so much replaced as diffused; that is, Christianity took its place under the broad rubric of "spirituality." This eclectic umbrella was sufficient to cover not only various types of Christianity but also forms of Hindu and Buddhist belief and practice, Jungianism (itself a form of religion and a mandate for eclecticism and syncretism[4]) and samplings of other cults.

Broadly speaking, the ethos tended toward mysticism with a strong emphasis on inwardness--making one's own "spiritual journey." A statement from the Spring 1978 Koinonia newsletter conveys the religious attitude that was fairly typical in our time, too:

> This is the season of Revelation; it is truly the beginning of the year. This is the time when the eternal message of Life resounds through the countryside; when layers of colorless snow give way to snowdrops, daffodils and tulips, forsythia and azalea. We go to the garden each day and ask, "Is it time, yet?" This is the season of Revelation; it is during this time of year that we recall how the Divine Presence led Israel out of bondage and into a covenant; it is at this time that the flow of dharma deposited the Buddha into our world; and it is also at this time that the Christ was nailed to the Tree of Life and rose--after days in darkness--to take upon Himself the task of the salvation of all beings. This is the season when the Will of the Transcendent manifests itself in our midst.

A related statement in the Summer 1978 course catalogue says: "While we promote no single theology or doctrine, we seek to realize in ourselves that common truth which informs all religious and humanist faiths."

Such statements pose several grave problems. First, to the student of religion the notion that all religions are essentially the same is, despite the wide credence given this idea, a very disputable proposition indeed. Further, this premise serves, I believe, to subvert genuine inter-religious dialogue where learning takes place as the hard edges of religious distinctiveness and particularity contact each other. To ignore or deny such particularity is to leach out the content of particular religions in a wash of individual subjectivity. I have already alluded to another problem in this area, namely the tension--more unspoken than explicit--between the Christian commitment of the older Koinonia staff and the "new spirituality" of many of the younger community members. Further, one may question whether an eclectic spirituality can provide an adequate basis for shaping a community's purposes and priorities; and whether the young can find in it a firm enough world view on which to cut the teeth of their own psychological and intellectual identities.

One incident is revealing in this discussion of religion and community identity. In the early 1970's Philip Berrigan, Elizabeth McAlister, and several friends were in the process of forming a community in Baltimore and approached Koinonia to discuss a joint venture. The staff, though not unanimous in the decision, turned the proposal down. Apparently a number felt that the Berrigan group would constitute a tight mini-community, and that their absences from Koinonia on speaking missions would also have a fragmenting effect. I believe that the clear religious and political commitments of the Berrigan group were also experienced as a threat to the fragile identity of Koinonia at the time. In my judgment a crucial and clarifying opportunity was lost.

This same incident serves to introduce another basic issue: the relation between the community and society at large. Fundamentally, this concerns the political status and function of the community. I take it for granted that any community, whether conventional or intentional, is a political unit that either replicates the larger political society or exists in a relation of tension or contradiction. Self-consciousness on this issue has of course been a hallmark of utopian thought and communities for centuries.

I do not recall Koinonia calling itself utopian, but it clearly and deliberately intended to be an alternative community that cultivated a life-style different from the conventional. There were many signs of this. One, obviously, was that the members had chosen to live in community rather than as isolated single or family units. Another was that the staff chose to live in relative poverty, eschewing the quest for wealth. A strong respect for nature was evident: appreciation for the physical gifts of the land and its life, and for natural products of weaving, pottery, and other crafts; a sensitivity to the seasons of the year; and perhaps above all the central and symbolic role of the large organic garden in the life of the community. Naturally, an ecological awareness accompanied this respect for nature. The food was simple and healthy, much of it grown on the premises, and junk food was scorned. Sensitivity to the arts-- poetry, drawing, photography, film, printing, music, and dance--was also quite evident. In ethos the community tried to avoid a hierarchy of power as much as possible and to reach decisions by consensus. Cooperation rather than competition was fostered. Sex roles were subject to experimentation, with women interested in tractors and pumps and men preparing food and minding children. On the political front militarism, nationalism, racism, violence, conspicuous consumption, and economic injustice were frequently criticized.

On the debit side of the ambiguity ledger there are several observations to be made. First is the matter of class and race. The members of the community in our time were predominantly white and middle class, and there was little awareness of class alienations in evidence. There were two black people on the staff, original Koinonians, who became good friends of our family; because of age and ailments, and also philosophical differences, their participation in the community was somewhat limited. Yet their presence should have served as a reminder of the ugliest sore on the nation's body politic. Nevertheless, I detected little raised consciousness about racism, and no effort to recruit more black members into the community.

On other political fronts the record was spotty. My wife, for example, organized a supper for some of Cesar Chavez's United Farm Workers (it was the time of the grape boycott); they were warmly welcomed and their presentation was received with interest. However, there was virtually no follow-up. And this initiative, and others like it, came from a semi-outsider, so to speak, and was not typical of the more permanent community. Political consciousness and activism, in the narrower sense of the term, was not typical--recall the story of the Berrigan overture.

Here, it is pertinent to recall another change from
the first to the second stage of Koinonia's history.  In the
beginning it was outward-looking and oriented to world need.
To be sure, this seems to have involved compassion and the
ideal of service rather than a tough political analysis.  But
in its second stage Koinonia turned inward, to focus on the
life of the community itself and the individual member's inward journey.  Obviously, this is a subjective and psychological attitude, not a political orientation.  Here, a great
irony stands revealed.  For all its efforts to cultivate an
alternative life-style, Koinonia fell prey to the prototypical
modern American temptation:  individualism and subjectiv-
ism. 5

If this is evidence concerning the predisposing power
of social conditioning and cultural habit, it also points to the
political challenge any serious alternative community must
face.  In short, if it intends to be an alternative, it needs
a thoroughgoing analysis of the society from which it wishes
to differ.  In particular it needs a raised consciousness on
precisely those political realities and cultural attitudes that
society takes for granted.  It must have critical expertise
in the infrastructure and must be able to demythologize society's orthodoxies in a systematic manner.

A couple of examples should illustrate this point.  If
a community wishes to develop an alternative form of life
from that of the ordinary nuclear family, it needs a solid
historical, sociological, and psychological critique of the
nuclear family.  The same goes for sex roles, education,
social class, and race.  Above all, an analysis of the economic system and its power relations is essential.  Furthermore, the systemic and interlocking character of these social factors must be probed and understood.  This is a task
of considerable intellectual rigor; superficial truisms are
quite inadequate.  And undertaking such analysis presupposes
some clear vision of a more just and humane society.
Naturally, systematic analysis is only the beginning of the
battle; a whole new set of personal and communal resources
will be necessary to create an alternative, even in micro-
cosm.  But without such analysis and raised consciousness
I fail to see how a community can generate a viable alternative; more likely it will fall prey to the very forces that it
neglects.

In 1977, Koinonia began reviewing its recent life
and program as part of a search for a new director.  Her

appointment presumably will lead to new directions and emphases. Whether the issues discussed here will be taken up by Koinonia is a matter, of course, for the community itself to decide. But as I review our two years of experience I see that it brought both opportunities and frustrations, though not regret. Among the many lessons we learned, perhaps the most encompassing is the complexity of community and the enormous challenge involved in creating an alternative community. It is to be hoped that the current movement that has given birth to so many experiments in community life will not founder on these complexities and challenges. For what is ultimately at stake in this movement, it seems to me, is not the private passions of groups of enthusiasts but a probing of the very foundation and future of our civilization itself. The community movement does not have a monopoly on this creative process. Yet, perhaps it can produce not more unrealistic fantasies of utopia but some viable paradigms for social transformation.

## Notes

[1] The Greek term has nuances of communion, fellowship, sharing, and participation; see, for example, Acts 2:42, I Cor. 10:16, Gal. 2:9, Phil. 2:1, 3:10, I John 1:3-7.

[2] Glenn Harding, "Background and Historical Notes on Koinonia Foundation"; mimeographed, unpublished, n.d. [1977]. Since his retirement Mr. Harding has continued to serve on the Koinonia board. (A later director, David Poist, comments that the picture sketched by Mr. Harding is somewhat idealized. Agreeing with Harding that Koinonia was united in its Christian focus for the first fifteen years, Poist says that records show significant tensions at times between those who favored the international training model and those who favored more a retreat model.)

[3] See Public Papers of the Presidents of the United States. Harry S. Truman, 1949 (Washington, D.C.: U.S. Government Printing Office, 1964), p. 114.

[4] See Philip Rieff, The Triumph of the Therapeutic (New York: Harper & Row, 1966), esp. Ch. 5.

[5] See Rieff, op. cit.; Russell Jacoby, Social Amnesia: A Critique of Conformist Psychology from Adler to Laing (Boston: Beacon Press, 1975); Christopher Lasch, "The

Narcissist Society, " New York Review of Books, September 30, 1976, pp. 5ff. , and especially his The Culture of Narcissism (New York: Norton, 1978). See also the recent writings of Robert N. Bellah, especially The Broken Covenant (New York: Seabury Press, 1975); "Grounds for a Value Consensus in America, " in The Search for a Value Consensus (New York: The Rockefeller Foundation, 1978); "Religion and Legitimation in the American Republic, " Society, May-June 1978; "New Religious Consciousness and the Crisis in Modernity, " in Glock and Bellah, eds. , The New Religious Consciousness (Berkeley: University of California, 1976); "Commentary and Proposed Agenda: The Normative Framework for Pluralism in America, " Soundings, Fall 1978.

# XII. THE ECONOMICS OF UTOPIA

## Ronald A. Krieger

Utopian thinking in economics always seems to focus on the construction of virtually complete, internally consistent, idealized economic systems. I would therefore like to start with some handy working definitions of a few idealized systems that have actually been put to the test in various places at one time or another. These come to us courtesy of the Financial Times of London and perhaps will serve us as useful benchmarks:

> Socialism: You have two cows, and you give one to
> your neighbor.
> Communism: You have two cows, and the govern-
> ment takes both of them and gives you milk.
> Fascism: You have two cows, and the government
> takes both of them and sells you milk.
> Capitalism: You have two cows, and you sell one of
> them and buy a bull.

These cynical definitions capture so succinctly the essence of some working socioeconomic models that I would not attempt to improve upon the statements by looking any further into those systems. Instead, I would like to direct your attention away from grim reality and in the direction of hopeful fantasy: the construction of idealized economic societies by American thinkers in the 1970's. I will restrict my remarks to the two main patterns of utopian thought that seem to be emerging--the individualist and the collectivist. Both patterns have powerful antecedents in the economic literature that has come down to us over the past two centuries, but both are now appearing in distinctively modern formulations. On the right, we have the libertarian philosophy as represented by the writings of Murray Rothbard, which must be distinguished from the more traditional, classical economic liberalism of such economists as Milton Friedman. On

194

the left, I will present the ideas of Jerome Shuchter, which differ considerably from the standard old/new-left formulations represented by such modern writers as Howard Sherman. I will attempt to let all of these authors speak to you in their own words as much as possible.

## Individualist Utopias:  Classical Liberalism

Although the libertarians would appear to be direct decendants of Adam Smith, the eighteenth-century prophet of self-interest and laissez-faire, they depart from Smith, and the nineteenth-century liberal philosophy that followed him, in a number of ways.  The two most important are Smith's concession of some coercive role to government, through taxation, and more fundamentally, his justification of free markets on utilitarian grounds.

In his enduring masterpiece, the Wealth of Nations--we have recently celebrated the bicentennial of its publication--Smith actually preaches the gospel of the public interest.  He contends, however, that the public is better served by selfish individuals vigorously pursuing their own self-interest than by any direct action taken in the name of promoting the general welfare.  "It is not from the benevolence of the butcher, the brewer, or the baker, that we expect our dinner, but from their regard to their own interest," Smith wrote.  "We address ourselves, not to their humanity, but to their self-love, and never talk to them of our necessities but of their advantages."  Again with his eye to the public interest, Smith endorses the neglect by business of action taken in the name of social responsibility.  Smith says of the businessman:

> He generally, indeed, neither intends to promote the public interest, nor knows how much he is promoting it.  By preferring the support of domestic to that of foreign industry, he intends only his own security; and by directing that industry in such a manner as its produce may be of the greatest value, he intends only his own gain, and he is in this, as in many other cases, led by an invisible hand to promote an end which was no part of his intention.  By pursuing his own interest he frequently promotes that of society more effectually than when he really intends to promote it.  I have never known much good done by those who affected

> to trade for the public good.... What is the
> species of domestic industry which his capital can
> best employ, and of which the produce is likely to
> be of greatest value, every individual, it is evi-
> dent, can, in his local situation, judge much bet-
> ter than any statesman or lawgiver can do for him.

Elsewhere in the Wealth of Nations Smith does advocate "the obvious and simple system of natural liberty," con-
demning all violations of it. Still, it is clear that this
eighteenth-century moral philosopher saw the primary justification for free markets in the utilitarian sense of promoting the general welfare of members of society as a whole.

Classical liberalism, as it developed in the century
after Smith, did emphasize freedom as the ultimate goal of
society. It supported laissez-faire as a means of reducing
the role of the State in economic affairs, and therefore en-
larging the role of the individual. The doctrine that has
come to be known as twentieth-century American liberalism
is more identified, in contrast, with the use of the power of
the State to promote welfare and equality. I will retain the
classical, nineteenth-century usage of the term "liberal,"
which is the way it appears in the development of economic
thought. But the nineteenth-century liberal, in common with
Adam Smith, also viewed economic freedom in a utilitarian
context--as a means of promoting welfare and equality rather
than as an alternative to them. To this end decentralization,
as opposed to centralization, of economic power and activity
was supported.

The role of freedom in liberal philosophy has been
well articulated by Nobel Laureate Milton Friedman, the
most prominent modern-day apostle of laissez-faire. "In a
society freedom has nothing to say about what an individual
does with his freedom; it is not an all-embracing ethic,"
says Friedman. "Indeed, a major aim of the liberal is to
leave the ethical problem for the individual to wrestle with."
The liberal, adds Friedman, conceives of women and men
as imperfect beings, with social organization concerned as
much with the negative problem of preventing "bad" people
from doing harm as with enabling "good" people to do good,
whoever and whatever the good or the bad might be.

For modern liberal descendants of Adam Smith, the
free-market system is justified as the best form of economic
organization for realizing the twin values of individual freedom and social welfare. In the words of Friedman:

Robert Owen's proposed Village

The basic problem of social organization is how to
coordinate the economic activities of large numbers of people. Even in relatively backward societies, extensive division of labor and specialization of function is required to make effective use
of available resources. In advanced societies, the
scale on which coordination is needed, to take full
advantage of the opportunities offered by modern
science and technology, is enormously greater.
Literally millions of people are involved in providing one another with their daily bread, let alone
with their yearly automobiles. The challenge to
the believer in liberty is to reconcile this widespread interdependence with individual freedom.

Liberals view the market mechanism as the ideal
means of reconciling the twin goals of economic society.
They see the only alternative coordinating mechanism as
that of central direction and coercion, which they fear would
negate both freedom and the efficient, effective promotion of
economic welfare. "The possibility of coordination through
voluntary cooperation rests on the elementary--yet frequently
denied--proposition that both parties to an economic transaction benefit from it, provided the transaction is bilaterally
voluntary and informed. "

That is, voluntary exchange can bring about coordination without coercion. Each household uses its resources to
produce goods and services that it exchanges for other goods

and services, indirectly satisfying its wants by producing for others.   As Smith pointed out two centuries ago the incentive for this is the increased production and income made possible by specialization.   The exchange is voluntary and uncoerced, with both parties cooperating in their self-interest.

Friedman argues that this simple household model can be extended with little modification to a complex, monetized, industrial economy.   "Cooperation is strictly individual and voluntary <u>provided</u>:   (a) that enterprises are private, so that the ultimate contracting parties are individuals and (b) that individuals are effectively free to enter or not to enter into any particular exchange, so that every transaction is strictly voluntary. "

In Friedman's view the absence of coercion is central to the functioning of the market mechanism, in the sense that it prevents one person from interfering with another in most of his or her activities.   "The consumer is protected from coercion by the seller because of the presence of other sellers with whom he can deal.   The seller is protected from coercion by the consumer because of other consumers to whom he can sell.   The employee is protected from coercion by the employer because of other employers for whom he can work, and so on.   And the market does this impersonally and without centralized authority. "

Opponents of the market mechanism often object to it precisely because it gives people what they want rather than what "a particular group thinks they ought to want, " says Friedman.   Thus, arguments against the free market are based in part on a lack of belief in freedom itself.

The role of government in this system is to serve as a forum for determining the rules and to enforce contracts-- a limited role that is further minimized by the effectiveness of the market.   "The characteristic feature of action through political channels is that it tends to require or enforce substantial conformity, " Friedman declares.   "The great advantage of the market, on the other hand, is that it permits wide diversity.   It is, in political terms, a system of proportional representation.   Each man can vote, as it were, for the color of tie he wants and get it; he does not have to see what color the majority wants and then, if he is in the minority, submit. "

These views are commonplace today in competitive

economic theory.   Who decides what gets produced?   Consumers do, by "voting" with their dollars.   But what insures
that it does get produced?   Profit incentives do, by offering
the probability of the highest returns in activities producing
those goods and services most desired by consumers.   By
the same token producers suffer financial penalties for not
allocating resources according to consumer preferences.
The system of incentives and penalties established by the
free market insures that labor and capital flow to the most
promising activities.   Millions of decentralized decisions result in what economists call a "Pareto optimum," in which
no one can be made better off unless someone else is made
worse off.

## Individualist Utopias:   Libertarianism

If Milton Friedman is the leading exponent of free markets
as a practical policy for modern industrial societies, Murray
Rothbard surely must rank as the outstanding individualist
utopian.   To an outsider their respective schools of thought
seem to stand for much the same thing; to liberals and libertarians, however, the differences between them are monu-
mental.   In Rothbard's utopian writings, best represented by
For a New Liberty, an idealized liberal society is constructed
without the slightest compromise with current political structures or social organization.   A fervent anti-statist, often to
the point of pure anarchism, Rothbard has little use for what
he considers the statist anti-communism of American con-
servatism.   He frequently condemns, in fact, what he alleges
to be the political authoritarianism and warmongering of the
American Right.

A crucial axiom of Rothbard's libertarianism asserts
that "no person or group of persons have the right to aggress
against the person or property of anyone else."   The libertarian advocacy of non-aggression puts Rothbard in with some
strange bedfellows.   He shares with the democratic Left in
America a devotion to civil liberties, including freedom of
speech and freedom to publish, assemble, and engage in
"victimless crimes."   Military conscription is slavery to
Rothbard, as would be any conscription for civilian purposes,
such as a "national service" corps.   On the other hand,
with the political Right that he so often opposes, Rothbard
shares a strong belief in economic liberties:   Government
should not interfere with property rights or with the free-
market economy through controls, regulation, subsidies, or
prohibitions.

> While opposing any and all private or group ag-
> gression against the rights of person and property,
> the libertarian sees that throughout history and into
> the present day, there has been one central, domi-
> nant, and overriding aggressor upon all of these
> rights: the State. In contrast to all other thinkers,
> left, right, or in-between, the libertarian refuses
> to give the State the moral sanction to commit ac-
> tions that almost everyone agrees would be im-
> moral, illegal, and criminal if committed by any
> person or group in society.... The State habitually
> commits mass murder, which it calls "war," or
> sometimes "suppression of subversion"; the State
> engages in enslavement into its military forces,
> which it calls "conscription"; and it lives and has
> its being in the practice of forcible theft, which it
> calls "taxation." The libertarian insists that
> whether or not such practices are supported by
> the majority of the population is not germane to
> their nature: that, regardless of popular sanction,
> War is Mass Murder, Conscription is Slavery, and
> Taxation is Robbery. The libertarian, in short,
> is almost completely the child in the fable, point-
> ing out insistently that the emperor has no clothes.

The libertarian philosophy opposes big business, placing upon it much of the responsibility for statism in the
twentieth century. This is in marked contrast to Friedman,
who regards problems of big business and monopoly as overstated and tangential. But while Friedman looks at the economic consequences of business concentration, Rothbard is
concerned with the political. For Rothbard big business
means the military-industrial complex, the very essence of
rampant, coercive statism.

Rothbard believes absolutely in the primacy of property rights in a very broad sense. In fact, he refuses to
accept the popular distinction that is often drawn between
"property rights" and "human rights." Should an individual
have the freedom to cry "fire" maliciously in a crowded
theater? No, answers Rothbard, but only because this is
a violation of the (broadly defined) property rights of the
theater owner and of other patrons.

Libertarians, therefore, want to establish "the absolute right to private property of every man: first, in his
own body, and second, in the previously unused natural

resources which he first transforms by his labor. " If, says
Rothbard, a person owns anything--his own person and labor
and land--"he then has the right to give away or exchange
these property titles to someone else, after which point the
other person also has absolute property title. " This right
to private property justifies both free contract and the free-
market economy. People may exchange both the tangible
objects they own and their own labor, which they also own.

For libertarians the utilitarian result of the free
market, so eloquently stressed by Adam Smith, is nothing
more than a positive side effect of the operation of free
markets. They refuse to accept its social utility as a justification of the market system. The primary justification
for the system "is moral, and is rooted in the natural rights
defense of private property, " asserts Rothbard. The market
is nothing more than a "vast network of voluntary and mu-
tually agreed-upon two-person exchanges. " When you buy
something from a vendor, the transaction takes place only
because the buyer prefers the product to the money, while
the seller prefers the money to the product. "Or, when I
teach at a university, I estimate that I prefer my salary to
not expending my labor of teaching, while the university
authorities calculate that they prefer gaining my teaching
services to not paying me the money. If the newsdealer insisted on charging more for the paper, I might well decide
that it isn't worth the price; similarly, if I should insist on
triply my present salary, the university might well decide to
dispense with my services. "

In similar fashion the libertarian uses the notion of
property rights to dismiss objections to inheritance of wealth,
concentrating not on the bonanza for the recipient but on the
freedom of the giver. The idea of property rights is fundamental to the libertarian definition of "freedom":

> Freedom is a condition in which a person's owner-
> ship rights in his own body and his legitimate
> material property are not invaded, are not ag-
> gressed against. A man who steals another man's
> property is invading and restricting the victim's
> freedom, as does the man who beats another over
> the head. Freedom and unrestricted property right
> go hand in hand. On the other hand, to the liber-
> tarian, "crime" is an act of aggression against a
> man's property right, either in his own person or
> his materially owned objects. Crime is an invasion,

by the use of violence, against a man's property
and therefore against his liberty. "Slavery"--the
opposite of freedom--is a condition in which the
slave has little or no right of self-ownership....
The libertarian, then, is clearly an individualist
but not an egalitarian. The only "equality" he
would advocate is the equal right of every man to
the property is his own person, to the property in
the unused resources he "homesteads," and to the
property of others he has acquired either through
voluntary exchange or gift.

The role of the State, in this construction, is that of
the collective criminal, or group plunderer. On the one
hand government forbids private murder and theft, but on
the other it engages in the same actions collectively through
war and taxation. According to Rothbard virtually every
social problem can be traced to government action. He regards war, for example, as a direct result of government
monopoly. The military-industrial complex, while fostered
by big business, is in the last analysis a creature of government.

Government does no better in the civil realm, in
Rothbard's formulation. Traffic congestion occurs solely on
government-owned streets and roads, illustrating the paradox that when everybody owns something through government,
then nobody owns it; everyone tramples on everyone else's
property rights. Other transportation problems--decaying
railroads, overpriced airlines, deficit-ridden mass-transit
systems--all result from government subsidization, regulation, and ownership.

Government fares no better with Rothbard in its
management of natural resources. Water pollution results
from rivers being kept in the public domain and from the
abominations of municipally owned sewage disposal systems.
"Government is at the same time the largest polluter, as
well as the careless 'owner' of the resource," he says.
The same goes for water shortages, air pollution, and power
shortages and blackouts resulting from government creation
and regulation of monopolies in public utilities. Likewise,
poor telephone and postal service and the blandness of tele-
vision result from government regulation.

Continuing his assault on the role of the State in the
economy, Rothbard blames government for the welfare system,

urban housing problems compounded by urban planning, zoning laws, property taxes, building codes, urban renewal, rent controls, and other alleged horrors of city life. Unions have gained the power to cripple the economy through special privileges afforded by the government, and the widely acknowledged failures of the public schools come from ownership and operation by government, backed by compulsory attendance laws. Finally, "high and rising taxes have crippled almost everyone, and are hampering productivity, incentives, and thrift, as well as the free energies of the people. Taxes, of course, are exclusively the province of the government. "

Rothbard's solutions, which he steadfastly denies are "utopian, " call for replacement of coercive government action in these and all other sectors of society with voluntary private action. There would be no taxation, no public schools, no welfare system, no compulsory testimony in legal actions, and no "involuntary servitude" or coercive government action in any social, legal, or economic spheres.

There are some obvious problems with the libertarian utopia, not the smallest of which is the task of winning over a society that is at least as suspicious of private gain and privilege as it is of government coercion. When it comes to getting converts, however, Rothbard sees little room for compromise on the principles of his utopia. His only concession is his counsel to fellow libertarians to work within the existing system for tax reductions and any other policies that might limit the role of government.

More fundamentally, Rothbard's obsession with the coercive role of the State blinds him to the possibilities of repression through private coercion, which has been, after all, one of the standard justifications for government intervention. Rothbard offers no alternative to government to restrain individuals from combining to coerce others. The logic of his system suggests that in the absence of countervailing government force, the strongest and wealthiest members of society will become like feudal barons, operating their own private coercive systems. It is easy to envision them maintaining their power through such devices as paramilitary troops, mercenary police forces, and vigilante groups. They would become, in effect, an unelected quasi-government filling the power vacuum left by the abdication of conventional government. To prevent unchecked property rights from giving some members of society the freedom to coerce or even enslave others, what solution is there other than the reinstatement of coercive governmental institutions? The choice does not seem to be between freedom and government, as in the libertarian construct, but between government co-ercion and quasi-governmental coercion by the powerful.

Ultimately, the realization of an individualist utopia, in which no persons commit aggression against any others, seems to rest more on a transformation of the human spirit than on the presence or absence of certain formal institu-tions. Barring the instant perfectability of humankind--the appearance of New Individualist Man, as it were--the liber-tarian utopia does not appear to be feasible or even desir-able.

## Collectivist Utopias: Socialism and the New Left

What Adam Smith did for individualism, liberalism, and libertarian thought, Karl Marx did for the socialist move-ment. Marx was not the first socialist, and indeed he came to public notice in the mid-nineteenth century as a vociferous critic of the utopian socialists of that period. But his is the version of socialism that still endures, the prophet whose revolutionary ideas still infuse the socialist movement today. Marx was certainly no utopian, and in fact his writings were devoid of any detailed construction of the idealized socialist or communist state. His concern was the indictment of capitalism and the foretelling of its inevitable destruction through its own internal contradictions: the accumulation of capital through expropriation of the surplus value of labor, the falling rate of profit, the pauperization of the working class, and a series of worsening business crises leading to the final bloody revolution. The workers would rise up to expropriate the expropriators, confiscate the means of pro-duction, and set up a dictatorship of the proletariat. After a suitable transition period this socialist state would wither away and a vaguely defined stage of pure communism would ensue, in which everyone would produce according to their abilities and receive according to their needs.

It has been left up to the followers of Marx in the twentieth century, from Lenin to the American New Left, to flesh out the details of the collectivist utopia that would re-sult from the overthrow of capitalism. The socialist indict-ment of capitalism still stands much as Marx proposed it a century ago, with the current attack of the New Left centering on inequitable distribution of income, poverty, unemployment, alienation of workers, maldistribution of power, and business crises. Capitalism also takes the blame for such social evils as racism, sexism, and pollution. Common to socialist solutions is some form of government ownership of the means of production, with resources allocated by central planners through state bureaucracies rather than by the market through its system of incentives and penalties.

A prominent classical Marxist, New Left economics professor Howard Sherman of the University of California at Riverside, carries his utopian conjecture beyond socialism to the final stage of the Marxian dialectic: pure communism. Assuming the label of Marxist-humanist, Sherman is a critic of both American capitalism and Soviet socialism, and calls himself the only member of the "worldwide Democratic Communist party."

U. S. capitalism is efficient within each enterprise to a large degree. It suffers, however, from extreme income inequality due to exploitation; considerable general unemployment; considerable inflation; pollution; inefficiency through waste, particularly advertising and military; monopoly high prices and excess profits; monopoly obstruction through planned obsolescence and holding back some inventions; racial, religious, and sexual discrimination; many forms of alienation; and imperialist activity leading to (limited?) wars. The majority of capitalist countries, particularly the underdeveloped ones, have political dictatorships.
Soviet socialism is probably somewhat less efficient within each enterprise. Income distribution, however, is much more equal and exploitation is very small in total amount. It has a high growth rate, no general unemployment, and very little inflation at present. It has no private monopoly, but a large inefficient bureaucracy. It has very little racial and sexual discrimination, but some discrimination against Jews. Its pollution level is much less than the U. S. level. It does dominate East Europe in an imperialist manner, but for reasons not directly economic. It has a repressive dictatorship, and very considerable alienation.

Sherman's ideal society would be one of "full communism," which in the economic sphere would solve the problems of poverty and income distribution while "political-ly, it offers hope for the end of police and prisons, wars and armies; socially, it offers hope for the eventual end of discrimination and alienation."

By full communism he means an economy in which all goods would be "free" in the sense of zero-priced, and "would be produced under public control and ownership, and consumed by everyone according to his desires." His goals include the establishment of a "non-commercialized coopera-tive society," and he therefore opposes such ideas as a guaranteed annual income as an alternative to free goods be-cause wages or other forms of money income would preserve "the present money-grubbing competitive psychology."

If establishment of full communism proves impracti-cal, Sherman is willing to settle for the reasonable proxy of "partial communism," where wages are still paid but 80 to 90 percent of all goods are priced at zero. "This system is workable," he says, and it would achieve "almost all the political and social advantages usually alleged in favor of full communism." He would eliminate prices and rationing for perhaps 80 percent of goods and services, retaining prices only for luxury items, and limiting demand by keep-ing aggregate wages constant. Sherman contemplates the eventual emergence of a new type of unselfish, noncompetitive individual in communist society, but "only when all consumer necessities have been free for some time under full commu-nism would any social scientist, Marxist or otherwise, expect that acquisitive behavior might begin to diminish very con-siderably." How would goods get produced under this sys-tem?

> The classic attack on pure communism is that, if all goods are free, there is insufficient incentive to work. Suppose, however, that there is a grad-ual change, with only a half percent of consumer goods per year passing from the monetary to the free goods sector. It seems unlikely that at some point, the ordinary worker would suddenly stop working. It may still be argued that he will grad-ually reduce his effort. Even at an 80 percent free goods level, however, differentiated wages (which could be used to buy the remaining, priced luxury goods) would probably be a more than suf-ficient incentive for those who still need such in-centives.

Economic planning would replace the market system in the allocation of resources. Planners would gather information on consumer preferences, alternative technologies, and available resources. "With these data, optimal programming can find the output combinations and technologies producing the maximum output."

Although consumer goods are given away in Sherman's partial communist economy, producer goods are still bought and sold in a market, and managers are instructed to maximize profits. The central government pays a specified price for the goods, based on market cost to the producers.

Sherman is less specific on the non-economic content of the communist system. "If the economics of communism consists of murky speculation in a utopian vein, its political and social analysis is pure science fiction," he admits. Nevertheless, he is willing to venture some predictions. The state would not totally wither away under communism, he says, but "the oppressive and violent side of government"-- police, prisons, courts, and armies--would disappear. Government would exist for purposes of economic planning and administration based on "non-coercive principles." Slower economic growth would mean less pollution. There would be no racism because the vested economic and political interests that foster it in capitalism and some socialist countries would be eliminated. Sexism would break down when free distribution of goods liberates women from "going into marriages for material gain."

A few comments are in order about Sherman's system, although I will not attempt at this time to present detailed critiques of any of the utopian writers. As in the case of the libertarians the disappearance of coercion appears to be a forlorn hope, although this time it is public force replacing the private variety. To base central economic planning and administration on "non-coercive principles" is a contradiction in terms. Unless the population can be totally pacified through repressive measures, zero pricing will lead to excess demand, waste, shortages, and inefficiencies. Coercive measures are inevitable. No planning body can hope to gather more than a fraction of the information generated by the market system, which gets its signals from prices based on millions of decentralized decisions, expressions of preference, and reflections of production costs and scarcity. Without market prices planners will have to proceed on the basis of ill-informed guesses about what prices might have been, and large and irreversible errors are a certainty. Allocation of goods and services under central planning would have to be performed by an authoritarian bureaucracy imposing the government's preferences--and mistakes--on a public that will have to be pacified by political repression, if it will not willingly accept whatever is offered.

Sherman is no more convincing on the supply side of his economy than on the demand side. With most goods free and differential wages available only for the purchase of a few luxuries, the rewards for initiative and industriousness seem minimal. It is difficult to see how more than a perfunctory effort will be forthcoming without a tightly controlled system of forced labor. As in the case of the libertarian utopia, the system could operate on a voluntary, uncoercive basis only in the event of a miraculous transformation of the human spirit--or the establishment, in this case, of a New Communist Man. Sherman indicates that long years of operation of the system will eventually lead to this transformation; yet it is difficult to see how the system can operate at all in its absence.

The political and social benefits ascribed to the collectivist utopia--elimination of sexism, racism, and the like--seem to be little more than wishful thinking, as Sherman comes close to admitting. It is likely that many human attitudes are quite independent of the particular social and economic setting.

Finally, the reduction of pollution that Sherman foresees under communism is another improbability. Whether Sherman's factory managers are maximizing profits or just meeting pre-assigned production quotas, there is little reason to expect them to risk missing their targets by reducing pollution. Indeed, in a society where the Marxian labor theory of value dominates economic thinking, natural resources are considered free goods, and the ravishing of the environment is likely to be even worse than under capitalism. There is some evidence of this in the experience of Soviet socialism.

Collectivist Utopias: Collectivist Reform

A much less traditional approach to the building of a collectivist utopia is the reformist model proposed by a creative

non-academic economist, Jerome Shuchter of Los Angeles.
Shuchter is a former business economist who more recently
was editor and publisher of the provocative economic newsletter Jeremiad. Shuchter has graciously shared with me a
draft of his manuscript, "Revolutionizing Reform," which
will be published, I trust, in the not-too-distant future.
The tract distinguishes him, in my view, as the least dogmatic and most innovative of the modern American utopians.

Despite a romantic sympathy for Marxism Shuchter
has designed a program of reformist gradualism, thus part-
ing company with the revolutionary socialists who deny that
worthwhile change can come about without some bloodletting.
Shuchter is willing to opt for "some real socialism now"
rather than wait for the ultimate bloody revolt that has become a "puerile fantasy." "If the path to revolution has
been bottled up," he says, "we have to seek reforms which
come to grips with the elements of power. It is the path to
tomorrow." Shuchter believes that his reforms "can be
wrung from the prevailing authority far short of revolutionary overthrow," and he agrees with Martin Buber that utopian forms of organized society "must be shaped as we go,
in the here and now." He feels that his reform has a
chance to succeed where others have failed because previous
reform programs "hardly even pretend to come to grips with
power itself, the economic power of the corporation."

Shuchter proposes a three-pronged program to tame
the coporate giant: a ceiling on total profits in the economy,
a progressive corporate income tax, and a restriction on
corporate investment overseas. The first prong thrusts the
deepest.

> The reform would start by freezing the profit-
> making sector of the nation at its present size.
> The mechanism for the freeze would be a ceiling
> on the aggregate of all business profits, set by
> Act of Congress. Once set, such a ceiling would
> remain fixed for many years.... Each business,
> corporate and noncorporate, would strive as now
> to maximize its earnings, but when books close at
> the end of the period, the combined gross earnings
> of all business would invariably be reduced to the
> ceiling fixed by Congress, the difference carted
> off to the U. S. Treasury.

The tax rate would be adjusted to the percentage

required to confine total profits to the dollar ceiling. The profit incentive would remain, since companies would divide total profits in proportion to their gross earnings. "The profit ceiling must be set low enough to draw furious squawks of outraged businessmen and even a little blood," says Shuchter. "Yet it must remain high enough to leave business in a congenial environment replete with entrepreneurial opportunities and a lively, competitive market." Thus, the most efficient industries would retain the highest profits and be able to expand, while the least efficient would fall by the wayside.

Shuchter sees a three-fold benefit emanating from the process. First, the profit ceiling would shift economic, social, and political power "from the business sector to some nonbusiness order." Second, it would "bring a halt to the expansion of output, stabilizing the economy at zero economic growth, while fostering within the business sector the elements of a wholesome competitive environment." Shuchter sees this zero-growth aspect of the program as "a self-disciplinary move by the nation to halt its hectic, inordinate consumption of the world's material resources." Finally, the profit ceiling would allow the emergence and flowering of a nonprofit sector.

> Picture something new, a liberated half of a nation embarking on a self-conscious mission to awaken and put to purpose a public spirit hitherto virtually ignored. Life would not, not in this sector, be printed on dollar bills. While the profit sector would continue to attract all those acculturated to the traditional forms of breadwinning, led by the bold enterprisers, the money-driven and the game-players, the new social sector would engage more vital and intriguing questions: how to master the riddle of poverty, how to fashion lives of creativity and harmony, how to deal unbureaucratically with the public's health and welfare, how to foster the worldwide solidarity of peoples--all this along with mundane questions of how a thoughtful society handles mail and trains and planetary exploration.

As corporations yield some of their power, says Shuchter, a "new social compact" would emerge in America, and a new sector would be added to the nation's economy: a socialist sector imbued with a "sane, humanist, altruist spirit."

The second reform in Shuchter's program is the
eventual replacement of the single-rate, across-the-board
profits tax with a progressive or graduated tax, much like
the sliding scale used today for personal income taxes.
"Large corporations with higher profits would pay a higher
percent of them as taxes," says Shuchter, "while lesser
competitors would enjoy lower rates. In effect there would
emerge a tax on monopoly per se as it reflects in profit
volume." Such a tax system, he believes, would encourage
smaller-scale business operations and an unraveling of con-
glomerates. It could also replace the clumsy antitrust ap-
paratus of the federal government. "The marketplace would
revert a step to its classical form of individually powerless
units acting under the suasion of the combined operations of
all companies, much like the free market of yore," he says.

Shuchter's third reform calls for the gradual divestment by multinational corporations of their foreign holdings.
"We would have all investments abroad subject to liquidation
at a steady pace, so that in due course every investment
would be rolled over, moving into the hands of host nation-
als, while our multinational corporation was off organizing
another industry elsewhere." For example, the company
might be required to sell off its investment at a rate of 2
percent per year, so that the host country would have majority control in twenty-five years and total ownership in
fifty years.

"By such means," he asserts, "the U.S. would pro-
claim itself to be an organizing force for industry in all
countries, the capitalist entrepreneur who gets the tough
startup work done, but without claim to permanent rights of
exploitation. The move defangs the imperialist motive in
U.S. commerce."

Shuchter's "socialist sector" would act as an employer
of last resort and often of first resort, absorbing all the nation's unemployment. "Ultimately there would be a standing
invitation for all of labor to shift allegiance to this noncompetitive sector guided by a developing socialist spirit."
This sector will "spawn new model forms of working relationships, production units designed for communal effort
rather than profit," he asserts. "Such cooperative enterprises would seek to establish humane conditions which would
enter into a kind of competition with the familiar optimizing
machine. A certain beneficiary would be labor in the competitive sector."

One of the components of the socialist sector in Shuchter's utopia would be a mass organization known as the Companions, offering compassionate assistance to the aged, infirm, and underprivileged. A neighborhood counterpart to the military or Peace Corps or Vista, Companions "would form the main base of the socialist community, made up in large measure of neophytes, the young, the unskilled. Companions would work in the slums and other urban areas, helping individuals and neighborhoods to improve their ways of life. The socialist sector would also take on the more common socialist tasks of centralized planning and managing publicly owned enterprises.

This brief sketch can no more do justice to the ideas of Shuchter than it has done for Friedman or Rothbard or Sherman. Their works really have to be read in their entirety, perhaps Shuchter's most of all, since it is at once the least conventional and the most complete, complex, and ingenious of the various systems.

As a utopian system that duly takes into account both the dynamism of private enterprise and compassionate social goals, Shuchter's reformism is certainly an intriguing blueprint for a new American economic society. More pragmatic than most utopian constructs, it is designed to be implemented in a series of steps that might someday even find a receptive atmosphere in the nation. It is not, however, without its problems.

More explicitly than any other utopia we have examined, Shuchter's system requires a transformation of the human spirit to make everything fall into place. Otherwise, there will not be enough room in the competitive, money-grubbing sector of the economy for the overwhelming majority of the population that wants a piece of the action. That attitude, in turn, reduces the desirability of zero economic growth, since the alleviation of poverty will have to depend more on increasing the size of the economic pie than on dividing up the slices more equally. In any event, it is not at all certain that the less-developed countries, which depend on an expanding American market for their raw materials, will welcome zero economic growth in the United States.

I also fear that without the "new socialist spirit" the planning and producing organs of the socialist sector will become nothing more than rigid bureaucracies centralizing a frightening concentration of power over the daily lives of the citizenry. The compassionate branch of the socialist sector is not likely to thrive under such circumstances. Of course, if the entire labor force does eventually accept Shuchter's invitation to join the nonprofit sector, the tax base to support it will go up in smoke along with the dynamic force of private initiative.

I would also take mild issue with Shuchter's dollar limitation on business profits, whether he means "real" dollars--adjusted for inflation--or nominal dollars, the value of which is eroded each year by a rising price level. Neither the real value of profits nor their share in national income has shown much tendency to grow in the past decade, and industrial concentration also does not seem to be on the rise. Neither is it clear to me that bigness by itself is necessarily bad or necessarily monopolistic. Economies of scale benefit consumers as well as producers, and large companies do not necessarily face less competition than small ones. The progressive element of the profits tax seems designed to penalize efficiency more than monopoly, rewarding the least able companies with lower tax rates.

The divestment proposal for foreign investment strikes me as the most immediately practical and desirable portion of the Shuchter program. Indeed, a similar idea is already being tested by the Andean group of South American countries. Divestment could actually increase the incentive for U. S. companies to invest in the economies of the Third World, since it would protect them from the threat of sudden expropriation. It would also, as Shuchter points out, do much to defuse the issue of the "imperialist" content of the U. S. overseas investment.

Whatever its practical problems, I must confess that I find Shuchter's vision of an ideal society to be an attractive one. In fact, I find much to celebrate in all the utopian societies I have considered. They all seem designed, in one way or another, to unleash the creative energies of the individual, respect her or his freedom, sustain material and spiritual needs, limit coercion, and put an end to war and imperialism. I hope it is not churlish to suggest, however, that the visions will remain strictly utopian in the absence of that all-too-necessary change of heart of most of the members of society. If humankind is not perfectable--in advance-- then it is doubtful that we shall ever see the perfect economic society.

## Bibliography

Catlin, Warren B.  The Progress of Economics:  A History of Economic Thought (New York:  Bookman, 1962).

Friedman, Milton.  Capitalism and Freedom (Chicago: University of Chicago Press, 1962).

Heilbroner, Robert L.  The Worldly Philosophers.  4th ed. (New York:  Simon and Schuster, 1972).

Laidler, Harry W.  Social-Economic Movements (New York: Crowell, 1949).

Rothbard, Murray N.  For a New Liberty (New York:  Macmillan, 1973).

Sherman, Howard.  Radical Political Economy (New York: Basic Books, 1972).

Shuchter, Jerome.  "Revolutionizing Reform."  (Los Angeles: Unpublished manuscript, 1977).

Smith, Adam.  An Inquiry into the Nature and Causes of the Wealth of Nations (1776) (New York:  Random House, 1937).

## XIII.  FROM UTOPIA TO DYSTOPIA: THE JONESTOWN TRAGEDY

### Gairdner B. Moment

Contemporary Americans will not soon forget the terrible events of the afternoon of November 18, 1978, when nearly 1000 women, men, and children, members of an agricultural commune in a remote corner of Guyana, either committed group suicide by drinking a fruit juice spiked with cyanide or were murdered.  With few if any exceptions they had migrated to a clearing in the jungle named Jonestown under the leadership of the Rev. Mr. Jim Jones, pastor of the Peoples Temple in San Francisco.

As in any complex event all the details will probably never be fully known.  Who was responsible for the fatal shooting of California Representative Leo Ryan who had gone to Guyana to gather information about alleged abuses?  Did Jim Jones shoot himself or did someone else?  How much did the two lawyers in Jones's employ really know?  Who now owns the money, perhaps over $10 million, which Jones had deposited in Nova Scotian and Swiss banks in Panama?  Such questions have their importance of course, but for the student of utopias they are very largely irrelevant.  The same holds true for the other "intentional societies" discussed in this book.  What does it matter now what individuals were responsible for the mob violence that drove the "Perfectionists" out of Putney, Vermont, and resulted in their settlement in Oneida, New York?  How important is it in historical perspective to learn the names of the individuals who set fire to a Mormon's barn or who killed whom in the "massacre of Maun's Hill," where some twenty Mormons died?

For those interested in utopias either as testing grounds and omens of a more humane and rational society or simply as examples of the range of human behavior, the Jonestown experience carries a wider significance.  Once the initial shock and surge of grief for these people, shown with their children lying with legs extended, face down, dead by the hundreds, had begun to subside, a rush of tough and far more searching questions demanded answers. Certainly, these very recent events in Jonestown hold up no "distant mirror" to our age, such as Barbara Tuchman, one of our most notable living historians, found in the bloody and turbulent fourteenth century, when knighthood was in flower and the landscape dotted with romantic castles, each with its own torture chamber. Rather, this is an up-close view through a terrifying lens of exceedingly high power. A symptomatic part, and probably far more than most of us would like admit, of our present is magnified here to gigantic proportions. And like any lens these sad and terrible events highlight both much of the best and the worst of our present world with equal impartiality.

Finding the right questions to ask is one of the most central and also most difficult acts in the entire scientific enterprise, as in many other fields of learning. After having uplifted the spirits of so many people both rich and poor, black and white, what went wrong with the Peoples Temple? Is the whole affair a case of some bizarre pathology of utopias? Does it shed any light on catastrophes to which any social organization is potentially susceptible? What does it tell us about our contemporary form of religion? And about contemporary social, political, and economic life? Indeed, what does it reveal about human nature that we may have tried to deny? More important is the task of identifying the real tragedy. Is the greatest tragedy the harsh fact that so many committed suicide, or were there prior calamities of which those appalling events in Jonestown were the inexorable consequences? From so costly a sacrifice, what can be learned to aid the rest of us?

Utopian Stigmata

Before proceeding further it is fair to ask whether either in San Francisco or in Jonestown the Peoples Temple movement bears more than a very superficial relationship to other American utopias. The Jonestown plantation commune was not only referred to as a utopia, Jones described it in utopian terms. In Guyana the true believers were told they would find an idyllic garden spot, trees laden with fruit, land waiting for the planting of the harvests to come, universal love among men and women of all faiths, all races, all educational and economic backgrounds. Although in San Francisco they had enjoyed working in a wide variety of handicrafts at Temple centers, how infinitely more rewarding to be taking part in a great common cause, the actual building of the Kingdom of God on earth? In Jonestown would be found a life of happy intercommunion among all God's children and a life of deeply satisfying work free from the striving for position and power and money--in short, free from the well-known competitive "rat-race" and all the follies and shallowness of modern "consumerism."

In other ways there were many important similarities between the Jim Jones phenomenon and many of the utopias discussed in this book. Most obvious perhaps is the presence of the charismatic leader. To realize how close to universal this figure is in utopian communities past and present, it is only necessary to recall Father Rapp and the communities he founded and led in Harmony and Economy, Robert Owen and New Harmony, John Humphrey Noyes and Oneida, "Mother Ann" and the Shakers, John Frederick Rock and then Michael Krausert of Amana, George Fox and the Quakers, Joseph Smith and later Brigham Young and the Mormons. In more recent times there was a celestial shower of charismatics connected with the Theosophical movement at Point Loma, Krotona, and Ojai Valley in California--Annie Besant, Krishnamurti, Katherine Tingly, even Maria and Aldous Huxley. In our own day Stephen Gaskin led his followers from the drug-ridden Haight-Ashbury section of San Francisco to the highly successful and still expanding Farm in Tennessee.

Another highly significant feature that links Jonestown with our other utopias is the strong religious impulse emphasized by the Rev. Mr. Jones. Such an impulse was clearly basic among the Shakers, Rappites, Mormons, Quakers, the Amana community and many others. In fact some claim, with much justification, that all successful utopias have enjoyed such a religious base, although Twin Oaks is at least a partial exception.

Almost without exception intentional communities find it desirable or necessary to draw apart and separate themselves from the general population from which their membership is derived. Again, one can list a dozen of our American utopias that did just that--Shakers, Oneidans, Harmonists, Perfectionists, Icarians, and, indeed, the Massachusetts Pilgrims and the founders of Rhode Island.

The present-day Farm in rural Tennessee, already mentioned, although located in a little-visited section, nevertheless maintains a gatekeeper who interviews, sometimes at
great length, anyone who wishes to enter the grounds even
for a very brief visit.  Mary Kilchenstein in Chapter 10 has
observed that the gatekeeper can be regarded as a reception-
ist in the front of an office or thought of as an army ser-
geant controlling ingress and egress from a military base.
However regarded, there is some justification for such with-
drawals from society.  Group loyalty and sense of mission
are intensified.  Distractions are reduced.  Worse yet, there
always seem to be people who are willing to go to great
lengths to insure that what they regard as dangerous experiments or models of social organization, life-styles, religious
beliefs, or economic systems do not succeed.  Perhaps they
seem dangerous just because they seem likely to succeed and
supplant the systems in which the attackers have, as psychol-
ogists say, a heavy emotional investment.  Perhaps the
motive is merely simple jealousy at someone else's good
fortune.  No matter; the result is the same.

Many utopian communities have sought to better the
relationships between the sexes through some kind of sexual
reformation.  For the Shakers it was total celibacy.  The
Oneidans developed a primitive, or at least subjective, form of
eugenics (which they called "stirpiculture") in an atmosphere of
Christian love and restraint.  All the children were regarded
as the children of all the adults in the community and accorded a full measure of love and devotion.  The Mormons
adopted what is usually called polygamy but which is more
accurately termed polygyny, the possession of more than one
wife by a single man.  This system they managed to integrate into their complex system of beliefs about life after
death and, indeed, life before birth.

Jim Jones did not attempt any systematic reformation
in sexual arrangement, and in that respect this utopia differs
from many other utopian communities.  However, Jones did
manipulate sexual behavior in the most brutal ways to control and exploit the helpless members of the commune.  His
lieutenants provided him with women of his choice, according
to testimony of several survivors of the Jonestown suicides.
There can be no doubt that families were broken up and
children turned against their parents, wives against husbands
and husbands against wives.  This was achieved partly by a
policy of sending some members of a family to Guyana first,
usually the children, and holding the remainder in California.

Parents complained that they were unable to see and talk
with their children even after they themselves had arrived
in Jonestown. Divorces were easily arranged with any settlement money going to the commune. Sex by itself was
used for blackmail and for material gain, according to surviving Temple members who were able to return to the
United States.

Historically, utopians have uniformly placed great
emphasis on work, not only to provide for the material needs
of the community but also as a means of spiritual development, almost as a sacrament, an ancient enough idea found
in the writings of St. Augustine and Calvin. "To work is to
pray. " For many utopians, notably among the Oneidans,
work in berry-picking and gardening "bees" and other forms
of group labor was a source of joyful, meaningful social
activity. In this respect our nineteenth- and twentiety-
century communes resemble the medieval orders of monks
and nuns, notably the Benedictines, whom Alfred North
Whitehead regarded as comparable to our present-day scientists, characterized as they were by the same three
traits: a serious purpose, a respect for learning, and a
belief in the value of manual labor (in the case of the scientist, laboratory work).

Work was also emphasized in the Jonestown commune.
The testimony is overwhelming for long hours, as much as
ten and twelve under a tropical sun, short lunch breaks,
meals of rice for breakfast, rice soup for lunch, rice or
beans and an egg for supper. While the Shakers, Mormons,
Oneidans, Amanans, and others saw the material rewards
of their work reflected in their own physical well-being,
nothing of the sort happened in Jonestown. One is reminded
of some nineteenth-century company-owned town where the
workers had to buy their food and clothing and rent their
housing from the company, which never paid them enough to
get out of debt, while at the same time amassing millions
of dollars in profits (although usually not deposited in Swiss
banks).

## In His Service

Members of the Temple, once they were in Guyana, were in
a no-exit situation, truly captives. All passports and all
possessions were taken from them, leaving little more than
the clothes on their backs; Social Security benefits were

signed over to Jim Jones.  For the converts it was total
commitment, an emotional "total immersion" in the cause.
They escaped from freedom to gain direction for their lives.
They felt deeply that Jim Jones, like Christ, had come that
they might have life and have it more abundantly.  They expected to find, in the words of the Episcopal Prayer Book,
that "in his service is perfect freedom."

They found plenty of service.  Many of the survivors
have complained bitterly of those long hours of work under
a tropical sun and of the meager and monotonous diet.  No
one but a traitor worthy of death, Jim Jones explained,
would consider leaving because all would be safe here in
Jonestown.  His camouflaged, armed guards, Jones told his
people, continually patrolled in the jungle surrounding the
community to keep out the enemies who were seeking to
destroy them and their work.  Such a reassuring message
must have carried a sinister double meaning.  In any case,
without a passport and without money to buy a plane ticket
home, what chance would a backslider have when there was
no road to anywhere except the relatively nearby commune
airstrip, and the nearest town was many long miles away
through dense jungle and swamps?  On top of all that Jones
told his followers that he had informants within the U.S.
Embassy in Georgetown, the capital of Guyana, who would
notify him of any renegade seeking to leave.  True or not,
apparently many of Jones's people believed it.  Under these
circumstances who could expect anyone to consider escape,
especially when they had originally joined the colony because
they found the Temple filled some deeply felt, even desperate, need, a need that life in their former homes had not
filled?

Much has been told of the evil in Jonestown, both by
survivors of the suicide-murders and by those who had managed to leave prior to those events:  systematic large-scale
destruction of self-respect and the ability for self-direction
and independent thought; the inculcation of a personality-
disintegrating sense of ingrained and ineradicable guilt, in
part through long and repeated self-analysis and mutual-
criticism sessions; the signing of incriminating documents
confessing to crimes of thought and action (Jones insisted
that everyone was bisexual and also a potential political
revolutionary willing to kill); humiliation of adults for a
variety of reasons by stripping them naked before a group
to be ridiculed and in some cases to be severely beaten;
children and adults lined up and beaten with paddle boards

("boards of education" they were called) until tears and even screams resulted. All this was commonplace and seems to indicate a psychopathology involving both sadism and masochism.

The thought and perhaps even more the photographic views of those mass-suicide and murder victims have made such an overwhelming impression on the minds of most people that more needs to be said about them. First of all it should be remembered that, as incredible as it may appear to most people, human history right down into our own day offers many examples of group suicide, sometimes among religious fanatics but by no means always. In World War II hundreds of patriotic Japanese civilians jumped to their deaths from high cliffs on Saipan rather than surrender to the approaching Americans. Large numbers of a Russian evangelical sect of Christians related to the Dukhobors destroyed themselves in the last century. After the fall of Jerusalem in A.D. 70, the Jewish zealots on the mountaintop fortress of Masada killed themselves rather than live under Roman rule. As every school child used to know, any Roman solider worth his salt would fall on his sword rather than surrender.

If you truly believe in personal immortality, much of the sting is removed from these suicides in what the participants believed was a noble cause. Furthermore, there is no explicit prohibition regarding suicide to be found in the Bible, although there are passages that can perhaps be so interpreted.

Suicide drills were held in preparation for a "White Night," when all would drink of the deadly fruit juice and enter a new life. These drills had been frightening, but there was no poison in the drink, and Jones assured his followers that these drills were a test of ultimate loyalty. They were, so to speak, the equivalent to lifeboat drills, to be used as a last resort if the enemies of the community should some day close in on them. In his latter days, when Jones began to talk and perhaps even think of himself as a reincarnation of Jesus Christ or else of Nikolai Lenin, he spoke more and more in long harangues over the commune loudspeakers of "the enemies." Suicide, he insisted, might be the only possible response to those enemies who were always seeking their destruction, the only possible option available to demonstrate to a hostile and unbelieving world the validity of their faith in the Kingdom of God. All without exception, Jones demanded, must drink the cup of poison if that time should come, because he would find it intolerable to discover that a single member of his great family had been left behind when they were all reunited in life after death.

In San Francisco membership in the Peoples Temple yielded real benefits to its adherents. These benefits were spiritual, psychological if you prefer, and material as well. Jones himself was an official with the housing agencies of the city. It is unquestionable that he and his followers were an influence for good in the area. However, fraud and force appeared well before Jones moved his group to Guyana. Several ex-converts have described some of the fake cures that characterized his ministry. A member of Jones's inner circle would hold a foul-smelling, partly decayed and bloody chicken gizzard wrapped in a white towel in her hand and thrust it far down a patient-accomplice's throat. On withdrawing the hand the "healer" would open the towel and hold its contents aloft for all to see. She would then walk up and down the ailes to show the "cancer" that had been removed by divine intervention. At the same time Jones would keep warning people not to get too close because that "cancer" might be contagious. When former Temple members were asked before a televised audience why they did not expose these fraudulent cures in which they had taken part, their replies were simple--and have been heard before in the long history of religions. Such apparently miraculous healings, they said, of throat and uterine cancers, and the sudden releasing of the paralyzed so that they could leap from their aluminum wheelchairs in joyous abandon, were highly effective in winning new converts and besides, it was all in such a good cause.

In both San Francisco and in Guyana Jones rode in an armored car and was always surrounded by an armed guard. This would not have seemed so puzzling had it been known at the time that Jones held millions of dollars in cash and in other valuables. As it turned out it was the presence of those bodyguards that finally aroused the press corps in San Francisco and Representative Ryan to look into the Jones Cult. In fact things might have happened very differently in Guyana, when Jones gave the call for the "White Night" of suicide, if it had not been for the presence of armed enforcers to assist those whose faith was weak. It was such armed men who shot Ryan and others on the airstrip just as they were about to leave Jonestown. These guards were in

addition to a group of elite riflemen, who also doubled as
the basketball team, and who were in the capital, Georgetown, where planes left for the U.S., at the very time of
the visit of Ryan and the press.   Since a defecting mother
and her three children were killed in Georgetown at this
time, one can only wonder if basketball was the team's only
intended mission.

## A Death Cult?

The meaning of these tragic events has been interpreted
largely in terms of some kind of a "Cult of Death," the
words Time magazine superimposed over the photograph of
dead bodies on the front cover of its December 4, 1978 number.   One respected newspaper called it a chilling view into
the pit of bestiality.   Even the New York Times (January 7)
ran an article on the Jones cult entitled "The Appeal of the
Death Trap."   All these perceptions are true.   Yet they are
far from the whole truth.   Rather, such appellations, while
not exactly calling names, point away from some of the most
significant aspects of the entire story, significant, that is, if
the rest of us are to learn much from  what happened.

        As already pointed out in this chapter, the bait that
attracted converts into the Peoples Temple and on to Jonestown was not any fascination with death.   These men and
women came that they might find what the Owenites in New
Harmony, over a century ago, called "The Valley of Love
and Delight."   True, there are said to be tapes recording
Temple members shouting their willingness to die for the
cause at the call of their commander.   But is this any more
than what is expected of any good patriot?

        The Peoples Temple exodus to Jonestown is the story
of a trek to a promised land that turned out to be a prison
of servitude.   How did it happen?   The reasons are many.
We have already told of some of the ways Jim Jones held his
people captive.   There were others, more instructive for
those of us still living outside such prisons, and to these we
now turn.

## The Problem of Power

High at one end of a large assembly room and mess hall in
Jonestown hung a sign reading, "Those who do not remember

the past are condemned to repeat it. " What this familiar quotation, from the Harvard philosopher George Santayana's Reason and Common Sense, was intended to mean or in reality did mean to the members of the Temple is unknown. Perhaps it was supposed to remind the members of the commune of the meaninglessness of their frustrated lives before they found life and joy with Jim Jones. For us it carries a nice irony, for it suggests that to forget the dangers of the kind of complete self-surrender to a charismatic leader such as Jim Jones, who is now part of our own past, might condemn us to a similar experience. One does not have to look far to recognize that such fatal hazards threaten other ideal-istic organizations regardless of how noble or evil the ideals may be. Witness Synanon, a community organized by a former alcoholic, Charles Dederich, for the reform of drug (including alcohol) addicts, but which has become a ruthless dictatorship; or think back to the rise of Hitler or of Stalin, both of whom held ideals some of which even their bitterest critics have to admit were good. Nixon demonstrated how close we all are to such hazards.

The unfortunate inhabitants of Jonestown lost their lives because, while "remembering their past, " they had forgotten Lord Acton's principle, from Historical Essays and Studies: "Power tends to corrupt and absolute power cor-rupts absolutely. "

The governance of utopias in this country has been only more or less democratic. At the contemporary Twin Oaks commune in Virginia, which certainly ranks among the most humane and most intelligently organized and run, mem-bers report that perhaps too much time is devoted to long-drawn-out planning sessions. However, the actual legal ownership and control of many communes, even of Twin Oaks, remains very vague. The charismatic founder-leader is re-garded as a benign dictator, someone very like yourself only more intensely dedicated to the same ideals that motivate your own life. He, or in rare instances, she, possesses greater wisdom and higher vision. No solemn oath of pov-erty and obedience is exacted, as was and still is in monas-tic orders. None is necessary, for the converts have been released from lives of futility, alienation, and spiritual deprivation into the company of the saved. All the same, in Jonestown Jim Jones wielded close to absolute power, power enforced, when psychological methods failed, by a cadre of armed men and the administration of tranquilizing drugs introduced into sandwiches and other food.

Many Americans who are impatient for quick results tend to forget that one of the essential buttresses of our liberties is the system of checks and balances built into our form of government. This is the separation of the powers of the legislative, executive, and judicial branches of the government. It is a legacy, historian Samuel Eliot Morison tells us, from English settlers whose experience under four totalitarian regimes in the seventeenth century (Charles I, the Long Parliament, Cromwell, and James II) had convinced them that one and the same body should not make the laws, carry them out, and interpret them.

One of the great unsolved problems facing communism in Russia, China, and elsewhere lies exactly here. How can the leadership be prevented from becoming tyrannical and yet remain effective? How can dissent be handled? Karl Marx, when he was living in England and writing Das Kapital, was much interested in the natural sciences, and his friends liked to compare him with his contemporary, Charles Darwin. Marx thought at that time, and perhaps always, that under communism problems of industrial development and social life in general would be solved the way they are in the natural sciences, by discussion and the free determination of a consensus. The "State," he believed, would "wither away." Obviously the reverse has occurred. There is no single reason, but surely one is the seductive appeal of power. In one of his writings Bertrand Russell notes that "power is sweet; it is a drug the desire for which increases with habit." Shakespeare puts a similar thought in the words of Ulysses in the first act of his Troilus and Cressida, explaining how power gets into the will and becomes an appetite that grows into a "universal wolf." When the shepherd develops a taste for lamb, woe to the sheep!

The most insidious part of the seduction is that it is only human to feel convinced that what you believe is correct and altogether righteous. The views of others are then mistaken, even pernicious. Why permit error to flourish when you have the power to prevent it? Like fake cures, the exercise of your power to crush dissent would be in a good cause. The trouble, of course, is that such are the complexities of this universe that it is always conceivable that you might be wrong. The realization that ultimate wisdom does not reside with any one group has been as hard for college and university faculties to attain as for boards of trustees or many students. The problem of power is an ancient one. Ever since Plato wrote his Republic, the first

utopia, thoughtful people have asked who will guard the
guardians. In Jonestown the answer was "no one."


## The Vacuum

The people who joined the Jim Jones Temple represented a
broad spectrum of the American scene in financial, racial,
religious, and educational status and to a considerable extent geographical range. There was, for example, the family of a biochemist who contributed several hundred thousand
dollars, but most were middle class or poor, and many were
black. They were drawn in by the charismatic leader. But
even the strongest charisma can only act on susceptible material just as a magnet no matter how powerful can only reveal its influence in the presence of the right metal, iron.

What was the void in the converts that made them
ready recipients for the Jim Jones message? Because Jones
relied very heavily on a Christian, largely Protestant, base,
as have most of our utopians, it seems important to ask how
Christianity appeared to potential cult members. Did they
see the church as an adjunct of the business community, the
handmaiden of a dogmatic economic philosophy, capitalism?
Did they see it as a captive of segregation and racism? Of
nationalism? Did drink, gambling, and adultery emerge as
the only sins to worry very much about?

Probably more pertinent than these questions are
others related to them. In the communities from which
these alienated men and women came, had they felt that
"immortal love, forever free, forever shared, forever whole,
a never ending sea" about which the Quaker poet John Green-
leaf Whittier wrote in his hymn? Had any converts heard
congregations sing the "new morality" hymn that James Russell Lowell wrote a century ago, "New occasions teach new
duties, Time makes ancient good uncouth, They must upward
still and onward Who would keep abreast of truth," and yet
had seen these same churches remain as backward-looking
as Lot's wife? The Rev. Mr. Jim Jones left Indianapolis
with his little flock because at the time it was a hotbed of
racial bigotry with the Ku Klux Klan using the cross of Christ
as its symbol. Surely any of Jones's converts in that city
would have held any church there worth only a horse laugh
when John Oxenham's hymn was sung. "In Christ there is
no east or west, In him no south or north, But one great
fellowship of love, Throughout the whole wide earth."

A Measure of Tragedy and of Success

The extent of the Jonestown tragedy cannot be measured by the deaths of 1000 women, men, and children. The real tragedy lies outside of that pathetic little jungle clearing. It occurred back in the United States and was a double-headed one: first, the social, economic, and, most significantly, the spiritual life of the communities from which the Peoples Temple converts were drawn had failed them. Second, when these sore beset people turned for help in finding a more fulfilling life, a religion that did not seem a pious sham, they were taken in by such a leader as the Rev. Mr. Jones.

Jones himself is a tragic figure. He was undeniably a man of great talents, although perhaps from the very start of his ministry he suffered from a flawed psyche. Certain it is that his disease of mind and soul was progressive, and it seems likely that his continual use of drugs was a major factor in his intellectual and emotional deterioration. In the end, when he fell victim to his own Götterdämmerung impulse and died like a mini-Hitler in his lair, he seemed autointoxicated with his own rhetoric and power. Perhaps if the "legitimate" churches in Indianapolis and in California had given the people he attracted the support they evidently needed so desperately, the whole story would have been very different for the Rev. Mr. Jones and for them.

The success of the Peoples Temple was likewise a two-fold one. Jones and his followers in San Francisco did help the poor in estate and in mind and heart. They provided a center for creative and healing activity in woodwork, photography, painting, and other crafts. The Temple was a place that offered fellowship and shelter to the lonely and alienated. Above all, Jones himself offered an exciting vision that lifted up the hearts of thousands of the discouraged, of those for whom life seemed utterly drab and without a worthy challenge, merely tawdry, a wretched plastic existence.

The emotional and intellectual conversion of these people to the Jones cult and their eventual deaths in Guyana demonstrated, well before they left for Jonestown, that people of diverse races, faiths, and social backgrounds will and can live together and work together in the continuing quest to bring nearer to reality the "Kingdom of God." In this, of course, they were by no means unique. The same kind of spirit motivated the thousands of somewhat naive American youth who congregated near Woodstock in rural New York some years ago to "celebrate life." A similar, although violent, manifestation of the same spirit of determination to break through the incrustations of established forms into a new world has occurred in Europe, notably in the student riots at the University of Paris at about the same time. There is, of course, no reason whatever to suppose that conditions of life or the general outlook of our present times will be any more permanent than those of any previous age. The terrible events at Jonestown, unlike those of Tuchman's fourteenth century, are no distant mirror of our times. They are a part of it. But perhaps we can see in them a hope like the one that Tuchman's mirror shows us, for out of that turbulent and calamatous fourteenth century was born the Renaissance.

## Bibliography

Kilduff, Marshall, and Ron Javers. The Suicide Cult: An Inside Story of the Peoples Temple Sect and the Massacre in Guyana (New York: Bantam, 1978). (Kilduff was the investigative reporter in San Francisco whose story helped precipitate Jones's move to Guyana. Javers suffered gunshot wounds on the Jonestown airstrip. Both are staff correspondents of the San Francisco Chronicle.)

Krause, Charles A. Guyana Massacre: Eyewitness Account (New York: Berkeley, 1978). (Krause was wounded on the Jonestown airstrip. He is a reporter for the Washington Post.)

Mills, Jeannie. Six Years with God (New York: A&W, 1979). (Jeannie Mills and her husband Al were members of the prestigious Temple Planning Committee and she was head of the Publications Office. They escaped with many photographs and written documents.)

Thielmann, Bonnie, with Dean Merrill. The Broken God (Elgin, Ill., and Weston, Ont.: D. C. Cook, 1979). (The story told by Jones's adopted daughter.)

# XIV. YESTERDAY'S DREAM, TOMORROW'S NECESSITY

## Fontaine Maury Belford

The study of utopias is a study of the uses of time. We look to the past to see what has been hoped for the future, and through this to understand the present. When we reverse this process of examination, and thereby explore the present, through the tool of the past, to discover what the future will be, we join the ranks of that species known as "futurist."

The discovery of the future is never disinterested; it is determined by how we understand the present and by how we use the past. Any projection of the future is purposeful. As we examine the various directions from which futurists see the future unfolding we realize that each of their prophecies achieves its power from a vision of what it is in human experience that has value, that must be preserved if life is not only to endure but sustain us. And these visions, of a past that the present threatens in the future to condemn, are in the profoundest sense utopian.

In writing a scenario for the ideal present, futurists look backward to the utopias of the past. The irony that defines us is that we live in a moment that was once the locus of a visionary's dream; that the present is the past's future. In the graveyard of visions that constitutes our culture is there a key to our present self-destruction? What kind of present would ensure the future for which we seek? In the Hebrew language there is no present tense. Transformed by the lived moment, immeasurable because never static, time is in a continuum from future to past. But the past is inaccessible to change, and the revolution that might transform the future must occur now, however ephemeral this moment may be. Thus, in the realm of visionaries, futurists are passionate exhorters, subversive, programmatic, political, suspect by both the worldly and the other-worldly.

229

History is rarely discontinuous. The spectre of tomorrow is simply the logical fulfillment of yesterday. There are levels of toleration that, in a potentially toxic situation, permit life to thrive. Once these levels have been violated the inevitable will occur. The messianic fervor that characterizes the most secular of futurists is grounded in a conviction that we have stepped over some of these boundaries already, and that we may not be able to step back. The question has become not, how do we flourish, but how shall we perish?

Perhaps because this conviction--that we have already set in action those forces that will call the human experiment to a close; that we have lost the capacity to dominate our destiny--has become so pervasive in our culture, the literature of the past fifty years has been marked by the emergence of a new sub-genre, the dystopia. Four of these scenarios for the beginning of the end of time provide, in particular, powerful metaphoric statements about the uses of time.

In Aldous Huxley's Brave New World, published in 1932, we find a vision of a world in which technology has taken complete control. Genetic manipulation, response conditioning, the omnipresent pill have defined the perimeter of possible experience. Of course, said Huxley in Brave New World Revisited, published in 1958, we are still generations away from the development of this kind of technology. But in only ten years, by 1968, we had nearly every single capability he had projected. Given the right political climate a Brave New World is ours....

George Orwell's 1984 describes a world in which time itself has been consumed in the maw of the great totalitarian machine. Every gesture, every attitude is monitored by the omnipresent Big Brother. Double think and Newspeak--"Hate is Love," "War is Peace"--manifest the devastation of judgment, of the integrity that is the only thing the state need fear. Stalin's Russia, Franco's Spain, Papa Doc's Haiti, Nixon's America--each proclaims Orwell a prophet; proclaims the clear and present danger that 1984 articulated three decades ago.

In The Day of the Locust Nathanael West renders the Apocalypse in the guise of Hollywood. Life is a freak show, a cheap trick, a sellout, a plastic nonstop party that shrivels, as is the wont of plastics, at the drop of an ash. The world is destroyed by its own lack of substance, by that

reality no one can bear very much of, by the circuses the
Roman emperors staged to make the people forget they had
no bread, by the hollow, trumpery underside of the great
American dream factory.   As the world comes to an end in
front of Grauman's Chinese Theatre there is no way to distance oneself from it.   Evel Knievel's pseudo-leap over the
Snake River Canyon, as drunks passed fifteen-year-old girls
overhead to one another, comes to mind.   The Academy
Awards come to mind.   The fact that we spend more on
cosmetics than on foreign aid comes to mind.   And the
laughing, mad faces of Charles Manson's girls, of all our
assassins and would-be assassins....   Surely The Day of
the Locust is at hand.

      B. F. Skinner's Walden Two is presented as a utopia
in the old genre and thus is perhaps the most chilling vision
of all.   In this pseudo-novel the psychologist sets forth the
"promised land" of a particular brand of social scientist.
Through careful conditioning human beings lose the capacity
to feel guilt, anger, jealousy, indignation, terror--a whole
range of the emotional spectrum has been eliminated.   People live in an ecologically sound, politically secure, emotionally safe environment.   And all it cost them was what
tradition has defined as their humanity.   Perhaps that's
cheap.   There are now four Walden Two communes--
flourishing, their inhabitants say, and growing all the time.
But in all that placidity there is a horror more final than
Big Brother, or soma, or plastic dreams in plastic cities.
Walden Two is the anesthetic of the soul, that ether we
smell daily in our streets, in our schools....   The sequel
to Walden Two was called Beyond Freedom and Dignity.

      There are other scenarios underway--no less un-
speakable for being unspoken.   Anthony Burgess's The Want-
ing Seed is a horror novel of an overpopulated world, which
finally follows the lead of Jonathan Swift's Modest Proposal,
solving its problem with cannibalism.   Nevil Shute's On the
Beach gives us the last days on earth of a nation waiting for
the aftermath of nuclear holocaust to catch up with it.   J. G.
Ballard imagines in a series of futuristic horror novels:   we
could all suffocate; we could all die of thirst....

      The point a futurist would make from these novels,
these passionately felt data, is that the future is here; Brave
New World is here, and 1984 is here, and The Day of the
Locust is here, and Walden Two is here.   The dystopian
scenario grows out of seeds that are already sprouting.   The

challenge this poses is unnerving: we look to the present to
see what the future will be. What are the signs of the times
that we should be discerning?

A clear-eyed look reveals a number of frightening
hints about our future. Five years ago, in Baltimore, it
was nothing to wait in line three hours for gasoline, a fact
well publicized in the local media. What was not publicized
was that 11,000 of the city's poor were living in the armory
because they had been frozen out of their oil-heated tenements.
Shortages are a commonplace to the housewife. One week there
are no cloves to be had, the next no paraffin. For months sugar
can only be purchased at scandalous prices and canning lids
are not to be had at all. We are faced with the paradox of
sky-high prices coupled with highest-ever unemployment. It
took us a long time to be able to perceive this because we
had all learned in Economics 100 that you do not have de-
pression and inflation simultaneously. There is the disturb-
ingly assertive behavior of the underdeveloped nations, who
begin to resent the famine and infant mortality and crippling
disease under which they have lived since time began. It
was one thing to send them hula hoops. But now they have
developed a taste for meat, and their babies are living long
enough to produce more babies, and they need electricity to
light their houses and gas for their tractors and nitrogen for
fertilizers, and suddenly they have become competitors for
our rapidly diminishing supply of resources, and people begin to mutter that we should have stuck with hula hoops.

The anomalies of the American way of life are legion.
We are become a sad country. On a hungry planet we pay
farmers not to plant crops. Our rates of cancer, heart
disease, alcoholism, suicide, and mental illness are stagger-
ing. We have discovered through the Marshall Plan and the
United Nations that we not only cannot buy love, we cannot
even buy loyalty. The more we have the more we want, the
more we consume the hungrier we grow, and the pursuit of
happiness has become, as Becker has pointed out in his book,
The Denial of Death, a headlong race against mortality.
More it seems, in all of its measurable forms, is less.

In order to look to the present to find the future we
must also look to the past. For the assertion that everything is a part of everything else is as true of time as it
is of ecology. If we are to live responsibly in this moment
we must live with a commitment to the future. But our
capacity to plan for the day after tomorrow is largely

contingent on what happened the day before yesterday. To
live in time is to transcend it, to be able to stand outside
of it when we need to.

As Alvin Toffler points out in Future Shock, for the
first 10,000 years of human civilization almost nothing
changed. From 8000 B.C., which marks the beginning of
commercial agricultural cultivation, to 1776, people didn't
get much richer, and this steady-state economy was an outgrowth of a steady-state life. Values were passed on from
one generation to another, essentially unquestioned, because
in the long haul very little changed. The average per capita
annual income from the birth of Christ until the Declaration
of Independence remained at $100. The population went from
250 million to 700 million. Energy sources were animal
muscle, wind, and water. Life expectancy was from the
late 30's to the early 40's. Transportation was by foot,
small sailing vessel, and horse. From the birth of Christ
to the Fourth of July there were only two technological advances that radically changed the way people lived: the inventions of gunpowder and the printing press.

However, between 1776 and 1976 the world population
has increased six-fold; the gross world product, eighty-fold;
the distance one can travel in a day, a thousand-fold; killing
power, a million-fold; the amount of energy that can be released from a pound of matter, fifty-million-fold; and the
range and volume of information technology, several billion-
fold. In 1850, when the Crimean War was brewing, the
population of the world reached one billion. In 1929, as
Wall Street was crashing about our ears, the population
reached two billion. In 1960, when John Fitzgerald Kennedy
entered the White House, it reached three billion. In 1975,
as thousands flocked to Concord to commemorate the shot
heard round the world, it reached four billion.

What has the impact of all this been? The first and
most obvious fact is that we simply cannot adjust to change
this quickly. We live in a world with which we feel ever
more unable to cope, which seems to move by its own momentum, carrying us passively along. Our old patterns are
irrelevant to this new life, and no new patterns have emerged
to take their place. Thus, our society has a sense of aim-
lessness ("Where are you going?" "Out." "What are you
doing?" "Nothing."), of loss ("You can get anything you
want / At Alice's restaurant." But the cops closed it and
there's nowhere else to go), of desperation (in Clockwork

Orange Beethoven's Ninth accompanies a gang of young
toughs as they kick in an old man's head), of alienation
(Thomas Pynchon recently announced that the reason no one
had really understood his novel Gravity's Rainbow, was that
it was written from the point of view of a nostril)--these
pervade our literature, art, music, culture.  The decibel
level at rock concerts, well above the level of pain, is
rendering a generation of young people deaf.  Blowing your
mind is no longer a euphemism.

Sigmund Freud describes the process of maturation as
one whereby individuals are gradually forced to conform to
the Reality Principle.  What this means, in effect, is that
they give up more and more to gain less and less.  But unless they are willing to go along with this sacrifice they risk
becoming deviants, risk standing forever outside of all that
society has to offer.  Precisely what "reality" is is never
spelled out.

In a sense this is a paradigm for living in society.
In order to achieve certain things that are absolutely fundamental to human existence the individual gives up certain
other things--desirable in and of themselves perhaps, but
more expendable.  What are we supposed to get for all we
have given up?  What is it, then, that a society is meant to
provide?

First of all, minimally, it is supposed to provide
safety.  In my brief career as an archaeologist this was
always a factor that struck me.  Cities were fortresses--
surrounded by walls, or water, or unscalable cliffs.  Once
upon a time enemies were thought to come from without--to
be alien.  This is no longer the case.  Danger in America
comes from Americans--not in an abstract, philosophical
sense, but quite literally.  What could a stranger do to us
that we have not done to ourselves?  Our streets are not
safe to walk in, our food to eat, our air to breathe, our
water to drink.  Our property is subject to fire, theft, and
vandalism, ourselves to robbery, rape, and murder.  We
have one of the highest crime rates in the world, the highest rate of environmentally-related disease and job-related
injury.  More people have died on our highways than in all
the wars we have ever fought.  Eighty percent of our federal
budget goes to provide for our safety--that is, for life-
destroying activities.  In 1967 the total national budget for
education and culture constituted enough money to run the
Viet Nam war for eleven minutes.  And yet in America we

pay for our wealth with fear, a fear that is never assuaged. If the function of a society is to provide safety, then ours has failed.

A society is supposed to educate its children. In a study of children in a ghetto school in New York published in 1970 it was found that the average child forgot more in grades four through six than was learned in grades one through three--that is, sixth graders tested lower than entering first graders. Another recent survey indicated that only 30 percent of the American public was functionally literate-- that is, could balance a checkbook, read a newspaper, fill out a form. In 1965 the University of California at Berkeley devised a test to screen the language skills of its entering freshmen, in order to identify those who needed remediation. In 1975 80 percent of its freshman class fell below the cut- off point that ten years before had isolated the bottom 5 per- cent. As a corollary to this, juvenile crime--that is, of children under sixteen--has increased 800 percent in the last three years. As of now, children up to the age of fifteen commit one-third of the violent crime. If the function of a society is to educate its children, then ours has failed.

A society is supposed to give its citizens a sense of belonging, a niche, a role to play that is useful and that, because of this, gives their lives meaning. But America was founded by men and women who had uprooted themselves, who traded off whatever they had and whatever they were for a chance to have and be something else. Loneliness is indige- nous to America; it is as fundamental to our economy as war, colonialism, and unemployment. The carrot of "advance- ment" can only drive the workaholic donkeys if they regard their own personalities as more significant than the needs of family, friends, and community. They cannot afford the luxury of attachment to the past, or to a place, or to peo- ple. Philip Slater says in his book The Pursuit of Loneli- ness that "Americans are forced into making more choices per day, with fewer givens, more ambiguous criteria, less environmental stability and less social structural support, than any people in history. " But in exchange for giving these up we are free to do and be whatever we want. And this is the American dream. Or nightmare. For we have violated the infinite interconnectedness of all life, the pri- mordial need for community, for belonging, for boundaries, definitions, and limits. And in return we have become foreigners on earth, filled with emptiness, terrified by the resonances that silence finds within us. We are rich, and the richer we are the more solitude we buy; our own car, house, pool, tennis court, golf links, plane. We seek privacy because we feel alienated, and then feel more and more alienated when we get it. Our God speaks to us not out of the joy and abundance of our life, but out of its solitary anguish. If the function of society is to provide a sense of belonging, then our society has failed.

Futurists, those of us who have made a commitment to discerning the signs of the times, find ourselves in an odd place. The voice of the other, the lunatic fringe, is heard in the land. And those of us in the safe center have turned our heads to hear it. Hippies in communes, little old ladies in tennis shoes squeezing carrot juice, nuns with begging bowls at the entrance to Macy's, pacifists, antivivisectionists, vegetarians--these may be the, albeit improbable, edge of the future.

Where does this leave us? If we accept that unlimited growth is impossible, that we cannot sustain change at the rate to which we have been subjected to it, that scarcity is already present and will soon be omnipresent, that our society is no longer in many primary ways functional, where do we go? The price our ancestors paid to become Americans was the reconstruction of themselves. And the price we will pay if we are to survive the transition from growth to equilibrium, from glut to scarcity, may be precisely that. Once again we must reconstrue our understanding of what we are and what we are willing to give up to get it.

As a way of undertaking this re-vision we might affirm the fact that our vision of the "good life" must change. Bred into us, on every level of our experience, is not only a hierarchy of values, but the value of hierarchy itself. Milk is better than grass, cheese than milk, mice than cheese, cats than mice, and so on. We have only just begun to realize that fish have rights, and air has rights, and water has rights; and that the value of things is not totally contingent on their value to us. Socially, we have also internalized a pattern of value that we are now beginning to confront. Class, in our so-called classless society, is based, generally, not on birth but on possessions. And possession functions in the following way. If it is good to have one car it is better to have two. If it is good to have a big car it is better to have an even bigger car. If it is good to have a car one needs it is even better to have a car one does

not need.  Conspicuous consumption abides by the same
rules among the aborigines of the Australian outback and the
middle-management executives of Towson, Maryland.  To be
happy is to have reached the highest possible level of ownership of useless objects.

Another mark of happiness in our culture is "success."  Success is measured by the quantity and quality of
that which falls under our control.  To be a janitor is to
control only inanimate matter.  To be the building's super-
indendent is to control not only property but also the people
who maintain it.  To own the building....

These attitudes lie at the very heart of many of our
present problems.  They stand in the way of a sounder land-
use policy, of a more stable economic system, of the preservation of our environment.  Happiness is defined as what only
a high-growth economy can produce, and this precludes any
serious attempt at social change; makes discussion, for instance, of a steady-state economy unthinkable.  For this
conversion to a new vision to be able to occur, we must
create an image of the "good life" that is structured around
the recognition of three primary values.  We must indeed
come ourselves to believe in, not just to articulate, the joys
of Interdependence, Sustainability, and Simplification.  Any
envisioning of the "good life," not to mention any articula-
tion of public policy, that does not contain these admittedly
utopian values is by definition part of the problem, rather
than a step toward its solution.

I should like, now, to focus on these values one by
one.  Basic to everything else is the acceptance of interdependence.  Some three hundred years ago the poet/priest
John Donne wrote a meditation that began, "No man is an
island, entire of himself./  Each man is a piece of the continent, a part of the main...."  In 1980 a strike at a tin
mine in Chile paralyzes a textiles factory in Japan, causing
workers to be laid off at a power plant in Tennessee, pre-
cipitating a run on sugar in Marseilles....  There may be
nothing new under the sun, but things once true may become
more true; metaphysical conviction becomes economic hardship.  One of the problems that living in a Global Village
carries with it is that of magnification.  Behavior that may
pass unnoticed in New York City causes eyebrows to be
raised in Sioux City, conversation in Tupelo, outrage in
Monteagle, and complete social ostracism in White River
Junction.  The closer we are to one another the more effect

our actions have. The more crowded the lifeboat is, the less it takes to capsize it.

And yet we continue to behave as though we were discrete entities. As "rugged individuals" we exercise our constitutional right to do our own thing, feeling free in all but the narrowest sense of any sense of responsibility to or involvement with the World Out There. As our songs remind us, it's "You and me baby, you and me baby, you and me against the world." In the West our social organization has evolved from that of the tribe, to the clan, to the nuclear family, to the self. This development has reached its apogee in America, land of lonely joiners, where, as a British critic once pointed out, we invite anyone into our houses, and no one into our lives. Our national literature locates itself in the image of a youth floating down the Mississippi on a raft; a man in leathern breeches striding off into the wilderness with his dog.

A young country, feeling itself free of the constraints of history (time) and geography (space), we used up in a century a frontier Jefferson predicted would sustain us "unto the hundredth generation." Our leitmotif became "The impossible is our most important product." We advertised ourselves as a refuge for the refuse of Europe's teeming shores; in the great Melting Pot of America we latter-day alchemists could make gold out of dross. Any boy might travel that road from the log cabin to the White House. As Horatio Alger was eager to remind us, the only limitations we had to deal with were those that came from our own inadequacies. And these inadequacies were the products of sin. Passivity, lack of ambition, intellect, introspection, passion, sensitivity, "womanliness" were qualities that could only lead to failure. And failure, as we all know, like ugliness, old age, illness, and death, is un-American. The only thing, after all, that a real American needs to fear is fear itself!

As Henry James revealed and Henry Adams bemoaned, without a past we had no means of assessing ourselves. Perspective only occurs within a matrix of relationships. Without Aunt Sally in the foreground of the snapshot we have no way of determining the size of the giant redwood behind her. Because we had never had to function within the constraints of a highly defined social complex we never had the experience of discovering what it means to live in relationship to constraints that are beyond our control. In con-

frontation with Europe's subtlety James's Americans, with
all of their energy and confidence, were not only abashed
but destroyed.

Yet the Europe of the nineteenth century, with which
we could not deal, has come home to us here in the America of the twentieth century.  Time and space have caught up
with us very fast, so fast that we have not had time to
measure our footsteps to them.  Living on a tiny lifeboat
where every gesture needs to be coordinated for us to survive, we continue to behave as though we were standing at
the edge of a vast prairie, all alone.  Our self-image and
our life-gestalt no longer have any real relationship to each
other.  And the circle is closing.  If we are to keep it
from trapping us then we must clearly repudiate the images
with which we have been nurtured and seek to find one that
celebrates the joyousness of the interconnections that bind us
to one another, not to constrain but to support.  We must
seek again to foster a communal sense of life.

In a small world there is little room for big heroes.
What makes a community function is sacrifice of self-interest
(and sometimes what we call freedom is just that); the subordination of the individual to the welfare of the group.  The
consciousness of the future must be focused on a sense of
the totality of life.  No one of us is autonomous.  No one of
us ever has been, and we have paid dearly for our illusions
to the contrary.  Everything is linked to everything else.
That is the beginning of the vision of a sustainable system,
and the beginning of a sense of the kind of happiness we
might find within it.  No longer do we need to function as
though we were our own last resort.  After all, a community, like a body, is an organism.  The heart has only to
pump blood, the lungs only to breathe, the stomach only to
digest.  Each is part of a whole, and the whole sustains
each.  Nothing has to, nothing can, function all alone.  So,
although in a sustainable society we would certainly find our
personal freedom greatly circumscribed and our possibilities
for self-development in some ways limited, what we would
gain would be a community.  We would have a social context
in which we would achieve definition and through which we
might derive meaning.  Most profoundly, we would learn to
live in face of the interconnectedness of all life.  We are a
young race on an old planet in an insignificant galaxy in a
system about which we know almost nothing.  "What is man
that thou art mindful of him?"  At the root of any sustainable
society must lie the reestablishment of a sense of community.

Community is built on a sense of the interrelatedness of all things. And the fruit of this is the liberation of humility.

Human beings yearn for a sense of engagement with a reality that is not simply an extension of their own egos. Contemporary literature redounds with the horror to which Sartre gave voice in his play No Exit. Reality is nothing but a reflection of our selves. We are the boundary of all that we can know. Our thought, our art, our relationships are nothing but the trap of the self writ large. There is no escape. We are all there is. This is an expression, and a profound one, of the alienation that characterizes our civilization. It is a manifestation of what happens when we are dependent on no one. It is another clue to the kind of happiness that living in a sustainable society might provide. For in community, in a system, there is no way in which the welfare of an individual can be separated from the welfare of all. To live in community is to put oneself, on a very profound level, in the hands of others. It is, in all humility, to admit that we do not stand alone. This is to engage oneself with another, with the otherness of all life, by acknowledging that one cannot stand alone.

In the wealth in which we have been rolling it has been possible to pretend that we have been liberated from the bondage of need, that we are free from having to interact with anyone, that thus we have acquired integrity, wholeness. Like Prometheus we have challenged the gods, stolen their fire. Like Prometheus's our heroism is a short-lived glory. He spends eternity alone, bound to a rock, the birds of prey tearing at his entrails. Money is powerful. It doesn't change reality, but it does disguise it. In the poverty that awaits us what we will come to see is not a new reality, but what has been there all along. "No man is an island, entire of himself, each man is a piece of the continent, a part of the main"--John Donne knew about it three hundred years ago.

The next value we must seek to articulate is that of sustainability. Central to this notion, as well as to that of community, is the fact that we are part of a finite system, that we must work within its boundaries if we are not to destroy it altogether. Some of the implications of this notion are, on the surface, fairly clear. If there are ten houses and forty people, equity demands that each house shelter four souls. If five individuals each own one house, then thirty-five people must crowd into the remaining five houses. Up until now our answer has been simply to build more houses. But if we have reached the conviction that the system cannot sustain any more construction then we must face the problem of equity. And equity, in this instance redistribution, is never a simple matter.

From the moment the first pilgrim set foot on Plymouth Rock, freedom, individual freedom, however defined, has been central to our understanding of our own value. What constraints will freedom have to face once we assert sustainability as a primary value? What does it mean to act for the good of the system instead of for the good of the self? Will we be able to accept the trade-off, giving up something tangible (driving our car to work) for something as intangible as the notion of fuel conservation? To talk about a sustainable society we must in fact have a society we want to sustain. No people who are hungry and depressed and out of work and overwhelmed by the fragility of their support systems are going to be one bit interested in sustainability. Society must learn to sustain them better before they are going to have any commitment to sustaining it. And dare we, the affluent, struggling to give up a second car, we who come from generations of car owners, tell them that they must give up the dream--which we have given them--of ever owning their own automobiles, or whatever other ecologically unsound, systemically dangerous possession they have set their hearts on? Sustainability is going to be as hard to sell to the poor as equity will be to sell to the rich. And until we find a way to do both of these, to make it as much our heart's desire as peace, we will not have begun to solve the future.

The final value that seems to me to underlie what we are trying to reach is that of simplicity. Thoreau performed a life's experiment in this, and the Buddhists have long embraced it. If I am happy with two cars, might I not be even more happy with one? If I can manage with one car, could I not manage even better with none? Everything that we own takes energy to maintain. Traditionally, the purchase of goods has been the role of men and the preservation of goods the role of women. But women are rebelling against washing and ironing and waxing and polishing and mending and all that their traditional role has meant. The less we have the freer we are to be what we want, to do what we want. How minimal can necessity be? We have asked for generation now, "How much does it take to make me happy?" And the more

we have had the sadder we have become.  Maybe we should
ask now, "How little does it take to make me happy?" and
focus our explorations at the other end of the spectrum.
For until we can come to feel that less really is more we
are either going to be trapped in a runaway-growth economy
or we are going to have to try to institutionalize radical in-
equity.  And that is something we'll never get away with for
long.

As we try to imagine what a sustainable society might
be like, and what kind of life it might hold for us, we must
keep always before us the knife edge of these realities.  The
society in which we live is, for many of us, the only one we
know.  Thus, our society assumes a kind of inevitability.
But it is not inevitable; it is unique to our culture and
bears the marks of its particular history and geography.
As we examine its characteristics we can begin to see,
as with a mirror image, what the contour of a sustainable society might be.

As Frederick Jackson Turner pointed out, our consciousness was shaped by the frontier.  Problems never had
to be confronted--the solution was simply to move on.
There was always an "away" to go to, and this away, our
limitless horizon, made it possible for us to develop a national habit of evasion, of avoidance, of escape.  As a college president once explained to me, in the middle of a
student strike, "My job is not to 'solve problems,' it's to
displace tensions."  Philip Slater talks in somewhat less
elegant terms than Turner, but to similar effect.  We have,
he says, a flush toilet approach to life.  Prior to the invention of this most useful of conveniences nothing miraculously
vanished--neither physical waste nor social problems.  But
now, occupational specialization and plumbing have exerted a
kind of censorship over our understanding of the world we
live in and how it operates.  For a long time we have dealt
with poverty and old age and illness and death by hiding them.

The notion of limits was meaningless in a country in
which it has taken these limits three hundred years to become apparent.  No one interested in moderation, discre-
tion, or finiteness would have been interested in mastering
a wilderness, or creating a nation out of a fistful of immigrants.  It was the seduction of the impossible dream, the
secret love for the infinite, which the finite world could
neither contain nor fulfill, that provided the life force that

shaped and sustained our country. It is these same qualities that are now destroying it.

The natural world, for the American settlers, was a world to be conquered--to be transformed into a habitat fit for farming, for business, for industry. It was a metaphor for their own souls, conceived of as a darkness of conflicting passions, unspeakable desires, terrors and dangers ever threatening to rise up and engulf them. As their spiritual task was to subdue and master the beast within, so was their physical task to impose that internal order on the wild, primitive world in which they found themselves. As Michael Novak points out in his The Rise of the Unmeltable Ethnics, the Anglo-Saxon (and by this he means, in fact, the assimilated American) is not at home in the world and therefore must conquer it. Thus, we are an anxious people, and because anxious, successful, achieving, and unsatisfied. The needs and desires that drive us cannot be answered within the context in which we now live. But they are very good for business. We strive toward Cadillacs, Chivas Regal, Benson and Hedges, whatever the iconic representations of happiness in our particular niche happen to be. But the hungry sheep look up and are not fed. We are trapped in an exponential spiral in which the more we have the more we want and our hunger grows and grows. Possessions generate scarcity. Once the concept exists that there is not enough, people deprive one another of what there is. Like Ugolino and his sons trapped in their tower in Dante's Hell, we have eaten one another, we now begin to gnaw upon ourselves.

Orwell says, "Who controls the past controls the future: who controls the present controls the past." Huxley says, "Was and will make me ill. I take a gram and only am." We cannot see the forest of history, of what was and what will be, while we are trying to make our way through the trees of the present. We do live in the woods; this is the realm in which we are given to act. But as human beings we are also given the capacity to transcend the trees, to stand above the forest--to see over its end, beyond its beginning. The root of the word "relevant" is not the Latin referre--to relate, but releváre, to lift up. The function of the utopian/dystopian vision is to enable us to stand outside of time; to see time and thus to be saved from it.

For the first time in history our capacity to do has outstripped our capacity to imagine doing. No single vision, not the sufferings in hell of Dante's damned, nor the frenzied curses of Goethe's Faust, not even the intricate tortures of the Marquis De Sade gave warning of what humankind would actually create in the concentration camps of Auschwitz, in the fire storms at Dresden, in the obliteration of Hiroshima. There is no artistic precedent for these horrors. The mind cannot encircle them, hold them, domesticate them. On some level they have not taught us anything because we cannot imagine them, because they are too big to bring into our consciousness, because they are too much to deal with.

If we can't imagine something we can't fear it. And if we can't imagine something we can't see it. And if we can't imagine something we can't believe in it. And if we can't imagine something it might as well not exist. The problem is that our imaginations do not control what is, but only how we deal with what is. The fact that I cannot imagine a world in which there will not be enough fuel to run our cars and heat our houses--not to mention a world without industry, without trains, planes, and ships--does not control the fact that I had to go to three service stations today to fill up my car's gas tank. I cannot imagine mass starvation. I cannot imagine the creation of life in a test tube. I cannot imagine a world in which we choke to death on the air we breathe and are poisoned by the water we drink, where humanity is added to the list of endangered species. Our world has become too hard to imagine. It has become unimaginable.

But what is not imaginable is possible, and it is this we must remember. The science fiction of Jules Verne has been proved prophecy. What of the science fiction of our own time? Will it prove prophecy? Shall we have the thought control of 1984? The genetic manipulation of Brave New World? These are worlds imagined in a world grown inimaginable. If our world stays unimaginable what is now possible will become probable will become fact. Orwell and Huxley will indeed prove prophetic. But it will be too late to care.

Until the imagination has taught us to imagine the unimaginable all of the harried, if prophetic, voices of those who document the seeds of the present, will echo uselessly in the wilderness. And this is why in the study of utopias we must engage ourselves not only in the history we know, but in the history that is to come. To design a utopia is to engage in an act of vision. It entails pressing beyond the constraints of the crises in which we live and moving into a new order of possibility. Visionary activity is not an <u>extra</u> in society any longer, if it ever was. It is the only thing that has any chance of carrying us from the world in which we presently live--which is destroying itself at such a rate that life within it cannot long be a possibility--to a world that is informed by new values and a new understanding of being. For this transformation cannot take place in think tanks and high-powered conferences. It will be brought about by a revolution in our imagination's exercise; by the dreaming up of new utopias. Plato, Thomas More, Bronson Alcott projected the perfection of human personality. We, more modestly, cherish the hope of survival.

## Bibliography

Meadows, D. L., and Donella Meadows, eds. <u>Toward Global Equilibrium</u> (Cambridge, Mass.: MIT, 1973).

Meadows, Donella, et al. <u>The Limits to Growth: A Report for the Club of Rome's Project on the Predicament of Mankind</u>, 2nd ed. (New York: Universe, 1974).

Pirages, D. C., and P. R. Ehrlich. <u>Ark Two: Social Response to Environmental Imperatives</u> (San Francisco: W. H. Freeman, 1974).